STATUTORY SUPPLEMENT

to

CASES AND MATERIALS

ON

EMPLOYMENT LAW

FIFTH EDITION

By

MARK A. ROTHSTEIN
Herbert F. Boehl Chair of Law and Medicine
University of Louisville

LANCE LIEBMAN
William S. Beinecke Professor of Law
Columbia University

FOUNDATION PRESS
New York, New York
2003

THOMSON
WEST

 *TEXT IS PRINTED ON 10% POST CONSUMER RECYCLED PAPER*

EDITORS' NOTE

This Statutory Supplement contains the relevant portions of the key federal employment laws considered in the casebook, as well as some representative state statutes. They have been arranged in the Supplement to correspond with their order of presentation in the casebook. The Supplement contains one unenacted statute: the Model Employment Termination Act. It is included because of its relevance to material discussed in the casebook.

Some of the enacted laws, such as the National Labor Relations Act and the Occupational Safety and Health Act, are often referred to by their statutory section numbers. For these laws, the statutory section number is followed by the United States Code section number in parentheses. For other laws, not usually referred to by their statutory section numbers, only the United States Code section numbers are given.

M.A.R.
L.L.

February 2003

*

TABLE OF CONTENTS

Page

EDITORS' NOTE -- iii

National Labor Relations Act --- 1
Labor Management Relations Act --- 12
Immigration Reform and Control Act -- 13
Employee Polygraph Protection Act -- 27
Civil Rights Act of 1964, Title VII --- 38
Civil Rights Act of 1991 --- 52
U.S. Constitution --- 56
42 U.S.C. § 1981, Revised Statutes § 1977A ------------------------------- 57
42 U.S.C. § 1983 -- 60
42 U.S.C. § 1985 -- 61
Age Discrimination in Employment Act ------------------------------------- 62
Rehabilitation Act -- 73
Americans With Disabilities Act --- 77
Fair Labor Standards Act -- 90
Portal to Portal Act -- 111
Family and Medical Leave Act -- 114
Health Insurance Portability and Accountability Act --------------------- 130
Occupational Safety and Health Act -- 146
Massachusetts Worker's Compensation Statute --------------------------- 167
Federal Old–Age, Survivors, and Disability Insurance Benefits Act
    (Social Security Act) -- 201
Montana Wrongful Discharge From Employment Act -------------------- 207
Model Employment Termination Act --------------------------------------- 211
Federal Unemployment Tax Act --- 223
California Unemployment Insurance Code --------------------------------- 226
Worker Adjustment and Retraining Notification Act --------------------- 244
Bankruptcy Act-- 251
Pension Law-- 259
Employee Retirement Income Security Act -------------------------------- 260
Older Workers Benefit Protection Act -------------------------------------- 289

*

STATUTORY SUPPLEMENT

to

CASES AND MATERIALS

ON

EMPLOYMENT LAW

*

NATIONAL LABOR RELATIONS ACT

29 U.S.C. §§ 151–169

RIGHTS OF EMPLOYEES

SEC. 7. **(§ 157)** Employees shall have the right to self-organization, to form, join, or assist labor organizations, to bargain collectively through representatives of their own choosing, and to engage in other concerted activities for the purpose of collective bargaining or other mutual aid or protection, and shall also have the right to refrain from any or all of such activities except to the extent that such right may be affected by an agreement requiring membership in a labor organization as a condition of employment as authorized in section 8(a)(3).

UNFAIR LABOR PRACTICES

SEC. 8. **(§ 158)** (a) It shall be an unfair labor practice for an employer—

(1) to interfere with, restrain, or coerce employees in the exercise of the rights guaranteed in section 7;

(2) to dominate or interfere with the formation or administration of any labor organization or contribute financial or other support to it: *Provided,* That subject to rules and regulations made and published by the Board pursuant to section 6, an employer shall not be prohibited from permitting employees to confer with him during working hours without loss of time or pay;

(3) by discrimination in regard to hire or tenure of employment or any term or condition of employment to encourage or discourage membership in any labor organization: *Provided,* That nothing in this Act, or in any other statute of the United States, shall preclude an employer from making an agreement with a labor organization (not established, maintained, or assisted by any action defined in this Act as an unfair labor practice) to require as a condition of employment membership therein on or after the thirtieth day following the beginning of such employment or the effective date of such agreement, whichever is the later, (i) if such labor organization is the representative of the employees as provided in section 9(a), in the appropriate collective-bargaining unit covered by such agreement when made, and (ii) unless following an election held as provided in section 9(e) within one year preceding the effective date of such agreement, the Board shall have certified that at least a majority of the employees eligible to vote in such election have voted

1

to rescind the authority of such labor organization to make such an agreement: *Provided further,* That no employer shall justify any discrimination against an employee for nonmembership in a labor organization (A) if he has reasonable grounds for believing that such membership was not available to the employee on the same terms and conditions generally applicable to other members, or (B) if he has reasonable grounds for believing that membership was denied or terminated for reasons other than the failure of the employee to tender the periodic dues and the initiation fees uniformly required as a condition of acquiring or retaining membership;

(4) to discharge or otherwise discriminate against an employee because he has filed charges or given testimony under this Act;

(5) to refuse to bargain collectively with the representatives of his employees, subject to the provisions of section 9(a).

(b) It shall be an unfair labor practice for a labor organization or its agents—

(1) to restrain or coerce (A) employees in the exercise of the rights guaranteed in section 7: *Provided,* That this paragraph shall not impair the right of a labor organization to prescribe its own rules with respect to the acquisition or retention of membership therein; or (B) an employer in the selection of his representatives for the purposes of collective bargaining or the adjustment of grievances;

(2) to cause or attempt to cause an employer to discriminate against an employee in violation of subsection (a)(3) or to discriminate against an employee with respect to whom membership in such organization has been denied or terminated on some ground other than his failure to tender the periodic dues and the initiation fees uniformly required as a condition of acquiring or retaining membership;

(3) to refuse to bargain collectively with an employer, provided it is the representative of his employees subject to the provisions of section 9(a);

(4)(i) to engage in, or to induce or encourage any individual employed by any person engaged in commerce or in an industry affecting commerce to engage in, a strike or a refusal in the course of his employment to use, manufacture, process, transport, or otherwise handle or work on any goods, articles, materials, or commodities or to perform any services; or (ii) to threaten, coerce, or restrain any person engaged in commerce or in an industry affecting commerce, where in either case an object thereof is:

2

(A) forcing or requiring any employer or self-employed person to join any labor or employer organization or to enter into any agreement which is prohibited by section 8(e);

(B) forcing or requiring any person to cease using, selling, handling, transporting, or otherwise dealing in the products of any other producer, processor, or manufacturer, or to cease doing business with any other person, or forcing or requiring any other employer to recognize or bargain with a labor organization as the representative of his employees unless such labor organization has been certified as the representative of such employees under the provisions of section 9: *Provided,* That nothing contained in this clause (B) shall be construed to make unlawful, where not otherwise unlawful, any primary strike or primary picketing;

(C) forcing or requiring any employer to recognize or bargain with a particular labor organization as the representative of his employees if another labor organization has been certified as the representative of such employees under the provisions of section 9;

(D) forcing or requiring any employer to assign particular work to employees in a particular labor organization or in a particular trade, craft, or class rather than to employees in another labor organization or in another trade, craft, or class, unless such employer is failing to conform to an order or certification of the Board determining the bargaining representative for employees performing such work:

Provided, That nothing contained in this subsection [8](b) shall be construed to make unlawful a refusal by any person to enter upon the premises of any employer (other than his own employer), if the employees of such employer are engaged in a strike ratified or approved by a representative of such employees whom such employer is required to recognize under this Act: *Provided further,* That for the purposes of this paragraph (4) only, nothing contained in such paragraph shall be construed to prohibit publicity, other than picketing, for the purpose of truthfully advising the public, including consumers and members of a labor organization, that a product or products are produced by an employer with whom the labor organization has a primary dispute and are distributed by another employer, as long as such publicity does not have an effect of inducing any individual employed by any person other than the primary employer in the course of his employment to refuse to pick up, deliver, or transport any goods, or not to perform any services, at the establishment of the employer engaged in such distribution;

(5) to require of employees covered by an agreement authorized under subsection (a)(3) the payment, as a condition precedent to becoming a member of such organization, of a fee in an amount which the Board finds excessive or discriminatory under all the circumstances. In making such a finding, the Board shall consider, among other relevant factors, the practices and customs of labor organizations in the particular industry, and the wages currently paid to the employees affected;

(6) to cause or attempt to cause an employer to pay or deliver or agree to pay or deliver any money or other thing of value, in the nature of an exaction, for services which are not performed or not to be performed; and

(7) to picket or cause to be picketed, or threaten to picket or cause to be picketed, any employer where an object thereof is forcing or requiring an employer to recognize or bargain with a labor organization as the representative of his employees, or forcing or requiring the employees of an employer to accept or select such labor organization as their collective bargaining representative, unless such labor organization is currently certified as the representative of such employees:

(A) where the employer has lawfully recognized in accordance with this Act any other labor organization and a question concerning representation may not appropriately be raised under section 9(c) of this Act,

(B) where within the preceding twelve months a valid election under section 9(c) of this Act has been conducted, or

(C) where such picketing has been conducted without a petition under section 9(c) being filed within a reasonable period of time not to exceed thirty days from the commencement of such picketing: *Provided,* That when such a petition has been filed the Board shall forthwith, without regard to the provisions of section 9(c)(1) or the absence of a showing of a substantial interest on the part of the labor organization, direct an election in such unit as the Board finds to be appropriate and shall certify the results thereof: *Provided further,* That nothing in this subparagraph (C) shall be construed to prohibit any picketing or other publicity for the purpose of truthfully advising the public (including consumers) that an employer does not employ members of, or have a contract with, a labor organization, unless an effect of such picketing is to induce any individual employed by any other person in the course of his employment, not to pick up, deliver or transport any goods or not to perform any services.

Nothing in this paragraph (7) shall be construed to permit any act which would otherwise be an unfair labor practice under this section 8(b).

(c) The expressing of any views, argument, or opinion, or the dissemination thereof, whether in written, printed, graphic, or visual form, shall not constitute or be evidence of an unfair labor practice under any of the provisions of this Act, if such expression contains no threat of reprisal or force or promise of benefit.

(d) For the purposes of this section, to bargain collectively is the performance of the mutual obligation of the employer and the representative of the employees to meet at reasonable times and confer in good faith with respect to wages, hours, and other terms and conditions of employment, or the negotiation of an agreement, or any question arising thereunder, and the execution of a written contract incorporating any agreement reached if requested by either party, but such obligation does not compel either party to agree to a proposal or require the making of a concession: *Provided,* That where there is in effect a collective bargaining contract covering employees in an industry affecting commerce, the duty to bargain collectively shall also mean that no party to such contract shall terminate or modify such contract, unless the party desiring such termination or modification—

(1) serves a written notice upon the other party to the contract of the proposed termination or modification sixty days prior to the expiration date thereof, or in the event such contract contains no expiration date, sixty days prior to the time it is proposed to make such termination or modification;

(2) offers to meet and confer with the other party for the purpose of negotiating a new contract or a contract containing the proposed modifications;

(3) notifies the Federal Mediation and Conciliation Service within thirty days after such notice of the existence of a dispute, and simultaneously therewith notifies any State or Territorial agency established to mediate and conciliate disputes within the State or Territory where the dispute occurred, provided no agreement has been reached by that time; and

(4) continues in full force and effect, without resorting to strike or lockout, all the terms and conditions of the existing contract for a period of sixty days after such notice is given or until the expiration date of such contract, whichever occurs later:

The duties imposed upon employers, employees, and labor organizations by paragraphs (2)–(4) of this subsection shall become inapplicable upon an intervening certification of the

Board, under which the labor organization or individual, which is a party to the contract, has been superseded as or ceased to be the representative of the employees subject to the provisions of section 9(a) of this Act, and the duties so imposed shall not be construed as requiring either party to discuss or agree to any modification of the terms and conditions contained in a contract for a fixed period, if such modification is to become effective before such terms and conditions can be reopened under the provisions of the contract. Any employee who engages in a strike within any notice period specified in this subsection, or who engages in any strike within the appropriate period specified in subsection (g) of this section, shall lose his status as an employee of the employer engaged in the particular labor dispute, for the purposes of sections 8 to 10 of this Act, but such loss of status for such employee shall terminate if and when he is reemployed by such employer. Whenever the collective bargaining involves employees of a health care institution, the provisions of this subsection shall be modified as follows:

(A) The notice of paragraph (1) of this subsection shall be ninety days; the notice of paragraph (3) of this subsection shall be sixty days; and the contract period of paragraph (4) of this subsection shall be ninety days.

(B) Where the bargaining is for an initial agreement following certification or recognition, at least thirty days' notice of the existence of a dispute shall be given by the labor organization to the agencies set forth in paragraph (3) of this subsection.

(C) After notice is given to the Federal Mediation and Conciliation Service under either clause (A) or (B) of this sentence, the Service shall promptly communicate with the parties and use its best efforts, by mediation and conciliation, to bring them to agreement. The parties shall participate fully and promptly in such meetings as may be undertaken by the Service for the purpose of aiding in a settlement of the dispute.

(e) It shall be an unfair labor practice for any labor organization and any employer to enter into any contract or agreement, express or implied, whereby such employer ceases or refrains or agrees to cease or refrain from handling, using, selling, transporting or otherwise dealing in any of the products of any other employer, or to cease doing business with any other person, and any contract or agreement entered into heretofore or hereafter containing such an agreement shall be to such extent unenforceable and void: *Provided,* That nothing in this subsection (e) shall apply to an agreement between a labor organization and an employer in the construction industry relating to the contracting or subcontracting of work to be done at the site of the construction, alteration, painting, or repair of a building, structure, or other work: *Provided further,* That for the purposes of this subsection (e) and section 8(b)(4)(B) the terms "any employer", "any person engaged in commerce or in industry affecting commerce", and "any person" when used in relation to the terms "any other producer, processor, or manufacturer", "any other employer", or "any other person" shall not include persons in the relation of a jobber, manufacturer, contractor, or subcontractor working on the goods or premises of the jobber or manufacturer or performing parts of an integrated process of production in the apparel and clothing industry: *Provided further,* That nothing in this Act shall prohibit the enforcement of any agreement which is within the foregoing exception.

(f) It shall not be an unfair labor practice under subsections (a) and (b) of this section for an employer engaged primarily in the building and construction industry to make an agreement covering employees engaged (or who, upon their employment, will be engaged) in the building and construction industry with a labor organization of which building and construction employees are members (not established, maintained, or assisted by any action defined in section 8(a) of this Act as an unfair labor practice) because (1) the majority status of such labor organization has not been established under the provisions of section 9 of this Act prior to the making of such agreement, or (2) such agreement requires as a condition of employment, membership in such labor organization after the seventh day following the beginning of such employment or the effective date of the agreement, whichever is later, or (3) such agreement requires the employer to notify such labor organization of opportunities for employment with such employer, or gives such labor organization an opportunity to refer qualified applicants for such employment, or (4) such agreement specifies minimum training or experience qualifications for employment or provides for priority in opportunities for employment based upon length of service with such employer, in the industry or in the particular geographical area: *Provided,* That nothing in this subsection shall set aside the final proviso to section 8(a)(3) of this Act: *Provided further,* That any agreement which would be invalid, but for clause (1) of this subsection, shall not be a bar to a petition filed pursuant to section 9(c) or 9(e).

(g) A labor organization before engaging in any strike, picketing, or other concerted refusal to work at any health care institution shall, not less than ten days prior to such action, notify the institution in writing and the Federal Mediation and Conciliation Service of that intention, except that in the case of bargaining for an initial agreement following certification or recognition the notice required by this subsection shall not be given until the expiration of the period specified in clause (B) of the last sentence of subsection (d) of this section. The notice shall state the date and time that such action will commence. The notice, once given, may be extended by the written agreement of both parties.

REPRESENTATIVES AND ELECTIONS

SEC. 9. (§ 159) (a) Representatives designated or selected for the purposes of collective bargaining by the majority of the employees in a unit appropriate for such purposes, shall be the exclusive representatives of all the employees in such unit for the purposes of collective bargaining in respect to rates of pay, wages, hours of employment, or other conditions of employment: *Provided,* That any individual employee or a group of employees shall have the right at any time to present grievances to their employer and to have such grievances adjusted, without the intervention of the bargaining representative, as long as the adjustment is not inconsistent with the terms of a collective-bargaining contract or agreement then in effect: *Provided further,* That the bargaining representative has been given opportunity to be present at such adjustment.

(b) The Board shall decide in each case whether, in order to assure to employees the fullest freedom in exercising the rights guaranteed by this Act, the unit appropriate for the purposes of collective bargaining shall be the employer unit, craft unit, plant unit, or subdivision thereof: *Provided,* That the Board shall not (1) decide that any unit is appropriate for such purposes if such unit includes both professional employees and employees who are not professional employees unless a majority of such professional employees vote for inclusion in such unit; or (2) decide that any craft unit is inappropriate for such purposes on the ground that a different unit has been established by a prior Board determination, unless a majority of the employees in the proposed craft unit vote against separate representation or (3) decide that any unit is appropriate for such purposes if it includes, together with other employees, any individual employed as a guard to enforce against employees and other persons rules to protect property of the employer or to protect the safety of persons on the employer's premises; but no labor organization shall be certified as the representative of employees in a bargaining unit of guards if such organization admits to membership, or is affiliated directly or indirectly with an organization which admits to membership, employees other than guards.

(c)(1) Wherever a petition shall have been filed, in accordance with such regulations as may be prescribed by the Board—

   (A) by an employee or group of employees or any individual or labor organization acting in their behalf alleging that a substantial number of employees (i) wish to be represented for collective bargaining and that their employer declines to recognize their representative as the representative defined in section 9(a), or (ii) assert that the individual or labor organization, which has been certified or is being currently recognized by their employer as the bargaining representative, is no longer a representative as defined in section 9(a);

(B) by an employer, alleging that one or more individuals or labor organizations have presented to him a claim to be recognized as the representative defined in section 9(a);

the Board shall investigate such petition and if it has reasonable cause to believe that a question of representation affecting commerce exists shall provide for an appropriate hearing upon due notice. Such hearing may be conducted by an officer or employee of the regional office, who shall not make any recommendations with respect thereto. If the Board finds upon the record of such hearing that such a question of representation exists, it shall direct an election by secret ballot and shall certify the results thereof.

(2) In determining whether or not a question of representation affecting commerce exists, the same regulations and rules of decision shall apply irrespective of the identity of the persons filing the petition or the kind of relief sought and in no case shall the Board deny a labor organization a place on the ballot by reason of an order with respect to such labor organization or its predecessor not issued in conformity with section 10(c).

(3) No election shall be directed in any bargaining unit or any subdivision within which, in the preceding twelve-month period, a valid election shall have been held. Employees engaged in an economic strike who are not entitled to reinstatement shall be eligible to vote under such regulations as the Board shall find are consistent with the purposes and provisions of this Act in any election conducted within twelve months after the commencement of the strike. In any election where none of the choices on the ballot receives a majority, a run-off shall be conducted, the ballot providing for a selection between the two choices receiving the largest and second largest number of valid votes cast in the election.

(4) Nothing in this section shall be construed to prohibit the waiving of hearings by stipulation for the purpose of a consent election in conformity with regulations and rules of decision of the Board.

(5) In determining whether a unit is appropriate for the purposes specified in subsection (b) the extent to which the employees have organized shall not be controlling.

9

(d) Whenever an order of the Board made pursuant to section 10(c) is based in whole or in part upon facts certified following an investigation pursuant to subsection (c) of this section and there is a petition for the enforcement or review of such order, such certification and the record of such investigation shall be included in the transcript of the entire record required to be filed under section 10(e) or 10(f), and thereupon the decree of the court enforcing, modifying, or setting aside in whole or in part the order of the Board shall be made and entered upon the pleadings, testimony, and proceedings set forth in such transcript.

(e)(1) Upon the filing with the Board, by 30 per centum or more of the employees in a bargaining unit covered by an agreement between their employer and a labor organization made pursuant to section 8(a)(3), of a petition alleging they desire that such authority be rescinded, the Board shall take a secret ballot of the employees in such unit and certify the results thereof to such labor organization and to the employer.

(2) No election shall be conducted pursuant to this subsection in any bargaining unit or any subdivision within which, in the preceding twelve-month period, a valid election shall have been held.

* * *

LIMITATIONS

SEC. 13. (**§ 163**) Nothing in this Act, except as specifically provided for herein, shall be construed so as either to interfere with or impede or diminish in any way the right to strike, or to affect the limitations or qualifications on that right.

SEC. 14. (**§ 164**) (a) Nothing herein shall prohibit any individual employed as a supervisor from becoming or remaining a member of a labor organization, but no employer subject to this Act shall be compelled to deem individuals defined herein as supervisors as employees for the purpose of any law, either national or local, relating to collective bargaining.

(b) Nothing in this Act shall be construed as authorizing the execution or application of agreements requiring membership in a labor organization as a condition of employment in any State or Territory in which such execution or application is prohibited by State or Territorial law.

(c)(1) The Board, in its discretion, may, by rule of decision or by published rules adopted pursuant to the Administrative Procedure Act, decline to assert jurisdiction over any labor dispute involving any class or category of employees, where, in the opinion of the Board, the effect of such labor dispute on commerce is not sufficiently substantial to warrant the exercise of its jurisdiction: *Provided,* That the Board shall not decline to assert jurisdiction over any labor dispute over which it would assert jurisdiction under the standards prevailing upon August 1, 1959.

(2) Nothing in this Act shall be deemed to prevent or bar any agency or the courts of any State or Territory (including the Commonwealth of Puerto Rico, Guam, and the Virgin Islands), from assuming and asserting jurisdiction over labor disputes over which the Board declines, pursuant to paragraph (1) of this subsection, to assert jurisdiction.

* * *

SEC. 19. (**§ 169**) Any employee who is a member of and adheres to established and traditional tenets or teachings of a bona fide religion, body, or sect which has historically held conscientious objections to joining or financially supporting labor organizations shall not be required to join or financially support any labor organization as a condition of employment; except that such employee may be required in a contract between such employees' employer and a labor organization in lieu of periodic dues and initiation fees, to pay sums equal to such dues and initiation fees to a nonreligious, nonlabor organization charitable fund exempt from taxation under section 501(c)(3) of Title 26, chosen by such employee from a list of at least three such funds, designated in such contract or if the contract fails to designate such funds, then to any such fund chosen by the employee. If such employee who holds conscientious objections pursuant to this section requests the labor organization to use grievance-arbitration procedure on the employee's behalf, the labor organization is authorized to charge the employee for the reasonable cost of using such procedure.

LABOR MANAGEMENT RELATIONS ACT

29 U.S.C. §§ 141–197

SUITS BY AND AGAINST LABOR ORGANIZATIONS

SEC. 301. **(§ 185)** (a) Suits for violation of contracts between an employer and a labor organization representing employees in an industry affecting commerce as defined in this Act, or between any such labor organizations, may be brought in any district court of the United States having jurisdiction of the parties, without respect to the amount in controversy or without regard to the citizenship of the parties.

* * *

SAVING PROVISION

SEC. 502. **(§ 143)** Nothing in this Act shall be construed to require an individual employee to render labor or service without his consent, nor shall anything in this act be construed to make the quitting of his labor by an individual employee an illegal act; nor shall any court issue any process to compel the performance by an individual employee of such labor or service, without his consent; nor shall the quitting of labor by an employee or employees in good faith because of abnormally dangerous conditions for work at the place of employment of such employee or employees be deemed a strike under this Act.

IMMIGRATION REFORM AND CONTROL ACT

8 U.S.C. §§ 1324a, 1324b

§ 1324a. Unlawful employment of aliens

(a) Making employment of unauthorized aliens unlawful

(1) In general

It is unlawful for a person or other entity—

(A) to hire, or to recruit or refer for a fee, for employment in the United States an alien knowing the alien is an unauthorized alien (as defined in subsection (h)(3) of this section) with respect to such employment, or

(B)(i) to hire for employment in the United States an individual without complying with the requirements of subsection (b) of this section or (ii) if the person or entity is an agricultural association, agricultural employer, or farm labor contractor (as defined in section 1802 of Title 29) to hire, or to recruit or refer for a fee, for employment in the United States an individual without complying with the requirements of subsection (b) of this section.

(2) Continuing employment

It is unlawful for a person or other entity, after hiring an alien for employment in accordance with paragraph (1), to continue to employ the alien in the United States knowing the alien is (or has become) an unauthorized alien with respect to such employment.

(3) Defense

A person or entity that establishes that it has complied in good faith with the requirements of subsection (b) of this section with respect to the hiring, recruiting, or referral for employment of an alien in the United States has established an affirmative defense that the person or entity has not violated paragraph (1)(A) with respect to such hiring, recruiting, or referral.

(4) Use of labor through contract

For purposes of this section, a person or other entity who uses a contract, subcontract, or exchange, entered into, renegotiated, or extended after the date of the enactment of this section, to obtain the labor of an alien in the United States knowing that the alien is

13

an unauthorized alien (as defined in subsection (h)(3) of this section) with respect to performing such labor, shall be considered to have hired the alien for employment in the United States in violation of paragraph (1)(A).

(5) Use of State employment agency documentation

For purposes of paragraphs (1)(B) and (3), a person or entity shall be deemed to have complied with the requirements of subsection (b) of this section with respect to the hiring of an individual who was referred for such employment by a State employment agency (as defined by the Attorney General), if the person or entity has and retains (for the period and in the manner described in subsection (b)(3)) appropriate documentation of such referral by that agency, which documentation certifies that the agency has complied with the procedures specified in subsection (b) of this section with respect to the individual's referral.

* * *

(b) Employment verification system

The requirements referred to in paragraphs (1)(B) and (3) of subsection (a) of this section are, in the case of a person or other entity hiring, recruiting, or referring an individual for employment in the United States, the requirements specified in the following three paragraphs:

(1) Attestation after examination of documentation

(A) In general

The person or entity must attest, under penalty of perjury and on a form designated or established by the Attorney General by regulation, that it has verified that the individual is not an unauthorized alien by examining—

(i) a document described in subparagraph (B), or

(ii) a document described in subparagraph (C) and a document described in subparagraph (D).

A person or entity has complied with the requirement of this paragraph with respect to examination of a document if the document reasonably appears on its face to be genuine. If an individual provides a document or combination of documents that reasonably appears on its face to be genuine and that is sufficient to meet the requirements of the first sentence of this paragraph, nothing in this paragraph shall be construed as requiring the person or entity to solicit the production of any other document or as requiring the individual to produce such another document.

(B) Documents establishing both employment authorization and identity

A document described in this subparagraph is an individual's—

(i) United States passport;

(ii) resident alien card, alien registration card, or other document designated by the Attorney General, if the document—

(I) contains a photograph of the individual and such other personal identifying information relating to the individual as the Attorney General finds, by regulation, sufficient for purposes of this subsection.

(II) is evidence of authorization of employment in the United States, and

(III) contains security features to make it resistant to tampering, counterfeiting, and fraudulent use.

(C) Documents evidencing employment authorization

A document described in this subparagraph is an individual's—

(i) social security account number card (other than such a card which specifies on the face that the issuance of the card does not authorize employment in the United States); or

(ii) other documentation evidencing authorization of employment in the United States which the Attorney General finds, by regulation, to be acceptable for purposes of this section.

(D) Documents establishing identity of individual

A document described in this subparagraph is an individual's—

(i) driver's license or similar document issued for the purpose of identification by a State, if it contains a photograph of the individual or such other personal identifying information relating to the individual as the Attorney General finds, by regulation, sufficient for purposes of this section; or

(ii) in the case of individuals under 16 years of age or in a State which does not provide for issuance of an identification document (other than a driver's license) referred to in clause (i), documentation of personal identity of such other type as the Attorney General finds, by regulation, provides a reliable means of identification.

(E) Authority to prohibit use of certain documents

If the Attorney General finds, by regulation, that any document described in subparagraph (B), (C), or (D) as establishing employment authorization or identity does not reliably establish such authorization or identity or is being used fraudulently to an unacceptable degree, the Attorney General may prohibit or place conditions on its use for purposes of this subsection.

(2) Individual attestation of employment authorization

The individual must attest, under penalty of perjury on the form designated or established for purposes of paragraph (1), that the individual is a citizen or national of the United States, an alien lawfully admitted for permanent residence, or an alien who is authorized under this chapter or by the Attorney General to be hired, recruited, or referred for such employment.

(3) Retention of verification form

After completion of such form in accordance with paragraphs (1) and (2), the person or entity must retain the form and make it available for inspection by officers of the Service, the Special Counsel for Immigration–Related Unfair Employment Practices, or the Department of Labor during a period beginning on the date of the hiring, recruiting, or referral of the individual and ending—

(A) in the case of the recruiting or referral for a fee (without hiring) of an individual, three years after the date of the recruiting or referral, and

(B) in the case of the hiring of an individual—

(i) three years after the date of such hiring, or

(ii) one year after the date the individual's employment is terminated,

whichever is later.

(4) Copying of documentation permitted

Notwithstanding any other provision of law, the person or entity may copy a document presented by an individual pursuant to this subsection and may retain the copy, but only (except as otherwise permitted under law) for the purpose of complying with the requirements of this subsection.

* * *

(e) Compliance

* * *

(4) Cease and desist order with civil money penalty for hiring, recruiting, and referral violations

With respect to a violation of subsection (a)(1)(A) or (a)(2) of this section, the order under this subsection—

(A) shall require the person or entity to cease and desist from such violations and to pay a civil penalty in an amount of—

(i) not less than $250 and not more than $2,000 for each unauthorized alien with respect to whom a violation of either such subsection occurred.

(ii) not less than $2,000 and not more than $5,000 for each such alien in the case of a person or entity previously subject to one order under this paragraph, or

(iii) not less than $3,000 and not more than $10,000 for each such alien in the case of a person or entity previously subject to more than one order under this paragraph; and

(B) may require the person or entity—

(i) to comply with the requirements of subsection (b) (or subsection (d) of this section if applicable) with respect to individuals hired (or recruited or referred for employment for a fee) during a period of up to three years, and

(ii) to take such other remedial action as is appropriate.

In applying this subsection in the case of a person or entity composed of distinct, physically separate subdivisions each of which provides separately for the hiring, recruiting, or referring for employment, without reference to the practices of, and not under the control of or common control with, another subdivision, each such subdivision shall be considered a separate person or entity.

(5) Order for civil money penalty for paperwork violations

With respect to a violation of subsection (a)(1)(B) of this section, the order under this subsection shall require the person or entity to pay a civil penalty in an amount of not less than $100 and not more than $1,000 for each individual with respect to whom such violation occurred. In determining the amount of the penalty, due consideration shall be given to the size of the business of the employer being charged, the good faith of the employer, the seriousness of the violation, whether or not the individual was an unauthorized alien, and the history of previous violations.

(6) Good faith compliance

(A) In general

Except as provided in subparagraphs (B) and (C), a person or entity is considered to have compiled with a requirement of this subsection notwithstanding a technical or procedural failure to meet such requirement if there was a good faith attempt to comply with the requirement.

(B) Exception if failure to correct after notice

Subparagraph (A) shall not apply if—

(i) the Service (or another enforcement agency) has explained to the person or entity the basis for the failure,

(ii) the person or entity has been provided a period of not less than 10 business days (beginning after the date of expiration) within which to correct the failure, and

(iii) the person or entity has not corrected the failure voluntarily within such period

(C) Exception for pattern or practice violators

Subparagraph (A) shall not apply to a person or entity that has or is engaging in a pattern or practice of violations of subsection (a)(1)(A) or (a)(2) of this section.

* * *

(f) Criminal penalties and injunctions for pattern or practice violations

(1) Criminal penalty

Any person or entity which engages in a pattern or practice of violations of subsection (a)(1)(A) or (a)(2) of this section shall be fined not more than $3,000 for each unauthorized alien with respect to whom such a violation occurs, imprisoned for not more than six months for the entire pattern or practice, or both, notwithstanding the provisions of any other Federal law relating to fine levels.

(2) Enjoining of pattern or practice violations

Whenever the Attorney General has reasonable cause to believe that a person or entity is engaged in a pattern or practice of employment, recruitment, or referral in violation of paragraph (1)(A) or (2) of subsection (a) of this section, the Attorney General may bring a civil action in the appropriate district court of the United States requesting such relief, including a permanent or temporary injunction, restraining order, or other order against the person or entity, as the Attorney General deems necessary.

* * *

§ 1324b.   Unfair immigration-related employment practices

(a) Prohibition of discrimination based on national origin or citizenship status

(1) General rule

It is an unfair immigration-related employment practice for a person or other entity to discriminate against any individual (other than an unauthorized alien, as defined in section 1324a(h)(3) of this section) with respect to the hiring, or recruitment or referral for a fee, of the individual for employment or the discharging of the individual from employment—

(A) because of such individual's national origin, or

(B) in the case of a protected individual (as defined in paragraph (3)), because of such individual's citizenship status.

(2) Exceptions

Paragraph (1) shall not apply to—

(A) a person or other entity that employs three or fewer employees,

(B) a person's or entity's discrimination because of an individual's national origin if the discrimination with respect to that person or entity and that individual is covered under section 2000e–2 of Title 42, or

(C) discrimination because of citizenship status which is otherwise required in order to comply with law, regulation, or executive order, or required by Federal, State, or local government contract, or which the Attorney General determines to be essential for an employer to do business with an agency or department of the Federal, State, or local government.

(3) Definition of protected individual

As used in paragraph (1), the term "protected individual" means an individual who—

    (A) is a citizen or national of the United States, or

    (B) is an alien who is lawfully admitted for permanent residence, is granted the status of an alien lawfully admitted for temporary residence under section 1160(a), or 1255a(a)(1) of this title, is admitted as a refugee under section 1157 of this title, or is granted asylum under section 1158 of this title; but does not include (i) an alien who fails to apply for naturalization within six months of the date the alien first becomes eligible (by virtue of period of lawful permanent residence) to apply for naturalization or, if later, within six months after November 6, 1986 and (ii) an alien who has applied on a timely basis, but has not been naturalized as a citizen within 2 years after the date of the application, unless the alien can establish that the alien is actively pursuing naturalization, except that time consumed in the Service's processing the application shall not be counted toward the 2–year period.

(4) Additional exception providing right to prefer equally qualified citizens

Notwithstanding any other provision of this section, it is not an unfair immigration-related employment practice for a person or other entity to prefer to hire, recruit, or refer an individual who is a citizen or national of the United States over another individual who is an alien if the two individuals are equally qualified.

(5) Prohibition of intimidation or retaliation

It is also an unfair immigration-related employment practice for a person or other entity to intimidate, threaten, coerce, or retaliate against any individual for the purpose of interfering with any right or privilege secured under this section or because the individual intends to file or has filed a charge or a complaint, testified, assisted, or participated in any manner in an investigation, proceeding, or hearing under this section. An individual so intimidated, threatened, coerced, or retaliated against shall be considered, for purposes of subsections (d) and (g) of this section, to have been discriminated against.

(6) Treatment of certain documentary practices as employ-ment practices

A person's or other entity's request, for purposes of satisfying the requirements of section 1324a(b) of this title, for more or different documents than are required under such section or refus-ing to honor documents tendered that on their face reasonably appear to be genuine shall be treated as an unfair immigration-related employment practice if made for the purpose or with the intent of discriminating against an individual in violation of para-graph (1).

(b) Charges of violations

(1) In general

Except as provided in paragraph (2), any person alleging that the person is adversely affected directly by an unfair immigration-related employment practice (or a person on that person's behalf) or an officer of the Service alleging that an unfair immigration-related employment practice has occurred or is occurring may file a charge respecting such practice or violation with the Special Counsel (ap-pointed under subsection (c) of this section). Charges shall be in writing under oath or affirmation and shall contain such informa-tion as the Attorney General requires. The Special Counsel by certified mail shall serve a notice of the charge (including the date, place, and circumstances of the alleged unfair immigration-related employment practice) on the person or entity involved within 10 days.

(2) No overlap with EEOC complaints

No charge may be filed respecting an unfair immigration-related employment practice described in subsection (a)(1)(A) of this section if a charge with respect to that practice based on the same set of facts has been filed with the Equal Employment Opportunity Com-mission under title VII of the Civil Rights Act of 1964 [42 U.S.C.A. § 2000e et seq.], unless the charge is dismissed as being outside the scope of such title. No charge respecting an employment practice may be filed with the Equal Employment Opportunity Commission under such title if a charge with respect to such practice based on the same set of facts has been filed under this subsection, unless the charge is dismissed under this section as being outside the scope of this section.

(c) Special Counsel

(1) Appointment

The President shall appoint, by and with the advice and consent of the Senate, a Special Counsel for Immigration–Related Unfair Employment Practices (hereinafter in this section referred to as the "Special Counsel") within the Department of Justice to serve for a term of four years. In the case of a vacancy in the office of the Special Counsel the President may designate the officer or employee who shall act as Special Counsel during such vacancy.

(2) Duties

The Special Counsel shall be responsible for investigation of charges and issuance of complaints under this section and in respect of the prosecution of all such complaints before administrative law judges and the exercise of certain functions under subsection (i)(1) of this section.

* * *

(d) Investigation of charges

(1) By Special Counsel

The Special Counsel shall investigate each charge received and, within 120 days of the date of the receipt of the charge, determine whether or not there is reasonable cause to believe that the charge is true and whether or not to bring a complaint with respect to the charge before an administrative law judge. The Special Counsel may, on his own initiative, conduct investigations respecting unfair immigration-related employment practices and, based on such an investigation and subject to paragraph (3), file a complaint before such a judge.

(2) Private actions

If the Special Counsel, after receiving such a charge respecting an unfair immigration-related employment practice which alleges knowing and intentional discriminatory activity or a pattern or practice of discriminatory activity, has not filed a complaint before an administrative law judge with respect to such charge within such 120–day period, the Special Counsel shall notify the person making the charge of the determination not to file such a complaint during such period and the person making the charge may (subject to paragraph (3)) file a complaint directly before such a judge within 90 days after the date of receipt of the notice. The Special Counsel's failure to file such a complaint within such 120–day period shall not affect the right of the Special Counsel to investigate the charge or to bring a complaint before an administrative law judge during such 90–day period.

(3) Time limitations on complaints

No complaint may be filed respecting any unfair immigration-related employment practice occurring more than 180 days prior to the date of the filing of the charge with the Special Counsel. This subparagraph shall not prevent the subsequent amending of a charge or complaint under subsection (e)(1) of this section.

(e) Hearings

(1) Notice

Whenever a complaint is made that a person or entity has engaged in or is engaging in any such unfair immigration-related employment practice, an administrative law judge shall have power to issue and cause to be served upon such person or entity a copy of the complaint and a notice of hearing before the judge at a place therein fixed, not less than five days after the serving of the complaint. Any such complaint may be amended by the judge conducting the hearing, upon the motion of the party filing the complaint, in the judge's discretion at any time prior to the issuance of an order based thereon. The person or entity so complained of shall have the right to file an answer to the original or amended complaint and to appear in person or otherwise and give testimony at the place and time fixed in the complaint.

(2) Judges hearing cases

Hearings on complaints under this subsection shall be considered before administrative law judges who are specially designated by the Attorney General as having special training respecting employment discrimination and, to the extent practicable, before such judges who only consider cases under this section.

(3) Complainant as party

Any person filing a charge with the Special Counsel respecting an unfair immigration-related employment practice shall be considered a party to any complaint before an administrative law judge respecting such practice and any subsequent appeal respecting that complaint. In the discretion of the judge conducting the hearing, any other person may be allowed to intervene in the proceeding and to present testimony.

* * *

(g) Determinations

(1) Order

The administrative law judge shall issue and cause to be served on the parties to the proceeding an order, which shall be final unless appealed as provided under subsection (i) of this section.

(2) Orders finding violations

(A) In general

If, upon the preponderance of the evidence, an administrative law judge determines that any person or entity named in the complaint has engaged in or is engaging in any such unfair immigration-related employment practice, then the judge shall state his findings of fact and shall issue and cause to be served on such person or entity an order which requires such person or entity to cease and desist from such unfair immigration-related employment practice.

(B) Contents of order

Such an order also may require the person or entity—

(i) to comply with the requirements of section 1324a(b) of this title with respect to individuals hired (or recruited or referred for employment for a fee) during a period of up to three years;

(ii) to retain for the period referred to in clause (i) and only for purposes consistent with section 1324a(b)(5) of this title, the name and address of each individual who applies, in person or in writing, for hiring for an existing position, or for recruiting or referring for a fee, for employment in the United States;

(iii) to hire individuals directly and adversely affected, with or without back pay;

(iv)(I) except as provided in subclauses (III) through (IV), to pay a civil penalty of not less than $250 and not more than $2,000 for each individual discriminated against,

(II) except as provided in subclauses (III) and (IV), in the case of a person or entity previously subject to a single

24

order under this paragraph, to pay a civil penalty of not less than $2,000 and not more than $5,000 for each individual discriminated against,

(III) except as provided in subclause (IV), in the case of a person or entity previously subject to more than one order under this paragraph, to pay a civil penalty of not less than $3,000 and not more than $10,000 for each individual discriminated against, and

(IV) in the case of an unfair immigration-related employment practice described in subsection (a)(6) of this section, to pay a civil penalty of not less than $100 and not more than $1,000 for each individual discriminated against;

(v) to post notices to employees about their rights under this section and employers' obligations under section 1324a of this title;

(vi) to educate all personnel involved in hiring and complying with this section or section 1324a of this title about the requirements of this section or such section;

(vii) to remove (in an appropriate case) a false performance review or false warning from an employee's personnel file; and

(viii) to lift (in an appropriate case) any restrictions on an employee's assignments, work shifts, or movements.

(C) Limitation on back pay remedy

In providing a remedy under subparagraph (B)(iii), back pay liability shall not accrue from a date more than two years prior to the date of the filing of a charge with the Special Counsel. Interim earnings or amounts earnable with reasonable diligence by the individual or individuals discriminated against shall operate to reduce the back pay otherwise allowable under such subparagraph. No order shall require the hiring of an individual as an employee or the payment to an individual of any back pay, if the individual was refused employment for any reason other than discrimination on account of national origin or citizenship status.

(D) Treatment of distinct entities

In applying this subsection in the case of a person or entity composed of distinct, physically separate subdivisions each of which provides separately for the hiring, recruiting, or referring for employment, without reference to the practices of, and not under the control of or common control with, another subdivision, each such subdivision shall be considered a separate person or entity.

* * *

(h) Awarding of attorney's fees

In any complaint respecting an unfair immigration-related employment practice, an administrative law judge, in the judge's discretion, may allow a prevailing party, other than the United States, a reasonable attorney's fee, if the losing party's argument is without reasonable foundation in law and fact.

(i) Review of final orders

(1) In general

Not later than 60 days after the entry of such final order, any person aggrieved by such final order may seek a review of such order in the United States court of appeals for the circuit in which the violation is alleged to have occurred or in which the employer resides or transacts business.

(2) Further review

Upon the filing of the record with the court, the jurisdiction of the court shall be exclusive and its judgment shall be final, except that the same shall be subject to review by the Supreme Court of the United States upon writ of certiorari or certification as provided in section 1254 of Title 28.

* * *

EMPLOYEE POLYGRAPH PROTECTION ACT

29 U.S.C. §§ 2001–2009

§ 2001. Definitions

As used in this chapter:

(1) Commerce.—The term "commerce" has the meaning provided by section 203(b) of this title.

(2) Employer.—The term "employer" includes any person acting directly or indirectly in the interest of an employer in relation to an employee or prospective employee.

(3) Lie detector.—The term "lie detector" includes a polygraph, deceptograph, voice stress analyzer, psychological stress evaluator, or any other similar device (whether mechanical or electrical) that is used, or the results of which are used, for the purpose of rendering a diagnostic opinion regarding the honesty or dishonesty of an individual.

(4) Polygraph.—The term "polygraph" means an instrument that—

   (A) records continuously, visually, permanently, and simultaneously changes in cardiovascular, respiratory, and electrodermal patterns as minimum instrumentation standards; and

   (B) is used, or the results of which are used, for the purpose of rendering a diagnostic opinion regarding the honesty or dishonesty of an individual.

(5) Secretary.—The term "Secretary" means the Secretary of Labor.

§ 2002. Prohibitions on lie detector use

Except as provided in sections 2006 and 2007 of this title, it shall be unlawful for any employer engaged in or affecting commerce or in the production of goods for commerce—

(1) directly or indirectly, to require, request, suggest, or cause any employee or prospective employee to take or submit to any lie detector test;

(2) to use, accept, refer to, or inquire concerning the results of any lie detector test of any employee or prospective employee;

(3) to discharge, discipline, discriminate against in any manner, or deny employment or promotion to, or threaten to take any such action against—

(A) any employee or prospective employee who refuses, declines, or fails to take or submit to any lie detector test, or

(B) any employee or prospective employee on the basis of the results of any lie detector test; or

(4) to discharge, discipline, discriminate against in any manner, or deny employment or promotion to, or threaten to take any such action against, any employee or prospective employee because—

(A) such employee or prospective employee has filed any complaint or instituted or caused to be instituted any proceeding under or related to this chapter,

(B) such employee or prospective employee has testified or is about to testify in any such proceeding, or

(C) of the exercise by such employee or prospective employee, on behalf of such employee or another person, of any right afforded by this chapter.

§ 2003. Notice of protection

The Secretary shall prepare, have printed, and distribute a notice setting forth excerpts from, or summaries of, the pertinent provisions of this chapter. Each employer shall post and maintain such notice in conspicuous places on its premises where notices to employees and applicants to employment are customarily posted.

§ 2004. Authority of the Secretary

(a) In general

The Secretary shall—

(1) issue such rules and regulations as may be necessary or appropriate to carry out this chapter;

(2) cooperate with regional, State, local, and other agencies, and cooperate with and furnish technical assistance to employers, labor organizations and employment agencies to aid in effectuating the purposes of this chapter; and

(3) make investigations and inspections and require the keeping of records necessary or appropriate for the administration of this chapter.

(b) Subpoena authority

For the purpose of any hearing or investigation under this chapter, the Secretary shall have the authority contained in sections 49 and 50 of Title 15.

§ 2005. Enforcement provisions

(a) Civil penalties

(1) In general

Subject to paragraph (2), any employer who violates any provision of this chapter may be assessed a civil penalty of not more than $10,000.

(2) Determination of amount

In determining the amount of any penalty under paragraph (1), the Secretary shall take into account the previous record of the person in terms of compliance, with this chapter and the gravity of the violation.

(3) Collection

Any civil penalty assessed under this subsection shall be collected in the same manner as is required by subsections (b) through (e) of section 1853 of this title with respect to civil penalties assessed under subsection (a) of such section.

(b) Injunctive actions by the Secretary

The Secretary may bring an action under this section to restrain violations of this chapter. The Solicitor of Labor may appear for and represent the Secretary in any litigation brought under this chapter. In any action brought under this section, the district courts of the United States shall have jurisdiction, for cause shown, to issued temporary or permanent restraining orders and injunctions to require compliance with this chapter, including such legal or equitable relief incident thereto as may be appropriate, including, but not limited to, employment, reinstatement, promotion, and the payment of lost wages and benefits.

(c) Private civil actions

(1) Liability

An employer who violated this chapter shall be liable to the employee or prospective employee affected by such violation. Such employer shall be liable for such legal or equitable relief as may be appropriate, including, but not limited to, employment, reinstatement, promotion, and the payment of lost wages and benefits.

(2) Court

An action to recover the liability prescribed in paragraph (1) may be maintained against the employer in any Federal or State court of competent jurisdiction by an employee or prospective employee for or on behalf of such employee, prospective employee, and other employees or prospective employees similarly situated. No such action may be commenced more than 3 years after the date of the alleged violation.

(3) Costs

The court, in its discretion, may allow the prevailing party (other than the United States) reasonable costs, including attorney's fees.

(d) Waiver of rights prohibited

The rights and procedures provided by this chapter may not be waived by contract or otherwise, unless such waiver is part of a written settlement agreed to and signed by the parties to the pending action or complaint under this chapter.

§ 2006. Exemptions

(a) No application to Governmental employers

This chapter shall not apply with respect to the United States Government, any State or local government, or any political subdivision of a State or local government.

(b) National defense and security exemption

(1) National defense

Nothing in this chapter shall be construed to prohibit the administration, by the Federal Government, in the performance of any counterintelligence function, of any lie detector test to—

    (A) any expert or consultant under contract to the Department of Defense or any employee of any contractor of such Department; or

    (B) any expert or consultant under contract with the Department of Energy in connection with the atomic energy defense activities of such Department or any employee of any contractor of such Department in connection with such activities.

(2) Security

Nothing in this chapter shall be construed to prohibit the administration, by the Federal Government, in the performance of any intelligence or counterintelligence function, of any lie detector test to—

    (A)(i) any individual employed by, assigned to, or detailed to, the National Security Agency, the Defense Intelligence Agency, or the Central Intelligence Agency,

(ii) any expert or consultant under contract to any such agency,

(iii) any employee of a contractor to any such agency,

(iv) any individual applying for a position in any such agency, or

(v) any individual assigned to a space where sensitive cryptologic information is produced, processed, or stored for any such agency; or

(B) any expert, or consultant (or employee of such expert or consultant) under contract with any Federal Government department, agency, or program whose duties involve access to information that has been classified at the level of top secret or designed as being within a special access program under the section 4.2(a) of Executive Order 12356 (or a successor Executive order).

(c) FBI contractors exemption

Nothing in this chapter shall be construed to prohibit the administration, by the Federal Government, in the performance of any counterintelligence function, of any lie detector test to an employee of a contractor of the Federal Bureau of Investigation of the Department of Justice who is engaged in the performance of any work under the contract with such Bureau.

(d) Limited exemption for ongoing investigations

Subject to sections 2007 and 2009 of this title, this chapter shall not prohibit an employer from requesting an employee to submit to a polygraph test if—

(1) the test is administered in connection with an ongoing investigation involving economic loss or injury to the employer's business, such as theft, embezzlement, misappropriation, or an act of unlawful industrial espionage or sabotage;

(2) the employee had access to the property that is the subject of the investigation;

(3) the employer has a reasonable suspicion that the employee was involved in the incident or activity under investigation; and

(4) the employer executes a statement, provided to the examinee before the test, that—

(A) sets forth with particularity the specific incident or activity being investigated and the basis for testing particular employees,

(B) is signed by a person (other than a polygraph examiner) authorized to legally bind the employer,

(C) is retained by the employer for at least 3 years, and

(D) contains at a minimum—

> **(i)** an identification of the specific economic loss or injury to the business of the employer,

> **(ii)** a statement indicating that the employee had access to the property that is the subject of the investigation, and

> **(iii)** a statement describing the basis of the employer's reasonable suspicion that the employee was involved in the incident or activity under investigation.

(e) Exemption for security services

(1) In general

Subject to paragraph (2) and sections 2007 and 2009 of this title, this chapter shall not prohibit the use of polygraph tests on prospective employees by any private employer whose primary business purpose consists of providing armored car personnel, personnel engaged in the design, installation, and maintenance of security alarm systems, or other uniformed or plainclothes security personnel and whose function includes protection of—

> **(A)** facilities, materials, or operations having a significant impact on the health or safety of any State or political subdivision thereof, or the national security of the United States, as determined under rules and regulations issued by the Secretary within 90 days after June 27, 1988, including—

>> **(i)** facilities engaged in the production, transmission, or distribution of electric or nuclear power,

>> **(ii)** public water supply facilities,

>> **(iii)** shipments or storage of radioactive or other toxic waste materials, and

>> **(iv)** public transportation, or

> **(B)** currency, negotiable securities, precious commodities or instruments, or proprietary information.

(2) Access

The exemption provided under this subsection shall not apply if the test is administered to a prospective employee who would not be employed to protect facilities, materials, operations, or assets referred to in paragraph (1).

(f) Exemption for drug security, drug theft, or drug diversion investigations

(1) In general

Subject to paragraph (2) and sections 2007 and 2009 of this title, this chapter shall not prohibit the use of a polygraph test by any employer authorized to manufacture, distribute, or dispense a controlled substance listed in schedule I, II, III, or IV of section 812 of Title 21.

(2) Access

The exemption provided under this subsection shall apply—

(A) if the test is administered to a prospective employee who would have direct access to the manufacture, storage, distribution, or sale of any such controlled substance; or

(B) in the case of a test administered to a current employee, if—

(i) the test is administered in connection with an ongoing investigation of criminal or other misconduct involving, or potentially involving, loss or injury to the manufacture, distribution, or dispensing of any such controlled substance by such employer, and

(ii) the employee had access to the person or property that is the subject of the investigation.

§ 2007. Restrictions on use of exemptions

(a) Test as basis for adverse employment action

(1) Under ongoing investigations exemption

Except as provided in paragraph (2), the exemption under subsection (d) of section 2006 of this title shall not apply if an employee is discharged, disciplined, denied employment or promotion, or otherwise discriminated against in any manner on the basis of the analysis of a polygraph test chart or the refusal to take a polygraph test, without additional supporting evidence. The evidence required by such subsection may serve as additional supporting evidence.

(2) Under other exemptions

In the case of an exemption described in subsection (e) or (f) of such section, the exemption shall not apply if the results of an analysis of a polygraph test chart are used, or the refusal to take a polygraph test is used, as the sole basis upon which an adverse employment action described in paragraph (1) is taken against an employee or prospective employee.

(b) Rights of examinee

The exemptions provided under subsections (d), (e), and (f) of section 2006 of this title shall not apply unless the requirements described in the following paragraphs are met:

(1) All phases

Throughout all phases of the test—

(A) the examinee shall be permitted to terminate the test at any time;

(B) the examinee is not asked questions in a manner designed to degrade, or needlessly intrude on, such examinee;

(C) the examinee is not asked any question concerning—

(i) religious beliefs or affiliations,

(ii) beliefs or opinions regarding racial matters,

(iii) political beliefs or affiliations,

(iv) any matter relating to sexual behavior; and

(v) beliefs, affiliations, opinions, or lawful activities regarding unions or labor organizations; and

(D) the examiner does not conduct the test if there is sufficient written evidence by a physician that the examinee is suffering from a medical or psychological condition or undergoing treatment that might cause abnormal responses during the actual testing phase.

(2) Pretest phase

During the pretest phase, the prospective examinee—

(A) is provided with reasonable written notice of the date, time, and location of the test, and of such examinee's right to obtain and consult with legal counsel or an employee representative before each phase of the test;

(B) is informed in writing of the nature and characteristics of the tests and of the instruments involved;

(C) is informed, in writing—

(i) whether the testing area contains a two-way mirror, a camera, or any other device through which the test can be observed,

(ii) whether any other device, including any device for recording or monitoring the test, will be used, or

(iii) that the employer or the examinee may (with mutual knowledge) make a recording of the test;

(D) is read and signs a written notice informing such examinee—

(i) that the examinee cannot be required to take the test as a condition of employment,

(ii) that any statement made during the test may constitute additional supporting evidence for the purposes of an adverse employment action described in subsection (a) of this section,

(iii) of the limitations imposed under this section,

(iv) of the legal rights and remedies available to the examinee if the polygraph test is not conducted in accordance with this chapter, and

(v) of the legal rights and remedies of the employer under this chapter (including the rights of the employer under section 2008(c)(2) of this title); and

(E) is provided an opportunity to review all questions to be asked during the test and is informed of the right to terminate the test at any time.

(3) Actual testing phase

During the actual testing phase, the examiner does not ask such examinee any question relevant during the test that was not presented in writing for review to such examinee before the test.

(4) Post-test phase

Before any adverse employment action, the employer shall—

(A) further interview the examinee on the basis of the results of the test; and

(B) provide the examinee with—

(i) a written copy of any opinion or conclusion rendered as a result of the test, and

(ii) a copy of the questions asked during the test along with the corresponding charted responses.

(5) Maximum number and minimum duration of tests

The examiner shall not conduct and complete more than five polygraph tests on a calendar day on which the test is given, and shall not conduct any such test for less than a 90-minute duration.

(c) Qualifications and requirements of examiners

The exemptions provided under subsections (d), (e), and (f) of section 2006 of this title shall not apply unless the individual who conducts the polygraph test satisfies the requirements under the following paragraphs:

(1) Qualifications

The examiner—

(A) has a valid and current license granted by licensing and regulatory authorities in the State in which the test is to be conducted, if so required by the State; and

(B) maintains a minimum of a $50,000 bond or an equivalent amount of professional liability coverage.

(2) Requirements

The examiner—

(A) renders any opinion or conclusion regarding the test—

(i) in writing and solely on the basis of an analysis of polygraph test charts,

(ii) that does not contain information other than admissions, information, case facts and interpretation of the charts relevant to the purpose and stated objectives of the test, and

(iii) that does not include any recommendation concerning the employment of the examinee; and

(B) maintains all opinions, reports, charts, written questions, lists, and other records relating to the test for a minimum period of 3 years after administration of the test.

§ 2008.　Disclosure of information

(a) In general

A person, other than the examinee, may not disclose information obtained during a polygraph test, except as provided in this section.

(b) Permitted disclosures

A polygraph examiner may disclose information acquired from a polygraph test only to—

(1) the examinee or any other person specifically designed in writing by the examinee;

(2) the employer that requested the test; or

(3) any court, governmental agency, arbitrator, or mediator, in accordance with due process of law, pursuant to an order from a court of competent jurisdiction.

(c) Disclosure by employer

An employer (other than an employer described in subsection (a), (b), or (c) of section 2006 of this title) for whom a polygraph test is conducted may disclose information from the test only to—

(1) a person in accordance with subsection (b) of this section; or

(2) a governmental agency, but only insofar as the disclosed information is an admission of criminal conduct.

§ 2009. Effect on other laws and agreements

Except as provided in subsections (a), (b), and (c) of section 2006 of this title, this chapter shall not preempt any provision of any State or local law or of any negotiated collective bargaining agreement that prohibits lie detector tests or is more restrictive with respect to lie detector tests than any provision of this chapter.

CIVIL RIGHTS ACT OF 1964, TITLE VII

42 U.S.C. §§ 2000e to 2000e–17

Sec. 701 (§ 2000e) Definitions

For the purposes of this subchapter—

(a) The term "person" includes one or more individuals, governments, governmental agencies, political subdivisions, labor unions, partnerships, associations, corporations, legal representatives, mutual companies, joint-stock companies, trusts, unincorporated organizations, trustees, trustees in cases under Title 11, or receivers.

(b) The term "employer" means a person engaged in an industry affecting commerce who has fifteen or more employees for each working day in each of twenty or more calendar weeks in the current or preceding calendar year, and any agent of such a person, but such term does not include (1) the United States, a corporation wholly owned by the Government of the United States, an Indian tribe, or any department or agency of the District of Columbia subject by statute to procedures of the competitive service (as defined in section 2102 of Title 5), or (2) a bona fide private membership club (other than a labor organization) which is exempt from taxation under section 501(c) of Title 26, except that during the first year after March 24, 1972, persons having fewer than twenty-five employees (and their agents) shall not be considered employers.

(c) The term "employment agency" means any person regularly undertaking with or without compensation to procure employees for an employer or to procure for employees opportunities to work for an employer and includes an agent of such a person.

(d) The term "labor organization" means a labor organization engaged in an industry affecting commerce, and any agent of such an organization, and includes any organization of any kind, any agency, or employee representation committee, group, association, or plan so engaged in which employees participate and which exists for the purpose, in whole or in part, of dealing with employers concerning grievances, labor disputes, wages, rates of pay, hours, or other terms or conditions of employment, and any conference, general committee, joint or system board, or joint council so engaged which is subordinate to a national or international labor organization.

* * *

38

(f) The term "employee" means an individual employed by an employer, except that the term "employee" shall not include any person elected to public office in any State or political subdivision of any State by the qualified voters thereof, or any person chosen by such officer to be on such officer's personal staff, or an appointee on the policy making level or an immediate adviser with respect to the exercise of the constitutional or legal powers of the office. The exemption set forth in the preceding sentence shall not include employees subject to the civil service laws of a State government, governmental agency or political subdivision. With respect to employment in a foreign country, such term includes an individual who is a citizen of the United States.

* * *

(j) The term "religion" includes all aspects of religious observance and practice, as well as belief, unless an employer demonstrates that he is unable to reasonably accommodate to an employee's or prospective employee's religious observance or practice without undue hardship on the conduct of the employer's business.

(k) The terms "because of sex" or "on the basis of sex" include, but are not limited to, because of or on the basis of pregnancy, childbirth, or related medical conditions; and women affected by pregnancy, childbirth, or related medical conditions shall be treated the same for all employment-related purposes, including receipt of benefits under fringe benefit programs, as other persons not so affected but similar in their ability or inability to work, and nothing in section 2000e–2(h) of this title shall be interpreted to permit otherwise. This subsection shall not require an employer to pay for health insurance benefits for abortion, except where the life of the mother would be endangered if the fetus were carried to term, or except where medical complications have arisen from an abortion: *Provided,* That nothing herein shall preclude an employer from providing abortion benefits or otherwise affect bargaining agreements in regard to abortion.

(*l*) The term "complaining party" means the Commission, the Attorney General, or a person who may bring an action or proceeding under this title.

(m) The term "demonstrates" means meets the burdens of production and persuasion.

(n) The term "respondent" means an employer, employment agency, labor organization, joint labor-management committee controlling apprenticeship or other training or retraining program, including an on-the-job training program, or Federal entity subject to section 717.

SEC. 702 (§ 2000e–1) **Subchapter not applicable to employment of aliens outside State and individuals for performance of activities of religious corporations, associations, educational institutions, or societies**

(a) This subchapter shall not apply to an employer with respect to the employment of aliens outside any State, or to a religious corporation, association, educational institution, or society with respect to the employment of individuals of a particular religion to perform work connected with the carrying on by such corporation, association, educational institution, or society of its activities.

(b) It shall not be unlawful under section 703 or 704 for an employer (or a corporation controlled by an employer), labor organization, employment agency, or joint labor-management committee controlling apprenticeship or other training or retraining (including on-the-job training programs) to take any action otherwise prohibited by such section, with respect to an employee in a workplace in a foreign country if compliance with such section would cause such employer (or such corporation), such organization, such agency, or such committee to violate the law of the foreign country in which such workplace is located.

(c)(1) If an employer controls a corporation whose place of incorporation is a foreign country, any practice prohibited by section 703 or 704 engaged in by such corporation shall be presumed to be engaged in by such employer.

(2) Sections 703 and 704 shall not apply with respect to the foreign operations of an employer that is a foreign person not controlled by an American employer.

(3) For purposes of this subsection, the determination of whether an employer controls a corporation shall be based on—

    (A) the interrelation of operations;

    (B) the common management;

    (C) the centralized control of labor relations; and

    (D) the common ownership or financial control, of the employer and the corporation.

SEC. 703 (§ 2000e–2) **Unlawful employment practices**

(a) Employer practices

It shall be an unlawful employment practice for an employer—

(1) to fail or refuse to hire or to discharge any individual, or otherwise to discriminate against any individual with respect to his compensation, terms, conditions, or privileges of employment, because of such individual's race, color, religion, sex, or national origin; or

(2) to limit, segregate, or classify his employees or applicants for employment in any way which would deprive or tend to deprive any individual of employment opportunities or otherwise adversely affect his status as an employee, because of such individual's race, color, religion, sex, or national origin.

(b) Employment agency practices

It shall be an unlawful employment practice for an employment agency to fail or refuse to refer for employment, or otherwise to discriminate against, any individual because of his race, color, religion, sex, or national origin, or to classify or refer for employment any individual on the basis of his race, color, religion, sex, or national origin.

(c) Labor organization practices

It shall be an unlawful employment practice for a labor organization—

(1) to exclude or to expel from its membership, or otherwise to discriminate against, any individual because of his race, color, religion, sex, or national origin;

(2) to limit, segregate, or classify its membership or applicants for membership, or to classify or fail or refuse to refer for employment any individual, in any way which would deprive or tend to deprive any individual of employment opportunities, or would limit such employment opportunities or otherwise adversely affect his status as an employee or as an applicant for employment, because of such individual's race, color, religion, sex, or national origin; or

(3) to cause or attempt to cause an employer to discriminate against an individual in violation of this section.

(d) Training programs

It shall be an unlawful employment practice for any employer, labor organization, or joint labor-management committee controlling apprenticeship or other training or retraining, including on-the-job training programs to discriminate against any individual because of his race, color, religion, sex, or national origin in admission to, or employment in, any program established to provide apprenticeship or other training.

(e) Businesses or enterprises with personnel qualified on basis of religion, sex, or national origin; educational institutions with personnel of particular religion

Notwithstanding any other provision of this subchapter, (1) it shall not be an unlawful employment practice for an employer to hire and employ employees, for an employment agency to classify, or refer for employment any individual, for a labor organization to classify its membership or to classify or refer for employment any individual, or for

41

an employer, labor organization, or joint labor-management committee controlling apprenticeship or other training or retraining programs to admit or employ any individual in any such program, on the basis of his religion, sex, or national origin in those certain instances where religion, sex, or national origin is a bona fide occupational qualification reasonably necessary to the normal operation of that particular business or enterprise, and (2) it shall not be an unlawful employment practice for a school, college, university, or other educational institution or institution of learning to hire and employ employees of a particular religion if such school, college, university, or other educational institution or institution of learning is, in whole or in substantial part, owned, supported, controlled, or managed by a particular religion or by a particular religious corporation, association, or society, or if the curriculum of such school, college, university, or other educational institution or institution of learning is directed toward the propagation of a particular religion.

(f) Members of Communist Party or Communist-action or Communist-front organizations

As used in this subchapter, the phrase "unlawful employment practice" shall not be deemed to include any action or measure taken by an employer, labor organization, joint labor-management committee, or employment agency with respect to an individual who is a member of the Communist Party of the United States or of any other organization required to register as a Communist-action or Communist-front organization by final order of the Subversive Activities Control Board pursuant to the Subversive Activities Control Act of 1950 [50 U.S.C.A. § 781 et seq.].

(g) National security

Notwithstanding any other provision of this subchapter, it shall not be an unlawful employment practice for an employer to fail or refuse to hire and employ any individual for any position, for an employer to discharge any individual from any position, or for an employment agency to fail or refuse to refer any individual for employment in any position, or for a labor organization to fail or refuse to refer any individual for employment in any position, if—

(1) the occupancy of such position, or access to the premises in or upon which any part of the duties of such position is performed or is to be performed, is subject to any requirement imposed in the interest of the national security of the United States under any security program in effect pursuant to or administered under any statute of the United States or any Executive order of the President; and

(2) such individual has not fulfilled or has ceased to fulfill that requirement.

(h) Seniority or merit system; quantity or quality of production; ability tests; compensation based on sex and authorized by minimum wage provisions

Notwithstanding any other provision of this subchapter, it shall not be an unlawful employment practice for an employer to apply different standards of compensation, or different terms, conditions, or privileges of employment pursuant to a bona fide seniority or merit system, or a system which measures earnings by quantity or quality of production or to employees who work in different locations, provided that such differences are not the result of an intention to discriminate because of race, color, religion, sex, or national origin, nor shall it be an unlawful employment practice for an employer to give and to act upon the results of any professionally developed ability test provided that such test, its administration or action upon the results is not designed, intended or used to discriminate because of race, color, religion, sex or national origin. It shall not be an unlawful employment practice under this subchapter for any employer to differentiate upon the basis of sex in determining the amount of the wages or compensation paid or to be paid to employees of such employer if such differentiation is authorized by the provisions of section 206(d) of Title 29.

(i) Businesses or enterprises extending preferential treatment to Indians

Nothing contained in this subchapter shall apply to any business or enterprise on or near an Indian reservation with respect to any publicly announced employment practice of such business or enterprise under which a preferential treatment is given to any individual because he is an Indian living on or near a reservation.

(j) Preferential treatment not to be granted on account of existing number or percentage imbalance

Nothing contained in this subchapter shall be interpreted to require any employer, employment agency, labor organization, or joint labor-management committee subject to this subchapter to grant preferential treatment to any individual or to any group because of the race, color, religion, sex, or national origin of such individual or group on account of an imbalance which may exist with respect to the total number or percentage of persons of any race, color, religion, sex, or national origin employed by any employer, referred or classified for employment by any employment agency or labor organization, admitted to membership or classified by any labor organization, or admitted to, or employed in, any apprenticeship or other training program, in comparison with the total number or percentage of persons of such race, color, religion, sex, or national origin in any community, State, section, or other area, or in the available work force in any community, State, section, or other area.

(k)(1)(A) An unlawful employment practice based on disparate impact is established under this title only if—

(i) a complaining party demonstrates that a respondent uses a particular employment practice that causes a disparate impact on the basis of race, color, religion, sex, or national origin and the respondent fails to demonstrate that the challenged practice is job related for the position in question and consistent with business necessity; or

(ii) the complaining party makes the demonstration described in subparagraph (C) with respect to an alternative employment practice and the respondent refuses to adopt such alternative employment practice.

(B)(i) With respect to demonstrating that a particular employment practice causes a disparate impact as described in subparagraph (A)(i), the complaining party shall demonstrate that each particular challenged employment practice causes a disparate impact, except that if the complaining party can demonstrate to the court that the elements of a respondent's decisionmaking process are not capable of separation for analysis, the decisionmaking process may be analyzed as one employment practice.

(ii) If the respondent demonstrates that a specific employment practice does not cause the disparate impact, the respondent shall not be required to demonstrate that such practice is required by business necessity.

(C) The demonstration referred to by subparagraph (A)(ii) shall be in accordance with the law as it existed on June 4, 1989, with respect to the concept of "alternative employment practice".

(2) A demonstration that an employment practice is required by business necessity may not be used as a defense against a claim of intentional discrimination under this title.

(3) Notwithstanding any other provision of this title, a rule barring the employment of an individual who currently and knowingly uses or possesses a controlled substance, as defined in schedules I and II of section 102(6) of the Controlled Substances Act (21 U.S.C. 802(6)), other than the use or possession of a drug taken under the supervision of a licensed health care professional, or any other use or possession authorized by the Controlled Substances Act or any other provision of Federal law, shall be considered an unlawful employment practice under this title only if such rule is adopted or applied with an intent to discriminate because of race, color, religion, sex, or national origin. * * *

(*l*) It shall be an unlawful employment practice for a respondent, in connection with the selection or referral of applicants or candidates for employment or promotion, to adjust the scores of, use different cutoff scores for, or otherwise alter the results of, employment related tests on the basis of race, color, religion, sex, or national origin.

* * *

(m) Except as otherwise provided in this title, an unlawful employment practice is established when the complaining party demonstrates that race, color, religion, sex, or national origin was a motivating factor for any employment practice, even though other factors also motivated the practice.

* * *

(n)(1)(A) Notwithstanding any other provision of law, and except as provided in paragraph (2), an employment practice that implements and is within the scope of a litigated or consent judgment or order that resolves a claim of employment discrimination under the Constitution or Federal civil rights laws may not be challenged under the circumstances described in subparagraph (B).

(B) A practice described in subparagraph (A) may not be challenged in a claim under the Constitution or Federal civil rights laws—

(i) by a person who, prior to the entry of the judgment or order described in subparagraph (A), had—

(I) actual notice of the proposed judgment or order sufficient to apprise such person that such judgment or order might adversely affect the interests and legal rights of such person and that an opportunity was available to present objections to such judgment or order by a future date certain; and

(II) a reasonable opportunity to present objections to such judgment or order; or

(ii) by a person whose interests were adequately represented by another person who had previously challenged the judgment or order on the same legal grounds and with a similar factual situation, unless there has been an intervening change in law or fact.

(2) Nothing in this subsection shall be construed to—

(A) alter the standards for intervention under rule 24 of the Federal Rules of Civil Procedure or apply to the rights of parties who have successfully intervened pursuant to such rule in the proceeding in which the parties intervened;

(B) apply to the rights of parties to the action in which a litigated or consent judgment or order was entered, or of members of a class represented or sought to be represented in such action, or of members of a group on whose behalf relief was sought in such action by the Federal Government;

(C) prevent challenges to a litigated or consent judgment or order on the ground that such judgment or order was obtained through collusion or fraud, or is transparently invalid or was entered by a court lacking subject matter jurisdiction; or

(D) authorize or permit the denial to any person of the due process of law required by the Constitution.

(3) Any action not precluded under this subsection that challenges an employment consent judgment or order described in paragraph (1) shall be brought in the court, and if possible before the judge, that entered such judgment or order. Nothing in this subsection shall preclude a transfer of such action pursuant to section 1404 of title 28, United States Code.

Sec. 704 (§ 2000e–3) Other unlawful employment practices

(a) Discrimination for making charges, testifying, assisting, or participating in enforcement proceedings

It shall be an unlawful employment practice for an employer to discriminate against any of his employees or applicants for employment, for an employment agency, or joint labor-management committee controlling apprenticeship or other training or retraining, including on-the-job training programs, to discriminate against any individual, or for a labor organization to discriminate against any member thereof or applicant for membership, because he has opposed any practice made an unlawful employment practice by this subchapter, or because he has made a charge, testified, assisted, or participated in any manner in an investigation, proceeding, or hearing under this subchapter.

(b) Printing or publication of notices or advertisements indicating prohibited preference, limitation, specification, or discrimination; occupational qualification exception

It shall be an unlawful employment practice for an employer, labor organization, employment agency, or joint labor-management committee controlling apprenticeship or other training or retraining, including on-the-job training programs, to print or publish or cause to be printed or published any notice or advertisement relating to employment by such an employer or membership in or any classification or referral for employment by such a labor organization, or relating to any classification or referral for employment by such an employment agency, or relating to admission to, or employment in, any program established to provide apprenticeship or other training by such a joint labor-management committee, indicating any preference, limitation, specification, or discrimination, based on race, color, religion, sex, or national origin, except that such a notice or advertisement may indicate a preference, limitation, specification, or discrimination based on religion, sex, or national origin when religion, sex, or national origin is a bona fide occupational qualification for employment.

SEC. 706 (§ 2000e–5) Enforcement provisions

(a) Power of Commission to prevent unlawful employment practices

The Commission is empowered, as hereinafter provided; to prevent any person from engaging in any unlawful employment practice as set forth in section 2000e–2 or 2000e–3 of this title.

(b) Charges by persons aggrieved or member of Commission of unlawful employment practices by employers, etc.; filing; allegations; notice to respondent; contents of notice; investigation by Commission; contents of charges; prohibition on disclosure of charges; determination of reasonable cause; conference, conciliation, and persuasion for elimination of unlawful practices; prohibition on disclosure of informal endeavors to end unlawful practices; use of evidence in subsequent proceedings; penalties for disclosure of information; time for determination of reasonable cause

Whenever a charge is filed by or on behalf of a person claiming to be aggrieved, or by a member of the Commission, alleging that an employer, employment agency, labor organization, or joint labor-management committee controlling apprenticeship or other training or retraining, including on-the-job training programs, has engaged in an unlawful employment practice, the Commission shall serve a notice of the charge (including the date, place and circumstances of the alleged unlawful employment practice) on such employer, employment agency, labor organization, or joint labor-management committee (hereinafter referred to as the "respondent") within ten days, and shall make an investigation thereof. Charges shall be in writing under oath or affirmation and shall contain such information and be in such form as the Commission requires. Charges shall not be made public by the Commission. If the Commission determines after such investigation that there is not reasonable cause to believe that the charge is true, it shall dismiss the charge and promptly notify the person claiming to be aggrieved and the respondent of its action. In determining whether reasonable cause exists, the Commission shall accord substantial weight to final findings and orders made by State or local authorities in proceedings commenced under State or local law pursuant to the requirements of subsections (c) and (d) of this section. If the Commission determines after such investigation that there is reasonable cause to believe that the charge is true, the Commission shall endeavor to eliminate any such alleged unlawful employment practice by informal methods of conference, conciliation, and persuasion. Nothing said or done during and as a part of such informal endeavors may be made public by the Commission, its officers or employees, or used as evidence in a subsequent proceeding without the written consent of the persons concerned. Any person who makes public information in violation of this subsection shall be fined not more than $1,000 or imprisoned for not more than one year, or both. The Commission shall make its determination on reasonable cause as promptly as possible and, so far as practicable, not later than one hundred and twenty days from the filing of the charge or, where applicable under subsection (c) or (d) of this section, from the date upon which the Commission is authorized to take action with respect to the charge.

(c)   State or local enforcement proceedings; notification of State or local authority; time for filing charges with Commission; commencement of proceedings

In the case of an alleged unlawful employment practice occurring in a State, or political subdivision of a State, which has a State or local law prohibiting the unlawful employment practice alleged and establishing or authorizing a State or local authority to grant or seek relief from such practice or to institute criminal proceedings with respect thereto upon receiving notice thereof, no charge may be filed under subsection (b) of this section by the person aggrieved before the expiration of sixty days after proceedings have been commenced under the State or local law, unless such proceedings have been earlier terminated, provided that such sixty-day period shall be extended to one hundred and twenty days during the first year after the effective date of such State or local law. If any requirement for the commencement of such proceedings is imposed by a State or local authority other than a requirement of the filing of a written and signed statement of the facts upon which the proceeding is based, the proceeding shall be deemed to have been commenced for the purposes of this subsection at the time such statement is sent by registered mail to the appropriate State or local authority.

(d)   State or local enforcement proceedings; notification of State or local authority; time for action on charges by Commission

In the case of any charge filed by a member of the Commission alleging an unlawful employment practice occurring in a State or political subdivision of a State which has a State or local law prohibiting the practice alleged and establishing or authorizing a State or local authority to grant or seek relief from such practice or to institute criminal proceedings with respect thereto upon receiving notice thereof, the

Commission shall, before taking any action with respect to such charge, notify the appropriate State or local officials and, upon request, afford them a reasonable time, but not less than sixty days (provided that such sixty-day period shall be extended to one hundred and twenty days during the first year after the effective day of such State or local law), unless a shorter period is requested, to act under such State or local law to remedy the practice alleged.

(e) Time for filing charges; time for service of notice of charge on respondent; filing of charge by Commission with State or local agency

(1) A charge under this section shall be filed within one hundred and eighty days after the alleged unlawful employment practice occurred and notice of the charge (including the date, place and circumstances of the alleged unlawful employment practice) shall be served upon the person against whom such charge is made within ten days thereafter, except that in a case of an unlawful employment practice with respect to which the person aggrieved has initially instituted proceedings with a State or local agency with authority to grant or seek relief from such practice or to institute criminal proceedings with respect thereto upon receiving notice thereof, such charge shall be filed by or on behalf of the person aggrieved within three hundred days after the alleged unlawful employment practice occurred, or within thirty days after receiving notice that the State or local agency has terminated the proceedings under the State or local law, whichever is earlier, and a copy of such charge shall be filed by the Commission with the State or local agency.

(2) For purposes of this section, an unlawful employment practice occurs, with respect to a seniority system that has been adopted for an intentionally discriminatory purpose in violation of this title (whether or not that discriminatory purpose is apparent on the face of the seniority provision), when the seniority system is adopted, when an individual becomes subject to the seniority system, or when a person aggrieved is injured by the application of the seniority system or provision of the system.

(f) Civil action by Commission, Attorney General, or person aggrieved; preconditions; procedure; appointment of attorney; payment of fees, costs, or security; intervention; stay of Federal proceedings; action for appropriate temporary or preliminary relief pending final disposition of charge; jurisdiction and venue of United States courts; designation of judge to hear and determine case; assignment of case for hearing; expedition of case; appointment of master

(1) If within thirty days after a charge is filed with the Commission or within thirty days after expiration of any period of reference under

subsection (c) or (d) of this section, the Commission has been unable to secure from the respondent a conciliation agreement acceptable to the Commission, the Commission may bring a civil action against any respondent not a government, governmental agency, or political subdivision named in the charge. In the case of a respondent which is a government, governmental agency, or political subdivision, if the Commission has been unable to secure from the respondent a conciliation agreement acceptable to the Commission, the Commission shall take no further action and shall refer the case to the Attorney General who may bring a civil action against such respondent in the appropriate United States district court. The person or persons aggrieved shall have the right to intervene in a civil action brought by the Commission or the Attorney General in a case involving a government, governmental agency, or political subdivision. If a charge filed with the Commission pursuant to subsection (b) of this section is dismissed by the Commission, or if within one hundred and eighty days from the filing of such charge or the expiration of any period of reference under subsection (c) or (d) of this section, whichever is later, the Commission has not filed a civil action under this section or the Attorney General has not filed a civil action in a case involving a government, governmental agency, or political subdivision, or the Commission has not entered into a conciliation agreement to which the person aggrieved is a party, the Commission, or the Attorney General in a case involving a government, governmental agency, or political subdivision, shall so notify the person aggrieved and within ninety days after the giving of such notice a civil action may be brought against the respondent named in the charge (A) by the person claiming to be aggrieved or (B) if such charge was filed by a member of the Commission, by any person whom the charge alleges was aggrieved by the alleged unlawful employment practice.
* * *

(2) Whenever a charge is filed with the Commission and the Commission concludes on the basis of a preliminary investigation that prompt judicial action is necessary to carry out the purposes of this Act, the Commission, or the Attorney General in a case involving a government, governmental agency, or political subdivision, may bring an action for appropriate temporary or preliminary relief pending final disposition of such charge. * * *

(3) Each United States district court and each United States court of a place subject to the jurisdiction of the United States shall have jurisdiction of actions brought under this subchapter. Such an action may be brought in any judicial district in the State in which the unlawful employment practice is alleged to have been committed, in the judicial district in which the employment records relevant to such practice are maintained and administered, or in the judicial district in which the

aggrieved person would have worked but for the alleged unlawful employment practice, but if the respondent is not found within any such district, such an action may be brought within the judicial district in which the respondent has his principal office. * * *

* * *

(g) Injunctions; appropriate affirmative action; equitable relief; accrual of back pay; reduction of back pay; limitations on judicial orders

(1) If the court finds that the respondent has intentionally engaged in or is intentionally engaging in an unlawful employment practice charged in the complaint, the court may enjoin the respondent from engaging in such unlawful employment practice, and order such affirmative action as may be appropriate, which may include, but is not limited to, reinstatement or hiring of employees, with or without back pay (payable by the employer, employment agency, or labor organization, as the case may be, responsible for the unlawful employment practice), or any other equitable relief as the court deems appropriate. Back pay liability shall not accrue from a date more than two years prior to the filing of a charge with the Commission. Interim earnings or amounts earnable with reasonable diligence by the person or persons discriminated against shall operate to reduce the back pay otherwise allowable.

(2)(A) No order of the court shall require the admission or reinstatement of an individual as a member of a union, or the hiring, reinstatement, or promotion of an individual as an employee, or the payment to him of any back pay, if such individual was refused admission, suspended, or expelled, or was refused employment or advancement or was suspended or discharged for any reason other than discrimination on account of race, color, religion, sex, or national origin or in violation of section 2000e–3(a) of this title.

(B) On a claim in which an individual proves a violation under section 703(m) and a respondent demonstrates that the respondent would have taken the same action in the absence of the impermissible motivating factor, the court—

(i) may grant declaratory relief, injunctive relief (except as provided in clause (ii)), and attorney's fees and costs demonstrated to be directly attributable only to the pursuit of a claim under section 703(m); and

(ii) shall not award damages or issue an order requiring any admission, reinstatement, hiring, promotion, or payment, described in subparagraph (A).

CIVIL RIGHTS ACT OF 1991

P.L. 102–166, 105 Stat. 1071

SEC. 1. SHORT TITLE.

This Act may be cited as the "Civil Rights Act of 1991".

SEC. 2. FINDINGS.

The Congress finds that—

(1) additional remedies under Federal law are needed to deter unlawful harassment and intentional discrimination in the workplace;

(2) the decision of the Supreme Court in Wards Cove Packing Co. v. Atonio, 490 U.S. 642 (1989) has weakened the scope and effectiveness of Federal civil rights protections; and

(3) legislation is necessary to provide additional protections against unlawful discrimination in employment.

SEC. 3. PURPOSES.

The purposes of this Act are—

(1) to provide appropriate remedies for intentional discrimination and unlawful harassment in the workplace;

(2) to codify the concepts of "business necessity" and "job related" enunciated by the Supreme Court in Griggs v. Duke Power Co., 401 U.S. 424 (1971), and in the other Supreme Court decisions prior to Wards Cove Packing Co. v. Atonio, 490 U.S. 642 (1989);

(3) to confirm statutory authority and provide statutory guidelines for the adjudication of disparate impact suits under title VII of the Civil Rights Act of 1964 (42 U.S.C. 2000e et seq.); and

(4) to respond to recent decisions of the Supreme Court by expanding the scope of relevant civil rights statutes in order to provide adequate protection to victims of discrimination. * * *

SEC. 116. LAWFUL COURT–ORDERED REMEDIES, AFFIRMATIVE ACTION, AND CONCILIATION AGREEMENTS NOT AFFECTED.

Nothing in the amendments made by this title shall be construed to affect court-ordered remedies, affirmative action, or conciliation agreements, that are in accordance with the law.

SEC. 117. COVERAGE OF HOUSE OF REPRESENTATIVES AND THE AGENCIES OF THE LEGISLATIVE BRANCH.

(a) COVERAGE OF THE HOUSE OF REPRESENTATIVES.—

(1) IN GENERAL.—Notwithstanding any provision of title VII of the Civil Rights Act of 1964 (42 U.S.C. 2000e et seq.) or of other law, the purposes of such title shall, subject to paragraph (2), apply in their entirety to the House of Representatives.

(2) EMPLOYMENT IN THE HOUSE.—

(A) APPLICATION.—The rights and protections under title VII of the Civil Rights Act of 1964 (42 U.S.C. 2000e et seq.) shall, subject to subparagraph (B), apply with respect to any employee in an employment position in the House of Representatives and any employing authority of the House of Representatives. * * *

(C) EXERCISE OF RULEMAKING POWER.—The provisions of subparagraph (B) are enacted by the House of Representatives as an exercise of the rulemaking power of the House of Representatives, with full recognition of the right of the House to change its rules, in the same manner, and to the same extent as in the case of any other rule of the House.

SEC. 301. GOVERNMENT EMPLOYEE RIGHTS ACT OF 1991.

(b) PURPOSE.—The purpose of this title is to provide procedures to protect the right of Senate and other government employees, with respect to their public employment, to be free of discrimination on the basis of race, color, religion, sex, national origin, age, or disability. * * *

SEC. 302. DISCRIMINATORY PRACTICES PROHIBITED.

All personnel actions affecting employees of the Senate shall be made free from any discrimination based on—

(1) race, color, religion, sex, or national origin, within the meaning of section 717 of the Civil Rights Act of 1964 (42 U.S.C. 2000e–16);

(2) age, within the meaning of section 15 of the Age Discrimination in Employment Act of 1967 (29 U.S.C. 633a); or

(3) handicap or disability, within the meaning of section 501 of the Rehabilitation Act of 1973 (29 U.S.C. 791) and sections 102–104 of the Americans with Disabilities Act of 1990 (42 U.S.C. 12112–14).

SEC. 303. ESTABLISHMENT OF OFFICE OF SENATE FAIR EMPLOYMENT PRACTICES.

(a) IN GENERAL.—There is established, as an office of the Senate, the Office of Senate Fair Employment Practices (referred to in this title as the "Office"), which shall—

(1) administer the processes set forth in sections 305 through 307;

(2) implement programs for the Senate to heighten awareness of employee rights in order to prevent violations from occurring.
* * *

SEC. 304. SENATE PROCEDURE FOR CONSIDERATION OF ALLEGED VIOLATIONS.

The Senate procedure for consideration of alleged violations consists of 4 steps as follows:

(1) Step I, counseling, as set forth in section 305.

(2) Step II, mediation, as set forth in section 306.

(3) Step III, formal complaint and hearing by a hearing board, as set forth in section 307.

(4) Step IV, review of a hearing board decision, as set forth in section 308 or 309.

* * *

SEC. 320. COVERAGE OF PRESIDENTIAL APPOINTEES.

(a) IN GENERAL.—

(1) APPLICATION.—The rights, protections, and remedies provided pursuant to section 302 and 307(h) of this title shall apply with respect to employment of Presidential appointees. * * *

SEC. 321. COVERAGE OF PREVIOUSLY EXEMPT STATE EMPLOYEES.

(a) APPLICATION.—The rights, protections, and remedies provided pursuant to section 302 and 307(h) of this title shall apply with respect to employment of any individual chosen or appointed, by a person elected to public office in any State or political subdivision of any State by the qualified voters thereof—

(1) to be a member of the elected official's personal staff;

(2) to serve the elected official on the policymaking level; or

(3) to serve the elected official as an immediate advisor with respect to the exercise of the constitutional or legal powers of the office. * * *

SEC. 323. PAYMENTS BY THE PRESIDENT OR A MEMBER OF THE SENATE.

The President or a Member of the Senate shall reimburse the appropriate Federal account for any payment made on his or her behalf out of such account for a violation committed under the provisions of this title by the President or Member of the Senate not later than 60 days after the payment is made.

U.S. CONSTITUTION

AMENDMENT XIV—CITIZENSHIP; PRIVILEGES AND IMMUNITIES; DUE
PROCESS; EQUAL PROTECTION; APPORTIONMENT OF REPRESEN-
TATION; DISQUALIFICATION OF OFFICERS; PUBLIC DEBT; EN-
FORCEMENT

Section 1. All persons born or naturalized in the United States,
and subject to the jurisdiction thereof, are citizens of the United States
and of the State wherein they reside. No State shall make or enforce
any law which shall abridge the privileges or immunities of citizens of
the United States; nor shall any State deprive any person of life, liberty,
or property, without due process of law; nor deny to any person within
its jurisdiction the equal protection of the laws. * * *

* * *

Section 5. The Congress shall have power to enforce, by appropriate legislation, the provisions of this article.

42 U.S.C. § 1981, REVISED STATUTES § 1977A

EQUAL RIGHTS UNDER THE LAW

(a) All persons within the jurisdiction of the United States shall have the same right in every State and Territory to make and enforce contracts, to sue, be parties, give evidence, and to the full and equal benefit of all laws and proceedings for the security of persons and property as is enjoyed by white citizens, and shall be subject to like punishment, pains, penalties, taxes, licenses, and exactions of every kind, and to no other.

(b) For purposes of this section, the term "make and enforce contracts" includes the making, performance, modification, and termination of contracts, and the enjoyment of all benefits, privileges, terms, and conditions of the contractual relationship.

(c) The rights protected by this section are protected against impairment by nongovernmental discrimination and impairment under color of State law.

SEC. 1977A. DAMAGES IN CASES OF INTENTIONAL DISCRIMINATION IN EMPLOYMENT

(a) RIGHT OF RECOVERY.—

(1) CIVIL RIGHTS.—In an action brought by a complaining party under section 706 or 717 of the Civil Rights Act of 1964 against a respondent who engaged in unlawful intentional discrimination (not an employment practice that is unlawful because of its disparate impact) prohibited under section 703, 704, or 717 of the Act, and provided that the complaining party cannot recover under section 1977 of the Revised Statutes (42 U.S.C. 1981), the complaining party may recover compensatory and punitive damages as allowed in subsection (b), in addition to any relief authorized by section 706(g) of the Civil Rights Act of 1964, from the respondent.

(2) DISABILITY.—In an action brought by a complaining party under the powers, remedies, and procedures set forth in section 706 or 717 of the Civil Rights Act of 1964 (as provided in section 107(a) of the Americans with Disabilities Act of 1990, and section 505(a)(1) of the Rehabilitation Act of 1973, respectively) against a respondent who engaged in unlawful intentional discrimination (not an employment practice that is unlawful because of its disparate impact) under section 501 of the Rehabilitation Act of 1973 and the regulations implementing section 501, or who violated the requirements of section 501 of the Act or the regulations implementing section 501

concerning the provision of a reasonable accommodation, or section 102 of the Americans with Disabilities Act of 1990, or committed a violation of section 102(b)(5) of the Act, against an individual, the complaining party may recover compensatory and punitive damages as allowed in subsection (b), in addition to any relief authorized by section 706(g) of the Civil Rights Act of 1964, from the respondent.

(3) REASONABLE ACCOMMODATION AND GOOD FAITH EFFORT.—In cases where a discriminatory practice involves the provision of a reasonable accommodation pursuant to section 102(b)(5) of the Americans with Disabilities Act of 1990 or regulations implementing section 501 of the Rehabilitation Act of 1973, damages may not be awarded under this section where the covered entity demonstrates good faith efforts, in consultation with the person with the disability who has informed the covered entity that accommodation is needed, to identify and make a reasonable accommodation that would provide such individual with an equally effective opportunity and would not cause an undue hardship on the operation of the business.

(b) COMPENSATORY AND PUNITIVE DAMAGES.—

(1) DETERMINATION OF PUNITIVE DAMAGES.—A complaining party may recover punitive damages under this section against a respondent (other than a government, government agency or political subdivision) if the complaining party demonstrates that the respondent engaged in a discriminatory practice or discriminatory practices with malice or with reckless indifference to the federally protected rights of an aggrieved individual.

(2) EXCLUSIONS FROM COMPENSATORY DAMAGES.—Compensatory damages awarded under this section shall not include backpay, interest on backpay, or any other type of relief authorized under section 706(g) of the Civil Rights Act of 1964.

(3) LIMITATIONS.—The sum of the amount of compensatory damages awarded under this section for future pecuniary losses, emotional pain, suffering, inconvenience, mental anguish, loss of enjoyment of life, and other nonpecuniary losses, and the amount of punitive damages awarded under this section, shall not exceed, for each complaining party—

> (A) in the case of a respondent who has more than 14 and fewer than 101 employees in each of 20 or more calendar weeks in the current or preceding calendar year, $50,000;

> (B) in the case of a respondent who has more than 100 and fewer than 201 employees in each of 20 or more calendar weeks in the current or preceding calendar year, $100,000; and

(C) in the case of a respondent who has more than 200 and fewer than 501 employees in each of 20 or more calendar weeks in the current or preceding calendar year, $200,000; and

(D) in the case of a respondent who has more than 500 employees in each of 20 or more calendar weeks in the current or preceding calendar year, $300,000.

(4) CONSTRUCTION.—Nothing in this section shall be construed to limit the scope of, or the relief available under, section 1977 of the Revised Statutes (42 U.S.C. 1981).

(c) JURY TRIAL.—If a complaining party seeks compensatory or punitive damages under this section—

(1) any party may demand a trial by jury; and

(2) the court shall not inform the jury of the limitations described in subsection (b)(3).

(d) DEFINITIONS.—As used in this section:

(1) COMPLAINING PARTY.—The term "complaining party" means—

(A) in the case of a person seeking to bring an action under subsection (a)(1), the Equal Employment Opportunity Commission, the Attorney General, or a person who may bring an action or proceeding under title VII of the Civil Rights Act of 1964 (42 U.S.C. 2000e et seq.); or

(B) in the case of a person seeking to bring an action under subsection (a)(2), the Equal Employment Opportunity Commission, the Attorney General, a person who may bring an action or proceeding under section 505(a)(1) of the Rehabilitation Act of 1973 (29 U.S.C. 794a(a)(1)), or a person who may bring an action or proceeding under title I of the Americans with Disabilities Act of 1990.

(2) DISCRIMINATORY PRACTICE.—The term "discriminatory practice" means the discrimination described in paragraph (1), or the discrimination or the violation described in paragraph (2) of subsection (a).

42 U.S.C. § 1983

CIVIL ACTION FOR DEPRIVATION OF RIGHTS

Every person who, under color of any statute, ordinance, regulation, custom, or usage, of any State or Territory or the District of Columbia, subjects, or causes to be subjected, any citizen of the United States or other person within the jurisdiction thereof to the deprivation of any rights, privileges, or immunities secured by the Constitution and laws, shall be liable to the party injured in an action at law, suit in equity, or other proper proceeding for redress. For the purposes of this section, any Act of Congress applicable exclusively to the District of Columbia shall be considered to be a statute of the District of Columbia.

42 U.S.C. § 1985

CONSPIRACY TO INTERFERE WITH CIVIL RIGHTS

* * *

Depriving persons of rights or privileges

(3) If two or more persons in any State or Territory conspire or go in disguise on the highway or on the premises of another, for the purpose of depriving, either directly or indirectly, any person or class of persons of the equal protection of the laws, or of equal privileges and immunities under the laws; or for the purpose of preventing or hindering the constituted authorities of any State or Territory from giving or securing to all persons within such State or Territory the equal protection of the laws; in any case of conspiracy set forth in this section, if one or more persons engaged therein do, or cause to be done, any act in furtherance of the object of such conspiracy, whereby another is injured in his person or property, or deprived of having and exercising any right or privilege of a citizen of the United States, the party so injured or deprived may have an action for the recovery of damages occasioned by such injury or deprivation, against any one or more of the conspirators.

AGE DISCRIMINATION IN EMPLOYMENT ACT

29 U.S.C. §§ 621–634

* * *

STATEMENT OF FINDINGS AND PURPOSE

SEC. 2 (**§ 621**) (a) The Congress hereby finds and declares that—

(1) in the face of rising productivity and affluence, older workers find themselves disadvantaged in their efforts to retain employment, and especially to regain employment when displaced from jobs;

(2) the setting of arbitrary age limits regardless of potential for job performance has become a common practice, and certain otherwise desirable practices may work to the disadvantage of older persons;

(3) the incidence of unemployment, especially long-term unemployment with resultant deterioration of skill, morale, and employer acceptability is, relative to the younger ages, high among older workers; their numbers are great and growing; and their employment problems grave;

(4) the existence in industries affecting commerce of arbitrary discrimination in employment because of age burdens commerce and the free flow of goods in commerce.

(b) It is therefore the purpose of this Act to promote employment of older persons based on their ability rather than age; to prohibit arbitrary age discrimination in employment; to help employers and workers find ways of meeting problems arising from the impact of age on employment.

* * *

SEC. 4 (§ 623) Prohibition of age discrimination

(a) It shall be unlawful for an employer—

(1) to fail or refuse to hire or to discharge any individual or otherwise discriminate against any individual with respect to his compensation, terms, conditions, or privileges of employment, because of such individual's age;

(2) to limit, segregate, or classify his employees in any which would deprive or tend to deprive any individual of employment opportunities or otherwise adversely affect his status as an employee, because of such individual's age; or

(3) to reduce the wage rate of any employee in order to comply with this chapter.

(b) It shall be unlawful for an employment agency to fail or refuse to refer for employment, or otherwise to discriminate against, any individual because of such individual's age, or to classify or refer for employment any individual on the basis of such individual's age.

(c) It shall be unlawful for a labor organization—

(1) to exclude or to expel from its membership, or otherwise to discriminate against, any individual because of his age;

(2) to limit, segregate, or classify its membership, or to classify or fail or refuse to refer for employment any individual, in any way which would deprive or tend to deprive any individual of employment opportunities, or would limit such employment opportunities or otherwise adversely affect his status as an employee or as an applicant for employment, because of such individual's age;

(3) to cause or attempt to cause an employer to discriminate against an individual in violation of this section.

(d) It shall be unlawful for an employer to discriminate against any of his employees or applicants for employment, for an employment agency to discriminate against any individual, or for a labor organization to discriminate against any member thereof or applicant for membership, because such individual, member or applicant for membership has opposed any practice made unlawful by this section, or because such individual, member or applicant for membership has made a charge, testified, assisted, or participated in any manner in an investigation, proceeding, or litigation under this chapter.

(e) It shall be unlawful for an employer, labor organization, or employment agency to print or publish, or cause to be printed or published, any notice or advertisement relating to employment by such an employer or membership in or any classification or referral for employment by such a labor organization, or relating to any classification or referral for employment by such an employment agency, indicating any preference, limitation, specification, or discrimination, based on age.

(f) It shall not be unlawful for an employer, employment agency, or labor organization—

(1) to take any action otherwise prohibited under subsections (a), (b), (c), or (e) of this section where age is a bona fide occupational qualification reasonably necessary to the normal operation of the particular business, or where the differentiation is based on reasonable factors other than age, or where such practices involve an employee in a workplace in a foreign country, and compliance with such subsections

would cause such employer, or a corporation controlled by such employer, to violate the laws of the country in which such workplace is located;

(2) to observe the terms of a bona fide seniority system or any bona fide employee benefit plan such as a retirement, pension, or insurance plan, which is not a subterfuge to evade the purposes of this chapter, except that no such employee benefit plan shall excuse the failure to hire any individual, and no such seniority system or employee benefit plan shall require or permit the involuntary retirement of any individual specified by section 631(a) of this title because of the age of such individual; or

(3) to discharge or otherwise discipline an individual for good cause.

(g)(1) For purposes of this section, any employer must provide that any employee aged 65 through 69, and any employee's spouse aged 65 through 69, shall be entitled to coverage under any group health plan offered to such employees under the same conditions as any employee, and the spouse of such employee, under age 65.

(2) For purposes of paragraph (1), the term "group health plan" has the meaning given to such term in section 162(i)(2) of Title 26.

(h)(1) If an employer controls a corporation whose place of incorporation is in a foreign country, any practice by such corporation prohibited under this section shall be presumed to be such practice by such employer.

(2) The prohibitions of this section shall not apply where the employer is a foreign person not controlled by an American employer.

(3) For the purpose of this subsection the determination of whether an employer controls a corporation shall be based upon the—

(A) interrelation of operations,

(B) common management,

(C) centralized control of labor relations, and

(D) common ownership or financial control, of the employer and the corporation.

(i)(1) Except as otherwise provided in this subsection, it shall be unlawful for an employer, an employment agency, a labor organization, or any combination thereof to establish or maintain an employee pension benefit plan which requires or permits—

(A) in the case of a defined benefit plan, the cessation of an employee's benefit accrual, or the reduction of the rate of an employee's benefit accrual, because of age, or

(B) in the case of a defined contribution plan, the cessation of allocations to an employee's account, or the reduction of the rate at which amounts are allocated to an employee's account, because of age.

(2) Nothing in this section shall be construed to prohibit an employer, employment agency, or labor organization from observing any provision of an employee pension benefit plan to the extent that such provision imposes (without regard to age) a limitation on the amount of benefits that the plan provides or a limitation on the number of years of service or years of participation which are taken into account for purposes of determining benefit accrual under the plan.

* * *

[Editor's note: Both the previous section and the following section were designated as Section 4(i) by the language of the public laws that added them.]

(i) It shall not be unlawful for an employer which is a State, a political subdivision of a State, an agency or instrumentality of a State or a political subdivision of a State, or an interstate agency to fail refuse to hire or to discharge any individual because of such individual's age if such action is taken—

(1) with respect to the employment of an individual as a firefighter or as a law enforcement officer and the individual has attained the age of hiring or retirement in effect under applicable State or local law on March 3, 1983, and

(2) pursuant to a bona fide hiring or retirement plan that is not a subterfuge to evade the purposes of this Act. [The preceding section was added by Public Law 99–592, effective January 1, 1987, through December 31, 1993. It does not apply to any causes of action arising under ADEA as in effect before January 1, 1987. Section 5 of Public Law 99–592 directed EEOC and the Labor Department to conduct a study and make recommendations on the use of physical and mental fitness tests to measure the ability and competence of police officers and firefighters. In addition, by November, 1991, EEOC must propose guidelines for the administration and use of such tests.]

* * *

ADMINISTRATION

SEC. 6 (§ 625) The Secretary shall have the power—

(a) to make delegations, to appoint such agents and employees, and to pay for technical assistance on a fee-for-service basis, as he deems necessary to assist him in the performance of his functions under this Act;

(b) to cooperate with regional, State, local, and other agencies, and to cooperate with and furnish technical assistance to employers, labor organizations, and employment agencies to aid in effectuating the purposes of this Act.

RECORDKEEPING, INVESTIGATION, AND ENFORCEMENT

SEC. 7 (§ 626) (a) The Equal Employment Opportunity Commission shall have the power to make investigations and require the keeping of records necessary or appropriate for the administration of this Act in accordance with the powers and procedures provided in sections 9 and 11 of the Fair Labor Standards Act of 1938, as amended (29 U.S.C. 209 and 211).

(b) The provisions of this Act shall be enforced in accordance with the powers, remedies, and procedures provided in sections 11(b), 16 (except for subsection (a) thereof), and 17 of the Fair Labor Standards Act of 1938, as amended (29 U.S.C. 211(b), 216, 217) and subsection (c) of this section. Any act prohibited under section 4 of this Act shall be deemed to be a prohibited act under section 15 of the Fair Labor Standards Act of 1938, as amended (29 U.S.C. 215). Amounts owing to an individual as a result of a violation of this Act shall be deemed to be unpaid minimum wages or unpaid overtime compensation for purposes of sections 16 and 17 of the Fair Labor Standards Act of 1938, as amended (29 U.S.C. 216, 217): Provided, that liquidated damages shall be payable only in cases of willful violations of this Act. In any action brought to enforce this Act the court shall have jurisdiction to grant such legal or equitable relief as may be appropriate to effectuate the purposes of this Act, including without limitation judgments compelling employment, reinstatement or promotion, or enforcing the liability for amounts deemed to be unpaid minimum wages or unpaid overtime compensation under this section. Before instituting any action under this section, the Equal Employment Opportunity Commission shall attempt to eliminate the discriminatory practice or practices alleged, and to effect voluntary compliance with the requirements of this Act through informal methods of conciliation, conference, and persuasion.

(c)(1) Any person aggrieved may bring a civil action in any court of competent jurisdiction for such legal or equitable relief as will effectuate the purposes of this Act: Provided, that the right of any person to bring such action shall terminate upon the commencement of an action by the Equal Employment Opportunity Commission to enforce the right of such person under this Act.

(2) In an action brought under paragraph (1), a person shall be entitled to a trial by jury of any issue of fact in any such action for recovery of amounts owing as a result of a violation of this Act,

regardless of whether equitable relief is sought by any party in such action.

(d) No civil action may be commenced by an individual under this section until 60 days after a charge alleging unlawful discrimination has been filed with the Equal Employment Opportunity Commission. Such a charge shall be filed—

(1) within 180 days after the alleged unlawful practice occurred; or

(2) in a case to which section 14(b) applies, within 300 days after the alleged unlawful practice occurred, or within 30 days after receipt by the individual of notice of termination of proceedings under State law, whichever is earlier.

Upon receiving such a charge, the Commission shall promptly notify all persons named in such charge as prospective defendants in the action and shall promptly seek to eliminate any alleged unlawful practice by informal methods of conciliation, conference, and persuasion.

(e)(1) Sections 6 and 10 of the Portal-to-Portal Act of 1947 shall apply to actions under this Act.

(2) For the period during which the Equal Employment Opportunity Commission is attempting to effect voluntary compliance with requirements of this Act through informal methods of conciliation, conference, and persuasion pursuant to subsection (b), the statute of limitations as provided in section 6 of the Portal-to-Portal Act of 1947 shall be tolled, but in no event for a period in excess of one year.

Notwithstanding section 7(e), a civil action may be brought under section 7 by the Commission or an aggrieved person, during the 540–day period beginning on the date of enactment of this Act [April 7, 1988] if—

(1) with respect to the alleged unlawful practice on which the claim in such civil action is based, a charge was timely filed under such Act with the Commission after December 31, 1983,

(2) the Commission did not, within the applicable period set forth in section 7(e) either—

(A) eliminate such alleged unlawful practice by informal methods of conciliation, conference, and persuasion, or

(B) notify such person, in writing, of the disposition of such charge and of the right of such person to bring a civil action on such claim,

(3) the statute of limitations applicable under such section 7(e) to such claim ran before the date of enactment of this Act, and

(4) a civil action on such claim was not brought by the Commission or such person before the running of the statute of limitations.

NOTICES TO BE POSTED

SEC. 8 **(§ 627)** Every employer, employment agency, and labor organization shall post and keep posted in conspicuous places upon its premises a notice to be prepared or approved by the Equal Employment Opportunity Commission setting forth information as the Commission deems appropriate to effectuate the purposes of this Act.

* * *

CRIMINAL PENALTIES

SEC. 10 **(§ 629)** Whoever shall forcibly resist, oppose, impede, intimidate, or interfere with a duly authorized representative of the Equal Employment Opportunity Commission while it is engaged in the performance of duties under this Act shall be punished by a fine of not more than $500 or by imprisonment for not more than one year, or by both: Provided, however, that no person shall be imprisoned under this section except when there has been a prior conviction hereunder.

DEFINITIONS

SEC. 11 **(§ 630)** For the purposes of this Act—

(a) The term "person" means one or more individuals, partnerships, associations, labor organizations, corporations, business trusts, legal representatives, or any organized groups of persons.

(b) The term "employer" means a person engaged in an industry affecting commerce who has twenty or more employees for each working day in each of twenty or more calendar weeks in the current or preceding calendar year: Provided, that prior to June 30, 1968, employers having fewer than fifty employees shall not be considered employers. The term also means (1) any agent of such a person, and (2) a State or political subdivision of a State and any agency or instrumentality of a State or a political subdivision of a State, and any interstate agency but such term does not include the United States, or a corporation wholly owned by the Government of the United States.

(c) The term "employment agency" means any person regularly undertaking with or without compensation to procure employees for an employer and includes an agent of such a person; but shall not include an agency of the United States.

(d) The term "labor organization" means a labor organization engaged in an industry affecting commerce, and any agent of such an organization, and includes any organization of any kind, any agency, or employee representation committee, group, association, or plan so engaged in which employees participate and which exists for the purpose, in whole or in part, of dealing with employers concerning grievances, labor disputes, wages, rates of pay, hours, or other terms or conditions of employment, and any conference, general committee, joint or system board, or joint council so engaged which is subordinate to a national or international labor organization.

(e) A labor organization shall be deemed to be engaged in an industry affecting commerce if (1) it maintains or operates a hiring hall or hiring office which procures employees for an employer or procures for employees opportunities to work for an employer, or (2) the number of its members (or, where it is a labor organization composed of other labor organizations or their representatives, if the aggregate number of the members of such other labor organization) is fifty or more prior to July 1, 1968, or twenty-five or more on or after July 1, 1968, and such labor organization—

(1) is the certified representative of employees under the provisions of the National Labor Relations Act, as amended, or the Railway Labor Act, as amended; or

(2) although not certified, is a national or international labor organization or a local labor organization recognized or acting as the representative of employees of an employer or employers engaged in an industry affecting commerce; or

(3) has chartered a local labor organization or subsidiary body which is representing or actively seeking to represent employees or employers within the meaning of paragraph (1) or (2); or

(4) has been chartered by a labor organization representing or actively seeking to represent employees within the meaning of paragraph (1) or (2) as the local or subordinate body through which such employees may enjoy membership or become affiliated with such labor organization; or

(5) is a conference, general committee, joint or system board or joint council subordinate to a national or international labor organization, which includes a labor organization engaged in an industry affecting commerce within the meaning of any of the preceding paragraphs of this subsection.

(f) The term "employee" means an individual employed by an employer except that the term "employee" shall not include any person elected to public office in any State or political subdivision of any State by the qualified voters thereof, or any person chosen by such officer to be on such officer's personal staff, or an appointee on the policy-making level or an immediate adviser with respect to the exercise of the constitutional or legal powers of the office. The exemption set forth in the preceding sentence shall not include employees subject to the civil service laws of a State government, governmental agency, or political subdivision. The term "employee" includes any individual who is a citizen of the United States employed by an employer in a workplace in a foreign country.

(g) The term "commerce" means trade, traffic, commerce, transportation, transmission, or communication among the several States, or between a State and any place outside thereof; or within the District of Columbia, or a possession of the United States, or between points in the same State but through a point outside thereof.

(h) The term "industry affecting commerce" means any activity, business, or industry in commerce or in which a labor dispute would hinder or obstruct commerce or the free flow of commerce and includes any activity or industry "affecting commerce" within the meaning of the Labor-Management Reporting and Disclosure Act of 1959.

(i) The term "State" includes a State of the United States, the District of Columbia, Puerto Rico, the Virgin Islands, American Samoa, Guam, Wake Island, the Canal Zone, and Outer Continental Shelf Lands defined in the Outer Continental Shelf Lands Act.

(j) The term "firefighter" means an employee, the duties of whose position are primarily to perform work directly connected with the control and extinguishment of fires or the maintenance and use of firefighting apparatus and equipment, including an employee engaged in this activity who is transferred to a supervisory or administrative position.

(k) The term "law enforcement officer" means an employee, the duties of whose position are primarily the investigation, apprehension, or detention of individuals suspected or convicted of offenses against the criminal laws of a State, including an employee engaged in this activity who is transferred to a supervisory or administration position. For the purpose of this subsection, "detention" includes the duties of employees assigned to guard individuals incarcerated in any penal institution.

LIMITATION

SEC. 12 (**§ 631**) (a) The prohibitions in this chapter shall be limited to individuals who are at least 40 years of age.

(b) In the case of any personnel action affecting employees or applicants for employment which is subject to the provisions of section 15 of this Act, the prohibitions established in section 15 of this Act shall be limited to individuals who are at least 40 years of age.

(c)(1) Nothing in this chapter shall be construed to prohibit compulsory retirement of any employee who has attained 65 years of age, and who, for the two-year period immediately before retirement, is employed in a bona fide executive or a high policymaking position, if such employee is entitled to an immediate nonforfeitable annual retirement benefit from a pension, profitsharing, savings, or deferred compensation plan, or any combination of such plans, of the employer of such employee, which equals, in aggregate, at least $44,000.

(2) In applying the retirement benefit test of paragraph (1) of this subsection, if any such retirement benefit is in a form other than a straight life annuity (with no ancillary benefits), or if employees contribute to any such plan or make rollover contributions, such benefit shall be adjusted in accordance with regulations prescribed by the Equal Employment Opportunity Commission, after consultation with the Secretary of the Treasury, so that the benefit is the equivalent of a straight life annuity (with no ancillary benefits) under a plan to which employees do not contribute and under which no rollover contributions are made.

(d) Nothing in this Act shall be construed to prohibit compulsory retirement of any employee who has attained 70 years of age, and who is serving under a contract of unlimited tenure (or similar arrangement providing for unlimited tenure) at an institution of higher education (as defined by section 1141(a) of Title 20).

* * *

FEDERAL–STATE RELATIONSHIP

SEC. 14   (§ 633) (a) Nothing in this Act shall affect the jurisdiction of any agency of any State performing like functions with regard to discriminatory employment practices on account of age except that upon commencement of an action under this Act such action shall supersede any State action.

(b) In the case of an alleged unlawful practice occurring in a State which has a law prohibiting discrimination in employment because of age and establishing or authorizing a State authority to grant or seek relief from such discriminatory practice, no suit may be brought under section 7 of this Act before the expiration of sixty days after proceedings have been commenced under the State law, unless such proceedings have been earlier terminated, provided that such sixty-day period shall be extended to one hundred and twenty days during the first year after the effective date of such State law. If any requirement for the commencement of such proceedings is imposed by a State authority other than a requirement of the filing of a written and signed statement of the facts upon which the proceeding is based, the proceeding shall be deemed to have been commenced for the purposes of this subsection at the time such statement is sent by registered mail to the appropriate State authority.

[Section 15 of the ADEA, 29 U.S.C. § 633a, prohibits discrimination on account of age in federal government employment, on bases similar to the rest of the Act.]

* * *

[In addition to the more widely known ADEA of 1967, the Age Discrimination Act of 1975, 42 U.S.C. § 6101 et seq., prohibits discrimination on the basis of age by recipients of federal financial assistance. This act does not in any way affect enforcement of the ADEA of 1967. The act does not specify age limits for coverage.]

REHABILITATION ACT

29 U.S.C. §§ 701–796i

SEC. 706   Definitions

For the purposes of this chapter:

* * *

(7)(A) Except as otherwise provided in subparagraph (B), the term "individual with a disability" means any individual who (i) has a physical or mental impairment which for such individual constitutes or results in a substantial impediment to employment and (ii) can benefit in terms of an employment outcome from vocational rehabilitation services provided pursuant to titles I, II, III, VI, and VIII of this Act.

(B) Subject to subparagraphs (C) and (D), (E) and (F), the term "individual with a disability" means, for purposes of sections 2, 14, and 15, and titles IV and V of this Act, any person who (i) has a physical or mental impairment which substantially limits one or more of such person's major life activities, (ii) has a record of such an impairment, or (iii) is regarded as having such an impairment.

(C)(i) For purposes of title V, the term "individual with a disability" does not include an individual who is currently engaging in the illegal use of drugs, when a covered entity acts on the basis of such use.

(ii) Nothing in clause (i) shall be construed to exclude as an individual with a disability an individual who—

(I) has successfully completed a supervised drug rehabilitation program and is no longer engaging in the illegal use of drugs, or has otherwise been rehabilitated successfully and is no longer engaging in such use;

(II) is participating in a supervised rehabilitation program and is no longer engaging in such use; or

(III) is erroneously regarded as engaging in such use, but is not engaging in such use;

except that it shall not be a violation of this Act for a covered entity to adopt or administer reasonable policies or procedures, including but not limited to drug testing, designed to ensure that an individual described in subclause (I) or (II) is no longer engaging in the illegal use of drugs.

(iii) Notwithstanding clause (i), for purposes of programs and activities providing health services and services provided under titles I, II, and III, an individual shall not be excluded from the benefits of such

73

programs or activities on the basis of his or her current illegal use of drugs if he or she is otherwise entitled to such services.

(iv) For purposes of programs and activities providing educational services, local educational agencies may take disciplinary action pertaining to the use or possession of illegal drugs or alcohol against any student who is an individual with a disability who currently is engaging in the illegal use of drugs or in the use of alcohol to the same extent that such disciplinary action is taken against students who are not individuals with disabilities. Furthermore, the due process procedures at 34 CFR 104.36 shall not apply to such disciplinary actions.

(v) For purposes of sections 503 and 504 as such sections relate to employment, the term "individual with a disability" does not include any individual who is an alcoholic whose current use of alcohol prevents such individual from performing the duties of the job in question or whose employment, by reason of such current alcohol abuse, would constitute a direct threat to property or the safety of others.

(D) For the purpose of sections 503 and 504, as such sections relate to employment, such term does not include an individual who has a currently contagious disease or infection and who, by reason of such disease or infection, would constitute a direct threat to the health or safety of other individuals or who, by reason of the currently contagious disease or infection, is unable to perform the duties of the job.

Sec. 501   (§ 791)   Employment of individuals with disabilities

* * *

(b) Federal agencies; affirmative action program plans

Each department, agency, and instrumentality (including the United States Postal Service and the Postal Rate Commission) in the executive branch shall, within one hundred and eighty days after September 26, 1973, submit to the Commission and to the Committee an affirmative action program plan for the hiring, placement, and advancement of individuals with disabilities in such department, agency, or instrumentality. Such plan shall include a description of the extent to which and methods whereby the special needs of employees who are individuals with disabilities are being met. Such plan shall be updated annually, and shall be reviewed annually and approved by the Commission, if the Office determines, after consultation with the Committee, that such plan provides sufficient assurances, procedures and commitments to provide adequate hiring, placement, and advancement opportunities for individuals with disabilities.

* * *

Sec. 503 (§ 793) Employment Under Federal Contracts

(a) Amount of contracts or subcontracts; provision for employment and advancement of qualified individuals with handicaps; regulations

Any contract in excess of $10,000 entered into by any Federal department or agency for the procurement of personal property and nonpersonal services (including construction) for the United States shall contain a provision requiring that the party contracting with the United States shall take affirmative action to employ and advance in employment qualified individuals with disabilities. The provisions of this section shall apply to any subcontract in excess of $10,000 entered into by a prime contractor in carrying out any contract for the procurement of personal property and nonpersonal services (including construction) for the United States. The President shall implement the provisions of this section by promulgating regulations within ninety days after September 26, 1973.

(b) Administrative enforcement; complaints; investigations; departmental action

If any individuals with a disability believes any contractor has failed or refused to comply with the provisions of a contract with the United States, relating to employment of individuals with disabilities, such individual may file a complaint with the Department of Labor. The Department shall promptly investigate such complaint and shall take such action thereon as the facts and circumstances warrant, consistent with the terms of such contract and the laws and regulations applicable thereto.

(c) Waiver by President; national interest special circumstances for waiver of particular agreements

(1) The requirements of this section may be waived, in whole or in part, by the President with respect to a particular contract or subcontract, in accordance with guidelines set forth in regulations which the President shall prescribe, when the President determines that special circumstances in the national interest so require and states in writing the reasons for such determination.

* * *

Sec. 504 (§ 794) Nondiscrimination under Federal grants and programs

(a) Promulgation of rules and regulations

No otherwise qualified individual with a disability in the United States, as defined in section 706(8) of this title, shall, solely by reason of her or his disability, be excluded from the participation in, be denied the benefits of, or be subjected to discrimination under any program or activity receiving Federal financial assistance or under any program or activity conducted by any Executive agency or by the United States Postal Service. The head of each such agency shall promulgate such regulations as may be necessary to carry out the amendments to this section made by the Rehabilitation, Comprehensive Services, and Developmental Disabilities Act of 1978. Copies of any proposed regulation shall be submitted to appropriate authorizing committees of the Congress, and such regulation may take effect no earlier than the thirtieth day after the date on which such regulation is so submitted to such committees.

(b) "Program or activity" defined

For the purposes of this section, the term "program or activity" means all of the operations of—

(1)(A) a department, agency, special purpose district, or other instrumentality of a State or of a local government; or

(B) the entity of such State or local government that distributes such assistance and each such department or agency (and each other State or local government entity) to which the assistance is extended, in the case of assistance to a State or local government;

(2)(A) a college, university, or other postsecondary institution, or a public system of higher education; or

(B) a local educational agency (as defined in section 2891(12) of Title 20) system of vocational education, or other school system;

(3)(A) an entire corporation, partnership, or other private organization, or an entire sole proprietorship—

(i) if assistance is extended to such corporation, partnership, private organization, or sole proprietorship as a whole; or

(ii) which is principally engaged in the business of providing education, health care, housing, social services, or parks and recreation; or

(B) the entire plant or other comparable, geographically separate facility to which Federal financial assistance is extended, in the case of any other corporation, partnership, private organization, or sole proprietorship; or

(4) any other entity which is established by two or more of the entities described in paragraph (1), (2), or (3);

any part of which is extended Federal financial assistance.

* * *

AMERICANS WITH DISABILITIES ACT

42 U.S.C. §§ 12101–12213

SECTION 3. (§ 12102) DEFINITIONS

As used in this Act:

* * *

(2) DISABILITY.—The term "disability" means, with respect to an individual—

(A) a physical or mental impairment that substantially limits one or more of the major life activities of such individual;

(B) a record of such an impairment; or

(C) being regarded as having such an impairment.

* * *

TITLE I—EMPLOYMENT

SECTION 101. (§ 12111) DEFINITIONS

As used in this title:

(1) COMMISSION.—The term "Commission" means the Equal Employment Opportunity Commission established by section 705 of the Civil Rights Act of 1964 (42 U.S.C. 2000e–4).

(2) COVERED ENTITY.—The term "covered entity" means an employer, employment agency, labor organization, or joint labor-management committee.

(3) DIRECT THREAT.—The term "direct threat" means a significant risk to the health or safety of others that cannot be eliminated by reasonable accommodation.

(4) EMPLOYEE.—The term "employee" means an individual employed by an employer. With respect to employment in a foreign country, such term includes an individual who is a citizen of the United States.

(5) EMPLOYER.—

(A) IN GENERAL.—The term "employer" means a person engaged in an industry affecting commerce who has 15 or more employees for each working day in each of 20 or more calendar weeks in the current or preceding calendar year, and any agent of such person, except that, for two years following the effective

77

date of this title, an employer means a person engaged in an industry affecting commerce who has 25 or more employees for each working day in each of 20 or more calendar weeks in the current or preceding year, and any agent of such person.

(B) EXCEPTIONS.—The term "employer" does not include—

(i) the United States, a corporation wholly owned by the government of the United States, or an Indian tribe; or

(ii) a bona fide private membership club (other than a labor organization) that is exempt from taxation under section 501(c) of the Internal Revenue Code of 1986.

(6) ILLEGAL USE OF DRUGS.—

(A) IN GENERAL.—The term "illegal use of drugs" means the use of drugs, the possession or distribution of which is unlawful under the Controlled Substances Act (21 U.S.C. 812). Such term does not include the use of a drug taken under supervision by a licensed health care professional, or other uses authorized by the Controlled Substances Act or other provisions of Federal law.

(B) DRUGS.—The term "drug" means a controlled substance, as defined in schedules I through V of section 202 of the Controlled Substances Act.

(7) PERSON, ETC.—The terms "person", "labor organization", "employment agency", "commerce", and "industry affecting commerce", shall have the same meaning given such terms in section 701 of the Civil Rights Act of 1964 (42 U.S.C. 2000e).

(8) QUALIFIED INDIVIDUAL WITH A DISABILITY.—The term "qualified individual with a disability" means an individual with a disability who, with or without reasonable accommodation, can perform the essential functions of the employment position that such individual holds or desires. For the purposes of this title, consideration shall be given to the employer's judgment as to what functions of a job are essential, and if an employer has prepared a written description before advertising or interviewing applicants for the job, this description shall be considered evidence of the essential functions of the job.

(9) REASONABLE ACCOMMODATION.—The term "reasonable accommodation" may include—

(A) making existing facilities used by employees readily accessible to and usable by individuals with disabilities; and

(B) job restructuring, part-time or modified work schedules, reassignment to a vacant position, acquisition or modification of equipment or devices, appropriate adjustment or modifications of examinations, training materials or policies, the provision of qualified readers or interpreters, and other similar accommodations for individuals with disabilities.

(10) UNDUE HARDSHIP.—

(A) IN GENERAL.—The term "undue hardship" means an action requiring significant difficulty or expense, when considered in light of the factors set forth in subparagraph (B).

(B) FACTORS TO BE CONSIDERED.—In determining whether an accommodation would impose an undue hardship on a covered entity, factors to be considered include—

(i) the nature and cost of the accommodation needed under this Act;

(ii) the overall financial resources of the facility or facilities involved in the provision of the reasonable accommodation; the number of persons employed at such facility; the effect on expenses and resources, or the impact otherwise of such accommodation upon the operation of the facility;

(iii) the overall financial resources of the covered entity; the overall size of the business of a covered entity with respect to the number of its employees; the number, type, and location of its facilities; and

(iv) the type of operation or operations of the covered entity, including the composition, structure, and functions of the workforce of such entity; the geographic separateness, administrative, or fiscal relationship of the facility or facilities in question to the covered entity.

SECTION 102. (§ 12112) DISCRIMINATION

(a) GENERAL RULE.—No covered entity shall discriminate against a qualified individual with a disability because of the disability of such individual in regard to job application procedures, the hiring, advancement, or discharge of employees, employee compensation, job training, and other terms, conditions, and privileges of employment.

(b) CONSTRUCTION.—As used in subsection (a), the term "discriminate" includes—

(1) limiting, segregating, or classifying a job applicant or employee in a way that adversely affects the opportunities or status of such applicant or employee because of the disability of such applicant or employee;

(2) participating in a contractual or other arrangement or relationship that has the effect of subjecting a covered entity's qualified applicant or employee with a disability to the discrimination prohibited by this title (such relationship includes a relationship with an employment or referral agency, labor union, an organization providing fringe benefits to an employee of the covered entity, or an organization providing training and apprenticeship programs);

(3) utilizing standards, criteria, or methods of administration—

(A) that have the effect of discrimination on the basis of disability; or

(B) that perpetuate the discrimination of others who are subject to common administrative control;

(4) excluding or otherwise denying equal jobs or benefits to a qualified individual because of the known disability of an individual with whom the qualified individual is known to have a relationship or association;

(5)(A) not making reasonable accommodations to the known physical or mental limitations of an otherwise qualified individual with a disability who is an applicant or employee, unless such covered entity can demonstrate that the accommodation would impose an undue hardship on the operation of the business of such covered entity; or

(B) denying employment opportunities to a job applicant or employee who is an otherwise qualified individual with a disability, if such denial is based on the need of such covered entity to make reasonable accommodation to the physical or mental impairments of the employee or applicant;

(6) using qualification standards, employment tests or other selection criteria that screen out or tend to screen out an individual with a disability or a class of individuals with disabilities unless the standard, test or other selection criteria, as used by the covered entity, is shown to be job-related for the position in question and is consistent with business necessity; and

(7) failing to select and administer tests concerning employment in the most effective manner to ensure that, when such test is administered to a job applicant or employee who has a disability that impairs sensory, manual, or speaking skills, such test results accurately reflect the skills, aptitude, or whatever other factor of such applicant or employee that such test purports to measure, rather than reflecting the impaired sensory, manual, or speaking skills of such employee or applicant (except where such skills are the factors that the test purports to measure).

(c) COVERED ENTITIES IN FOREIGN COUNTRIES.—

(1) IN GENERAL.—It shall not be unlawful under this section for a covered entity to take any action that constitutes discrimination under this section with respect to an employee in a workplace in a foreign country if compliance with this section would cause such covered entity to violate the law of the foreign country in which such workplace is located.

(2) CONTROL OF CORPORATION—

(A) PRESUMPTION.—If an employer controls a corporation whose place of incorporation is a foreign country, any practice that constitutes discrimination under this section and is engaged in by such corporation shall be presumed to be engaged in by such employer.

(B) EXCEPTION.—This section shall not apply with respect to the foreign operations of an employer that is a foreign person not controlled by an American employer.

(C) DETERMINATION.—For purposes of this paragraph, the determination of whether an employer controls a corporation shall be based on—

(i) the interrelation of operations;

(ii) the common management;

(iii) the centralized control of labor relations; and

(iv) the common ownership or financial control of the employer and the corporation.

(d) MEDICAL EXAMINATIONS AND INQUIRIES.—

(1) IN GENERAL.—The prohibition against discrimination as referred to in subsection (a) shall include medical examinations and inquiries.

(2) PREEMPLOYMENT.—

(A) PROHIBITED EXAMINATION OR INQUIRY.—Except as provided in paragraph (3), a covered entity shall not conduct a medical examination or make inquiries of a job applicant as to whether such applicant is an individual with a disability or as to the nature or severity of such disability.

(B) ACCEPTABLE INQUIRY.—A covered entity may make preemployment inquiries into the ability of an applicant to perform job-related functions.

(3) EMPLOYMENT ENTRANCE EXAMINATION.—A covered entity may require a medical examination after an offer of employment has been made to a job applicant and prior to the commencement of the employment duties of such applicant, and may condition an offer of employment on the results of such examination, if—

(A) all entering employees are subjected to such an examination regardless of disability;

(B) information obtained regarding the medical condition or history of the applicant is collected and maintained on separate forms and in separate medical files and is treated as a confidential medical record, except that—

(i) supervisors and managers may be informed regarding necessary restrictions on the work or duties of the employee and necessary accommodations;

(ii) first aid and safety personnel may be informed, when appropriate, if the disability might require emergency treatment; and

(iii) government officials investigating compliance with this Act shall be provided relevant information on request; and

(C) the results of such examination are used only in accordance with this title.

(4) EXAMINATION AND INQUIRY.—

(A) PROHIBITED EXAMINATIONS AND INQUIRIES.—A covered entity shall not require a medical examination and shall not make inquiries of an employee as to whether such employee is an individual with a disability or as to the nature or severity of the disability, unless such examination or inquiry is shown to be job-related and consistent with business necessity.

(B) ACCEPTABLE EXAMINATIONS AND INQUIRIES.—A covered entity may conduct voluntary medical examinations, including voluntary medical histories, which are part of an employee health program available to employees at that work site. A covered entity may make inquiries into the ability of an employee to perform job-related functions.

(C) REQUIREMENT.—Information obtained under subparagraph (B) regarding the medical condition or history of any employee are subject to the requirements of subparagraphs (B) and (C) of paragraph (3).

SECTION 103.   (§ 12113) DEFENSES

(a) IN GENERAL.—It may be a defense to a charge of discrimination under this Act that an alleged application of qualification standards, tests, or selection criteria that screen out or tend to screen out or otherwise deny a job or benefit to an individual with a disability has been shown to be job-related and consistent with business necessity, and such performance cannot be accomplished by reasonable accommodation, as required under this title.

(b) QUALIFICATION STANDARDS.—The term "qualification standards" may include a requirement that an individual shall not pose a direct threat to the health or safety of other individuals in the workplace.

(c) RELIGIOUS ENTITIES.—

(1) IN GENERAL.—This title shall not prohibit a religious corporation, association, educational institution, or society from giving preference in employment to individuals of a particular religion to perform work connected with the carrying on by such corporation, association, educational institution, or society of its activities.

(2) RELIGIOUS TENETS REQUIREMENT.—Under this title, a religious organization may require that all applicants and employees conform to the religious tenets of such organization.

(d) LIST OF INFECTIOUS AND COMMUNICABLE DISEASES.—

(1) IN GENERAL.—The Secretary of Health and Human Services, not later than 6 months after the date of enactment of this Act, shall—

(A) review all infectious and communicable diseases which may be transmitted through handling the food supply;

(B) publish a list of infectious and communicable diseases which are transmitted through handling the food supply;

(C) publish the methods by which such diseases are transmitted; and

(D) widely disseminate such information regarding the list of diseases and their modes of transmissability to the general public.

Such list shall be updated annually.

(2) APPLICATIONS.—In any case in which an individual has an infectious or communicable disease that is transmitted to others through the handling of food, that is included on the list developed by the Secretary of Health and Human Services under paragraph (1), and which cannot be eliminated by reasonable accommodation, a covered entity may refuse to assign or continue to assign such individual to a job involving food handling.

(3) CONSTRUCTION.—Nothing in this Act shall be construed to preempt, modify, or amend any State, county, or local law, ordinance, or regulation applicable to food handling which is designed to protect the public health from individuals who pose a significant risk to the health or safety of others, which cannot be eliminated by

reasonable accommodation, pursuant to the list of infectious or communicable diseases and the modes of transmissability published by the Secretary of Health and Human Services.

SECTION 104.   (§ 12114) ILLEGAL USE OF DRUGS AND ALCOHOL

(a) QUALIFIED INDIVIDUAL WITH A DISABILITY.—For purposes of this title, the term "qualified individual with a disability" shall not include any employee or applicant who is currently engaging in the illegal use of drugs, when the covered entity acts on the basis of such use.

(b) RULES OF CONSTRUCTION.—Nothing in subsection (a) shall be construed to exclude as a qualified individual with a disability an individual who—

(1) has successfully completed a supervised drug rehabilitation program and is no longer engaging in the illegal use of drugs, or has otherwise been rehabilitated successfully and is no longer engaging in such use;

(2) is participating in a supervised rehabilitation program and is no longer engaging in such use; or

(3) is erroneously regarded as engaging in such use, but is not engaging in such use;

except that it shall not be a violation of this Act for a covered entity to adopt or administer reasonable policies or procedures, including but not limited to drug testing, designed to ensure that an individual described in paragraph (1) or (2) is no longer engaging in the illegal use of drugs.

(c) AUTHORITY OF COVERED ENTITY.—A covered entity—

(1) may prohibit the illegal use of drugs and the use of alcohol at the workplace by all employees;

(2) may require that employees shall not be under the influence of alcohol or be engaging in the illegal use of drugs at the workplace;

(3) may require that employees behave in conformance with the requirements established under the Drug-Free Workplace Act of 1988 (41 U.S.C. 701 et seq.);

(4) may hold an employee who engages in the illegal use of drugs or who is an alcoholic to the same qualification standards for employment or job performance and behavior that such entity holds other employees, even if any unsatisfactory performance or behavior is related to the drug use or alcoholism of such employee; and

(5) may, with respect to Federal regulations regarding alcohol and the illegal use of drugs, require that—

(A) employees comply with the standards established in such regulations of the Department of Defense, if the employees of the covered entity are employed in an industry subject to such regulations, including complying with regulations (if any) that apply to employment in sensitive positions in such an industry, in the case of employees of the covered entity who are employed in such positions (as defined in the regulations of the Department of Defense);

(B) employees comply with the standards established in such regulations of the Nuclear Regulatory Commission, if the employees of the covered entity are employed in an industry subject to such regulations, including complying with regulations (if any) that apply to employment in sensitive positions in such an industry, in the case of employees of the covered entity who are employed in such positions (as defined in the regulations of the Nuclear Regulatory Commission); and

(C) employees comply with the standards established in such regulations of the Department of Transportation, if the employees of the covered entity are employed in a transportation industry subject to such regulations, including complying with such regulations (if any) that apply to employment in sensitive positions in such an industry, in the case of employees of the covered entity who are employed in such positions (as defined in the regulations of the Department of Transportation).

(d) DRUG TESTING.—

(1) IN GENERAL.—For purposes of this title, a test to determine the illegal use of drugs shall not be considered a medical examination.

(2) CONSTRUCTION.—Nothing in this title shall be construed to encourage, prohibit, or authorize the conducting of drug testing for the illegal use of drugs by job applicants or employees or making employment decisions based on such test results.

(e) TRANSPORTATION EMPLOYEES.—Nothing in this title shall be construed to encourage, prohibit, restrict, or authorize the otherwise lawful exercise by entities subject to the jurisdiction of the Department of Transportation of authority to—

(1) test employees of such entities in, and applicants for, positions involving safety-sensitive duties for the illegal use of drugs and for on-duty impairment by alcohol; and

(2) remove such persons who test positive for illegal use of drugs and on-duty impairment by alcohol pursuant to paragraph (1) from safety-sensitive duties in implementing subsection (c).

SECTION 105.   (§ 12115) POSTING NOTICES

Every employer, employment agency, labor organization, or joint labor-management committee covered under this title shall post notices in an accessible format to applicants, employees, and members describing the applicable provisions of this Act, in the manner prescribed by section 711 of the Civil Rights Act of 1964 (42 U.S.C. 2000e–10).

SECTION 106.   (§ 12116) REGULATIONS

Not later than 1 year after the date of enactment of this Act, the Commission shall issue regulations in an accessible format to carry out this title in accordance with subchapter II of chapter 5 of title 5, United States Code.

SECTION 107.   (§ 12117) ENFORCEMENT

(a) POWERS, REMEDIES, AND PROCEDURES.—The powers, remedies, and procedures set forth in sections 705, 706, 707, 709, and 710 of the Civil Rights Act of 1964 (42 U.S.C. 2000e–4, 2000e–5, 2000e–6, 2000e–8, and 2000e–9) shall be the powers, remedies, and procedures this title provides to the Commission, to the Attorney General, or to any person alleging discrimination on the basis of disability in violation of any provision of this Act, or regulations promulgated under section 106, concerning employment.

(b) COORDINATION.—The agencies with enforcement authority for actions which allege employment discrimination under this title and under the Rehabilitation Act of 1973 shall develop procedures to ensure that administrative complaints filed under this title and under the Rehabilitation Act of 1973 are dealt with in a manner that avoids duplication of effort and prevents imposition of inconsistent or conflicting standards for the same requirements under this title and the Rehabilitation Act of 1973. The Commission, the Attorney General, and the Office of Federal Contract Compliance Programs shall establish such coordinating mechanisms (similar to provisions contained in the joint regulations promulgated by the Commission and the Attorney General at part 42 of title 28 and part 1691 of title 29, Code of Federal Regulations, and the Memorandum of Understanding between the Commission and the Office of Federal Contract Compliance Programs dated January 16, 1981 (46 Fed. Reg. 7435, January 23, 1981)) in regulations implementing this title and the Rehabilitation Act of 1973 not later than 18 months after the date of enactment of this Act.

SECTION 108. (§ 12118) EFFECTIVE DATE

This title shall become effective 24 months after the date of enactment.

* * *

SUBCHAPTER IV—MISCELLANEOUS PROVISIONS

SECTION 501. (§ 12201) CONSTRUCTION

(a) IN GENERAL.—Except as otherwise provided in this Act, nothing in this Act shall be construed to apply a lesser standard than the standards applied under title V of the Rehabilitation Act of 1973 (29 U.S.C. 790 et seq.) or the regulations issued by Federal agencies pursuant to such title.

(b) RELATIONSHIP TO OTHER LAWS.—Nothing in this Act shall be construed to invalidate or limit the remedies, rights, and procedures of any Federal law or law of any State or political subdivision of any State or jurisdiction that provides greater or equal protection for the rights of individuals with disabilities than are afforded by this Act. Nothing in this Act shall be construed to preclude the prohibition of, or the imposition of restrictions on, smoking in places of employment covered by title I, in transportation covered by title II or III, or in places of public accommodation covered by title III.

(c) INSURANCE.—Titles I through IV of this Act shall not be construed to prohibit or restrict—

(1) an insurer, hospital or medical service company, health maintenance organization, or any agent, or entity that administers benefit plans, or similar organizations from underwriting risks, classifying risks, or administering such risks that are based on or not inconsistent with State law; or

(2) a person or organization covered by this Act from establishing, sponsoring, observing or administering the terms of a bona fide benefit plan that are based on underwriting risks, classifying risks, or administering such risks that are based on or not inconsistent with State law; or

(3) a person or organization covered by this Act from establishing, sponsoring, observing or administering the terms of a bona fide benefit plan that is not subject to State laws that regulate insurance.

Paragraphs (1), (2), and (3) shall not be used as a subterfuge to evade the purposes of title I and III.

(d) ACCOMMODATIONS AND SERVICES.—Nothing in this Act shall be construed to require an individual with a disability to accept an accommodation, aid, service, opportunity, or benefit which such individual chooses not to accept.

SECTION 502.   (§ 12202) STATE IMMUNITY

A State shall not be immune under the eleventh amendment to the Constitution of the United States from an action in Federal or State court of competent jurisdiction for a violation of this Act.   In any action against a State for a violation of the requirements of this Act, remedies (including remedies both at law and in equity) are available for such a violation to the same extent as such remedies are available for such a violation in an action against any public or private entity other than a State.

SECTION 503.   (§ 12203) PROHIBITION AGAINST RETALIA- TION AND COERCION

(a) RETALIATION.—No person shall discriminate against any individual because such individual has opposed any act or practice made unlawful by this Act or because such individual made a charge, testified, assisted, or participated in any manner in an investigation, proceeding, or hearing under this Act.

(b) INTERFERENCE, COERCION, OR INTIMIDATION.—It shall be unlawful to coerce, intimidate, threaten, or interfere with any individual in the exercises or enjoyment of, or on account of his or her having exercised or enjoyed, or on account of his or her having aided or encouraged any other individual in the exercise or enjoyment of, any right granted or protected by this Act.

(c) REMEDIES AND PROCEDURES.—The remedies and procedures available under sections 107, 203, and 308 of this Act shall be available to aggrieved persons for violations of subsections (a) and (b), with respect to title I, title II and title III, respectively.

* * *

SECTION 510.   (§ 12210) ILLEGAL USE OF DRUGS

(a) IN GENERAL.—For purposes of this Act, the term "individual with a disability" does not include an individual who is currently engaging in the illegal use of drugs, when the covered entity acts on the basis of such use.

(b) RULES OF CONSTRUCTION.—Nothing in subsection (a) shall be construed to exclude as an individual with a disability an individual who—

(1) has successfully completed a supervised drug rehabilitation program and is no longer engaging in the illegal use of drugs, or has otherwise been rehabilitated successfully and is no longer engaging in such use;

(2) is participating in a supervised rehabilitation program and is no longer engaging in such use; or

(3) is erroneously regarded as engaging in such use, but is not engaging in such use;

except that is shall not be a violation of this Act for a covered entity to adopt or administer reasonable policies or procedures, including but not limited to drug testing, designed to ensure that an individual described in paragraph (1) or (2) is no longer engaging in the illegal use of drugs; however, nothing in this section shall be construed to encourage, prohibit, restrict, or authorize the conducting of testing for the illegal use of drugs.

(c) HEALTH AND OTHER SERVICES.—Notwithstanding subsection (a) and section 511(b)(3), an individual shall not be denied health services, or services provided in connection with drug rehabilitation, on the basis of the current illegal use of drugs if the individual is otherwise entitled to such services.

(d) DEFINITION OF ILLEGAL USE OF DRUGS.—

(1) IN GENERAL.—The term "illegal use of drugs" means the use of drugs, the possession or distribution of which is unlawful under the Controlled Substances Act (21 U.S.C. 812). Such term does not include the use of a drug taken under supervision by a licensed health care professional, or other uses authorized by the Controlled Substances Act or other provisions of Federal law.

(2) DRUGS.—The term "drug" means a controlled substance, as defined in schedules I through V of section 202 of the Controlled Substances Act.

SECTION 511. (§ 12211) DEFINITIONS

(a) HOMOSEXUALITY AND BISEXUALITY.— For purposes of the definition of "disability" in section 3(2), homosexuality and bisexuality are not impairments and as such are not disabilities under this Act.

(b) CERTAIN CONDITIONS.—Under this Act, the term "disability" shall not include—

(1) transvestism, transsexualism, pedophilia, exhibitionism, voyeurism, gender identity disorders not resulting from physical impairments, or other sexual behavior disorders;

(2) compulsive gambling, kleptomania, or pyromania; or

(3) psychoactive substance use disorders resulting from current illegal use of drugs.

FAIR LABOR STANDARDS ACT

29 U.S.C. §§ 201–219

SEC. 202　Congressional finding and declaration of policy

(a) The Congress finds that the existence, in industries engaged in commerce or in the production of goods for commerce, of labor conditions detrimental to the maintenance of the minimum standard of living necessary for health, efficiency, and general well-being of workers (1) causes commerce and the channels and instrumentalities of commerce to be used to spread and perpetuate such labor conditions among the workers of the several States; (2) burdens commerce and the free flow of goods in commerce; (3) constitutes an unfair method of competition in commerce; (4) leads to labor disputes burdening and obstructing commerce and the free flow of goods in commerce; and (5) interferes with the orderly and fair marketing of goods in commerce. That Congress further finds that the employment of persons in domestic service in households affects commerce.

(b) It is declared to be the policy of this chapter, through the exercise by Congress of its power to regulate commerce among the several States and with foreign nations, to correct and as rapidly as practicable to eliminate the conditions above referred to in such industries without substantially curtailing employment or earning power.

SEC. 203　Definitions

As used in this chapter—

(a) "Person" means an individual, partnership, association, corporation, business trust, legal representative, or any organized group of persons.

* * *

(d) "Employer" includes any person acting directly or indirectly in the interest of an employer in relation to an employee and includes a public agency, but does not include any labor organization (other than when acting as an employer) or anyone acting in the capacity of officer or agent of such labor organization.

(e)(1) Except as provided in paragraphs (2), (3), and (4), the term "employee" means any individual employed by an employer.

* * *

90

(4)(A) The term "employee" does not include any individual who volunteers to perform services for a public agency which is a State, a political subdivision of a State, or an interstate governmental agency, if—

(i) the individual receives no compensation or is paid expenses, reasonable benefits, or a nominal fee to perform the services for which the individual volunteered; and

(ii) such services are not the same type of services which the individual is employed to perform for such public agency.

(B) An employee of a public agency which is a State, political subdivision of a State, or an interstate governmental agency may volunteer to perform services for any other State, political subdivision, or interstate governmental agency, including a State, political subdivision or agency with which the employing State, political subdivision, or agency has a mutual aid agreement.

* * *

(g) "Employ" includes to suffer or permit to work.

(h) "Industry" means a trade, business, industry, or other activity, or branch or group thereof, in which individuals are gainfully employed.

(i) "Goods" means goods (including ships and marine equipment), wares, products, commodities, merchandise, or articles or subjects of commerce of any character, or any part or ingredient thereof, but does not include goods after their delivery into the actual physical possession of the ultimate consumer thereof other than a producer, manufacturer, or processor thereof.

(j) "Produced" means produced, manufactured, mined, handled, or in any other manner worked on in any State; and for the purposes of this chapter an employee shall be deemed to have been engaged in the production of goods if such employee was employed in producing, manufacturing, mining, handling, transporting, or in any other manner working on such goods, or in any closely related process or occupation directly essential to the production thereof, in any State.

(k) "Sale" or "sell" includes any sale, exchange, contract to sell, consignment for sale, shipment for sale, or other disposition.

(*l*) "Oppressive child labor" means a condition of employment under which (1) any employee under the age of sixteen years is employed by an employer (other than a parent or a person standing in place of a parent employing his own child or a child in his custody under the age of sixteen years in an occupation other than manufacturing or mining or an occupation found by the Secretary of Labor to be particularly hazardous for the employment of children between the ages of sixteen and eighteen years or detrimental to their health or well-being) in any occupation, or (2) any employee between the ages of sixteen and eighteen years is employed by an employer in any occupation which the Chief of the Children's Bureau of the Department of Labor shall find and by order declare to be particularly hazardous for the employment of children between such ages or detrimental to their health or well-being; but oppressive child labor shall not be deemed to exist by virtue of the employment in any occupation of any person with respect to whom the employer shall have on file an unexpired certificate issued and held pursuant to regulations of the Chief of the Children's Bureau of the Department of Labor certifying that such person is above the oppressive child-labor age. The Chief of the Children's Bureau of the Department of Labor shall provide by regulation or by order that the employment of employees between the ages of fourteen and sixteen years in occupations other than manufacturing and mining shall not be deemed to constitute oppressive child labor if and to the extent that the Chief of the Children's Bureau of the Department of Labor determines that such employment is confined to periods which will not interfere with their schooling and to conditions which will not interfere with their health and well-being.

(m) "Wage" paid to any employee includes the reasonable cost, as determined by the Administrator, to the employer of furnishing such employee with board, lodging, or other facilities, if such board, lodging or other facilities are customarily furnished by such employer to his employees: *Provided,* That the cost of board, lodging, or other facilities shall not be included as a part of the wage paid to any employee to the extent it is excluded therefrom under the terms of a bona fide collective-bargaining agreement applicable to the particular employee: *Provided further,* That the Secretary is authorized to determine the fair value of such board, lodging, or other facilities for defined classes of employees and in defined areas, based on average cost to the employer or to groups of employers similarly situated, or average value to groups of employees, or other appropriate measures of fair value. Such evaluations, where applicable and pertinent, shall be used in lieu of actual measure of cost in determining the wage paid to any employee. In determining the wage of a tipped employee, the amount paid such employee by his employer shall be deemed to be increased on account of tips by an amount determined by the employer, but not by an amount in excess of (1) 45 percent of the applicable minimum wage rate during the year beginning April 1, 1990, and (2) 50 percent of the applicable minimum wage rate after March 31, 1991, except that the amount of the increase on account of tips determined by the employer may not exceed the value of tips actually received by the employee. The previous sentence shall not apply with respect to any tipped employee unless (1) such employee has been informed by the employer of the provisions of this subsection, and (2) all tips received by such employee have been retained by the employee, except that this subsection shall not be construed to prohibit the pooling of tips among employees who customarily and regularly receive tips.

* * *

(*o*) Hours Worked.—In determining for the purposes of sections 6 and 7 the hours for which an employee is employed, there shall be excluded any time spent in changing clothes or washing at the beginning or end of each workday which was excluded from measured working time during the week involved by the express terms of or by custom or practice under a bona fide collective-bargaining agreement applicable to the particular employee.

* * *

(r)(1) "Enterprise" means the related activities performed (either through unified operation or common control) by any person or persons for a common business purpose, and includes all such activities whether performed in one or more establishments or by one or more corporate or other organizational units including departments of an establishment operated through leasing arrangements, but shall not include the related activities performed for such enterprise by an independent contractor. Within the meaning of this subsection, a retail or service establishment which is under independent ownership shall not be deemed to be so operated or controlled as to be other than a separate and distinct enterprise by reason of any arrangement, which includes, but is not necessarily limited to, an agreement, (A) that it will sell, or sell only, certain goods specified by a particular manufacturer, distributor, or advertiser, or (B) that it will join with other such establishments in the same industry for the purpose of collective purchasing, or (C) that it will have the exclusive right to sell the goods or use the brand name of a manufacturer, distributor, or advertiser within a specified area, or by reason of the fact that it occupies premises leased to it by a person who also leases premises to other retail or service establishments. * * *

* * *

(s)(1) "Enterprise engaged in commerce or in the production of goods for commerce" means an enterprise that—

(A)(i) has employees engaged in commerce or in the production of goods for commerce, or that has employees handling, selling, or

93

otherwise working on goods or materials that have been moved in or produced for commerce by any person; and

(ii) is an enterprise whose annual gross volume of sales made or business done is not less than $500,000 (exclusive of excise taxes at the retail level that are separately stated);

(B) is engaged in the operation of a hospital, an institution primarily engaged in the care of the sick, the aged, or the mentally ill or defective who reside on the premises of such institution, a school for mentally or physically handicapped or gifted children, a preschool, elementary or secondary school, or an institution of higher education (regardless of whether or not such hospital, institution, or school is public or private or operated for profit or not for profit); or

(C) is an activity of a public agency.

(2) Any establishment that has as its only regular employees the owner thereof or the parent, spouse, child, or other member of the immediate family of such owner shall not be considered to be an enterprise engaged in commerce or in the production of goods for commerce or a part of such an enterprise. The sales of such an establishment shall not be included for the purpose of determining the annual gross volume of sales of any enterprise for the purpose of this subsection.

(t) "Tipped employee" means any employee engaged in an occupation in which he customarily and regularly receives more than $30 a month in tips.

Sec. 206   Minimum wages

(a) Employees engaged in commerce; home workers in Puerto Rico and Virgin Islands; employees in American Samoa; seamen on American vessels; agricultural employees

Every employer shall pay to each of his employees who in any workweek is engaged in commerce or in the production of goods for commerce, or is employed in an enterprise engaged in commerce or in the production of goods for commerce, wages at the following rates:

(1) except as otherwise provided in this section, not less than $4.25 an hour during the period ending September 30, 1996, not less than $4.75 an hour during the year beginning October 1, 1996, not less than $5.15 an hour beginning September 1, 1997.

* * *

(d) Prohibition of sex discrimination

(1) No employer having employees subject to any provisions of this section shall discriminate, within any establishment in which such employees are employed, between employees on the basis of sex by paying wages to employees in such establishment at a rate less than the rate at which he pays wages to employees of the opposite sex in such establishment for equal work on jobs the performance of which requires equal skill, effort, and responsibility, and which are performed under similar working conditions, except where such payment is made pursuant to (i) a seniority system; (ii) a merit system; (iii) a system which measures earnings by quantity or quality of production; or (iv) a differential based on any other factor other than sex: *Provided,* That an employer who is paying a wage rate differential in violation of this subsection shall not, in order to comply with the provisions of this subsection, reduce the wage rate of any employee.

(2) No labor organization, or its agents, representing employees of an employer having employees subject to any provisions of this section shall cause or attempt to cause such an employer to discriminate against an employee in violation of paragraph (1) of this subsection.

(3) For purposes of administration and enforcement, any amounts owing to any employee which have been withheld in violation of this subsection shall be deemed to be unpaid minimum wages or unpaid overtime compensation under this Act.

(4) As used in this subsection, the term "labor organization" means any organization of any kind, or any agency or employee representation committee or plan, in which employees participate and which exists for the purpose, in whole or in part, of dealing with employers concerning grievances, labor disputes, wages, rates of pay, hours of employment, or conditions of work.

SEC. 207 Maximum hours

(a) Employees engaged in interstate commerce; additional applicability to employees pursuant to subsequent amendatory provisions

(1) Except as otherwise provided in this section, no employer shall employ any of his employees who in any workweek is engaged in commerce or in the production of goods for commerce, or is employed in an enterprise engaged in commerce or in the production of goods for commerce, for a workweek longer than forty hours unless such employee receives compensation for his employment in excess of the hours above specified at a rate not less than one and one-half times the regular rate at which he is employed.

* * *

95

(b) Employment pursuant to collective bargaining agreement; employment by independently owned and controlled local enterprise engaged in distribution of petroleum products

No employer shall be deemed to have violated subsection (a) of this section by employing any employee for a workweek in excess of that specified in such subsection without paying the compensation for overtime employment prescribed therein if such employee is so employed—

(1) in pursuance of an agreement, made as a result of collective bargaining by representatives of employees certified as bona fide by the National Labor Relations Board, which provides that no employee shall be employed more than one thousand and forty hours during any period of twenty-six consecutive weeks; * * *

* * *

(e) Definition of "regular rate" of employment

As used in this section the "regular rate" at which an employee is employed shall be deemed to include all remuneration for employment paid to, or on behalf of, the employee, but shall not be deemed to include—

(1) sums paid as gifts; payments in the nature of gifts made at Christmas time or on other special occasions, as a reward for service, the amounts of which are not measured by or dependent on hours worked, production, or efficiency;

(2) payments made for occasional periods when no work is performed due to vacation, holiday, illness, failure of the employer to provide sufficient work, or other similar cause; reasonable payments for traveling expenses, or other expenses, incurred by an employee in the furtherance of his employer's interests and properly reimbursable by the employer; and other similar payments to an employee which are not made as compensation for his hours of employment;

(3) Sums paid in recognition of services performed during a given period if either, (a) both the fact that payment is to be made and the amount of the payment are determined at the sole discretion of the employer at or near the end of the period and not pursuant to any prior contract, agreement, or promise causing the employee to expect such payments regularly; or (b) the payments are made pursuant to a bona fide profit-sharing plan or trust or bona fide thrift or savings plan, meeting the requirements of the Administrator set forth in appropriate regulations which he shall issue, having due regard among other relevant factors, to the extent to which the amounts paid to the employee are determined without regard to hours of work, production, or efficiency; or (c) the payments are talent fees (as such talent fees are defined

and delimited by regulations of the Administrator) paid to performers, including announcers, on radio and television programs;

(4) contributions irrevocably made by an employer to a trustee or third person pursuant to a bona fide plan for providing old-age, retirement, life, accident, or health insurance or similar benefits for employees;

(5) extra compensation provided by a premium rate paid for certain hours worked by the employee in any day of workweek because such hours are hours worked in excess of eight in a day or in excess of the maximum workweek applicable to such employee under subsection (a) or in excess of the employee's normal working hours or regular working hours, as the case may be;

(6) extra compensation provided by a premium rate paid for work by the employee on Saturdays, Sundays, holidays, or regular days of rest, or on the sixth or seventh day of the workweek, where such premium rate is not less than one and one-half times the rate established in good faith for like work performed in nonovertime hours on other days;

(7) extra compensation provided by a premium rate paid to the employee, in pursuance of an applicable employment contract or collective-bargaining agreement, for work outside of the hours established in good faith by the contract or agreement as the basic, normal, or regular workday (not exceeding eight hours) or workweek (not exceeding the maximum workweek) applicable to such employee under subsection (a), where such premium rate is not less than one and one-half times the rate established in good faith by the contract or agreement for like work performed during such workday or workweek; or

(8) any value or income derived from employer-provided grants or rights provided pursuant to a stock option, stock appreciation right, or bona fide employee stock purchase program which is not otherwise excludable under any of paragraphs (1) through (7) if—

(A) grants are made pursuant to a program, the terms and conditions of which are communicated to participating employees either at the beginning of the employee's participation in the program or at the time of the grant;

(B) in the case of stock options and stock appreciation rights, the grant or right cannot be exercisable for a period of at least 6 months after the time of grant (except that grants or rights may become exercisable because of an employee's death, disability, retirement, or a change in corporate ownership, or other circumstances permitted by regulation), and the exercise price is at least 85 percent of the fair market value of the stock at the time of grant;

(C) exercise of any grant or right is voluntary; and

(D) any determinations regarding the award of, and the amount of, employer-provided grants or rights that are based on performance are—

(i) made based upon meeting previously established performance criteria (which may include hours of work, efficiency, or productivity) of any business unit consisting of at least 10 employees or of a facility, except that, any determinations may be based on length of service or minimum schedule of hours or days of work; or

(ii) made based upon the past performance (which may include any criteria) of one or more employees in a given period so long as the determination is in the sole discretion of the employer and not pursuant to any prior contract.

(f) Employment necessitating irregular hours of work

No employer shall be deemed to have violated subsection (a) by employing any employee for a workweek in excess of the maximum workweek applicable to such employee under subsection (a) if such employee is employed pursuant to a bona fide individual contract, or pursuant to an agreement made as a result of collective bargaining by representatives of employees, if the duties of such employee necessitate irregular hours of work, and the contract or agreement (1) specifies a regular rate of pay of not less than the minimum hourly rate provided in subsection (a) or (b) of section 6 (whichever may be applicable) and compensation at not less than one and one-half times such rate for all hours worked in excess of such maximum workweek, and (2) provides a weekly guaranty of pay for not more than sixty hours based on the rates so specified.

(g) Employment at piece rates

No employer shall be deemed to have violated subsection (a) by employing any employee for a workweek in excess of the maximum workweek applicable to such employee under such subsection if, pursuant to an agreement or understanding arrived at between the employer and the employee before performance of the work, the amount paid to the employee for the number of hours worked by him in such workweek in excess of the maximum workweek applicable to such employee under such subsection—

(1) in the case of an employee employed at piece rates, is computed at piece rates not less than one and one-half times the bona fide piece rates applicable to the same work when performed during non-overtime hours; * * * and if (i) the employee's average hourly earnings for the workweek exclusive of payments described in paragraphs (1) through (7) of subsection (e) are not less than the minimum hourly rate required by

applicable law, and (ii) extra overtime compensation is properly comput-ed and paid on other forms of additional pay required to be included in computing the regular rate.

* * *

(q) Maximum hour exemption for employees receiving reme-dial education.

Any employer may employ any employee for a period or periods of not more than 10 hours in the aggregate in any workweek in excess of the maximum workweek specified in subsection (a) without paying the compensation for overtime employment prescribed in such subsection, if during such period or periods the employee is receiving remedial edu-cation that is—

(1) provided to employees who lack a high school diploma or edu-cational attainment at the eighth grade level;

(2) designed to provide reading and other basic skills at an eighth grade level or below; and

(3) does not include job specific training.

Sec. **212   Child labor provisions**

(a) Restrictions on shipment of goods; prosecution; convic-tion

No producer, manufacturer, or dealer shall ship or deliver for shipment in commerce any goods produced in an establishment situated in the United States in or about which within thirty days prior to the removal of such goods therefrom any oppressive child labor has been employed: *Provided,* That any such shipment or delivery for shipment of such goods by a purchaser who acquired them in good faith in reliance on written assurance from the producer, manufacturer, or dealer that the goods were produced in compliance with the requirements of this section, and who acquired such goods for value without notice of any such violation, shall not be deemed prohibited by this subsection: *And provided further,* That a prosecution and conviction of a defendant for the shipment or delivery for shipment of any goods under the conditions herein prohibited shall be a bar to any further prosecution against the same defendant for shipments or deliveries for shipment of any such goods before the beginning of said prosecution.

(b) Investigations and inspections

The Secretary of Labor or any of his authorized representatives, shall make all investigations and inspections under section 211(a) of this title with respect to the employment of minors, and, subject to the direction and control of the Attorney General, shall bring all actions under section 217 of this title to enjoin any act or practice which is unlawful by reason of the existence of oppressive child labor, and shall administer all other provisions of this chapter relating to oppressive child labor.

(c) Oppressive child labor

No employer shall employ any oppressive child labor in commerce or in the production of goods for commerce or in any enterprise engaged in commerce or in the production of goods for commerce.

(d) Proof of age

In order to carry out the objectives of this section, the Secretary may by regulation require employers to obtain from any employee proof of age.

Sec. 213 Exemptions

(a) Minimum wage and maximum hour requirements

The provision of sections 6 (except subsection 6(d) in the case of paragraph (1) of this subsection) and section 7 of this title shall not apply with respect to—

(1) any employee employed in a bona fide executive, administrative, or professional capacity (including any employee employed in the capacity of academic administrative personnel or teacher in elementary or secondary schools), or in the capacity of outside salesman (as such terms are defined and delimited from time to time by regulations of the Secretary, subject to the provisions of the Administrative Procedure Act, except that an employee of a retail or service establishment shall not be excluded from the definition of employee employed in a bona fide executive or administrative capacity because of the number of hours in his workweek which he devotes to activities not directly or closely related to the performance of executive or administrative activities, if less than 40 per centum of his hours worked in the workweek are devoted to such activities); or

[(2) Repealed.]

(3) any employee employed by an establishment which is an amusement or recreational establishment organized camp, or religious or nonprofit educational conference center, if (A) it does not operate for more than seven months in any calendar year, or (B) during the preceding calendar year, its average receipts for any six months of such year were not more than 33⅓ per centum of its average receipts for the other six months of such year, except that the exemption from sections 6 and 7 provided by this paragraph does not apply with respect to any employee of a private entity engaged in providing services or facilities (other than, in the case of the exemption from section 6, a private entity engaged in providing services and facilities directly related to skiing) in a national

park or a national forest, or on land in the National Wildlife Refuge System, under a contract with the Secretary of the Interior or the Secretary of Agriculture; or

[(4) Repealed.]

(5) any employee employed in the catching, taking, propagating, harvesting, cultivating, or farming of any kind of fish, shellfish, crustacea, sponges, seaweeds, or other aquatic forms of animal and vegetable life, or in the first processing, canning or packing such marine products at sea as an incident to, or in conjunction with, such fishing operations, including the going to and returning from work and loading and unloading when performed by any such employee; or

(6) any employee employed in agriculture (A) if such employee is employed by an employer who did not, during any calendar quarter during the preceding calendar year, use more than five hundred mandays of agricultural labor, (B) if such employee is the parent, spouse, child, or other member of his employer's immediate family, (C) if such employee (i) is employed as a hand harvest laborer and is paid on a piece rate basis in an operation which has been, and is customarily and generally recognized as having been, paid on a piece rate basis in the region of employment, (ii) commutes daily from his permanent residence to the farm on which he is so employed, and (iii) has been employed in agriculture less than thirteen weeks during the preceding calendar year, (D) if such employee (other than an employee described in clause (C) of this subsection) (i) is sixteen years of age or under and is employed as a hand harvest laborer, is paid on a piece rate basis in an operation which has been, and is customarily and generally recognized as having been, paid on a piece rate basis in the region of employment, (ii) is employed on the same farm as his parent or person standing in the place of his parent, and (iii) is paid at the same piece rate as employees over age sixteen are paid on the same farm, or (E) if such employee is principally engaged in the range production of livestock; or

(7) any employee to the extent that such employee is exempted by regulations, order, or certificate of the Secretary issued under section 14; or

(8) any employee employed in connection with the publication of any weekly, semiweekly, or daily newspaper with a circulation of less than four thousand the major part of which circulation is within the county where published or counties contiguous thereto; or

[(9) Repealed.]

(10) any switchboard operator employed by an independently owned public telephone company which has not more than seven hundred and fifty stations; or

[(11) Repealed.]

(12) any employee employed as a seaman on a vessel other than an American vessel; or

[(13), (14) Repealed.]

(15) any employee employed on a casual basis in domestic service employment to provide babysitting services or any employee employed in domestic service employment to provide companionship services for individuals who (because of age or infirmity) are unable to care for themselves (as such terms are defined and delimited by regulations of the Secretary); or

(16) a criminal investigator who is paid availability pay under section 5545a of title 5, United States Code; or

(17) any employee who is a computer systems analyst, computer programmer, software engineer, or other similarly skilled worker, whose primary duty is—

(A) the application of systems analysis techniques and procedures, including consulting with users, to determine hardware, software, or system functional specifications;

(B) the design, development, documentation, analysis, creation, testing, or modification of computer systems or programs, including prototypes, based on and related to user or system design specifications;

(C) the design, documentation, testing, creation, or modification of computer programs related to machine operating systems; or

(D) a combination of duties described in subparagraphs (A), (B), and (C) the performance of which requires the same level of skills, and who, in the case of an employee who is compensated on an hourly basis, is compensated at a rate of not less than $27.63 an hour.

(b)   Maximum hour requirements

The provisions of section 207 of this title shall not apply with respect to—

(1) any employee with respect to whom the Secretary of Transportation has power to establish qualifications and maximum hours of service pursuant to the provisions of section 204 of the Motor Carrier Act, 1935; or

(2) any employee of an employer engaged in the operation of a rail carrier subject to part A of subtitle IV of title 49; or

(3) any employee of a carrier by air subject to the provisions of title II of the Railway Labor Act [45 U.S.C.A. § 181 et seq.]; or

[(4) Repealed.]

(5) any individual employed as an outside buyer of poultry, eggs, cream, or milk, in their raw or natural state; or

(6) any employee employed as a seaman; or

[(7), (8) Repealed.]

(9) any employee employed as an announcer, news editor, or chief engineer by a radio or television station the major studio of which is located (A) in a city or town of one hundred thousand population or less, according to the latest available decennial census figures as compiled by the Bureau of the Census, except where such city or town is part of a standard metropolitan statistical area, as defined and designated by the Office of Management and Budget, which has a total population in excess of one hundred thousand, or (B) in a city or town of twenty-five thousand population or less, which is part of such an area but is at least 40 airline miles from the principal city in such area; or

(10)(A) any salesman, partsman, or mechanic primarily engaged in selling or servicing automobiles, trucks, or farm implements, if he is employed by a nonmanufacturing establishment primarily engaged in the business of selling such vehicles or implements to ultimate purchasers; or

(B) any salesman primarily engaged in selling trailers, boats, or aircraft, if he is employed by a nonmanufacturing establishment primarily engaged in the business of selling trailers, boats, or aircraft to ultimate purchasers; or

(11) any employee employed as a driver or driver's helper making local deliveries, who is compensated for such employment on the basis of trip rates, or other delivery payment plan, if the Secretary shall find that such plan has the general purpose and effect of reducing hours worked by such employees to, or below, the maximum workweek applicable to them under section 7(a); or

(12) any employee employed in agriculture or in connection with the operation or maintenance of ditches, canals, reservoirs, or waterways, not owned or operated for profit, or operated on a sharecrop basis, and which are used exclusively for supply and storing of water for agricultural purposes during the preceding calendar year; or

(13) any employee with respect to his employment in agriculture by a farmer, notwithstanding other employment of such employee in connection with livestock auction operations in which such farmer is engaged as an adjunct to the raising of livestock, either on his own account or in conjunction with other farmers, if such employee (A) is primarily employed during his workweek in agriculture by such farmer, and (B) is paid for his employment in connection with such livestock auction

operations at a wage rate not less than that prescribed by section 6(a)(1); or

(14) any employee employed within the area of production (as defined by the Secretary) by an establishment commonly recognized as a country elevator, including such an establishment which sells products and services used in the operation of a farm, if no more than five employees are employed in the establishment in such operations; or

(15) any employee engaged in the processing of maple sap into sugar (other than refined sugar) or syrup; or

(16) any employee engaged (A) in the transportation and preparation for transportation of fruits or vegetables, whether or not performed by the farmer, from the farm to a place of first processing or first marketing within the same State, or (B) in transportation, whether or not performed by the farmer, between the farm and any point within the same State of persons employed or to be employed in the harvesting of fruits or vegetables; or

(17) any driver employed by an employer engaged in the business of operating taxicabs; or

[(18), (19) Repealed.]

(20) any employee of a public agency who in any workweek is employed in fire protection activities or any employee of a public agency who in any workweek is employed in law enforcement activities (including security personnel in correctional institutions), if the public agency employs during the workweek less than 5 employees in fire protection or law enforcement activities, as the case may be; or

(21) any employee who is employed in domestic service in a household and who resides in such household; or

[(22), (23) Repealed.]

(24) any employee who is employed with his spouse by a nonprofit educational institution to serve as the parents of children—

 (A) who are orphans or one of whose natural parents is deceased, or

 (B) who are enrolled in such institution and reside in residential facilities of the institution, while such children are in residence at such institution, if such employee and his spouse reside in such facilities, receive, without cost, board and lodging from such institution, and are together compensated, on a cash basis, at an annual rate of not less than $10,000; or

[(25), (26) Repealed.]

(27) any employee employed by an establishment which is a motion picture theater; or

(28) any employee employed in planting or tending trees, cruising, surveying, or felling timber, or in preparing or transporting logs or other forestry products to the mill, processing plant, railroad, or other transportation terminal, if the number of employees employed by his employer in such forestry or lumbering operations does not exceed eight; or

(29) any employee of an amusement or recreational establishment located in a national park or national forest or on land in the National Wildlife Refuge System if such employee (A) is an employee of a private entity engaged in providing services or facilities in a national park or national forest, or on land in the National Wildlife Refuge System, under a contract with the Secretary of the Interior or the Secretary of Agriculture, and (B) receives compensation for employment in excess of fifty-six hours in any workweek at a rate not less than one and one-half times the regular rate at which he is employed; or

(30) A criminal investigator who is paid availability pay

(c) Child labor requirements under section 5545(a) of title 5, United States Code.

(1) Except as provided in paragraph (2) or (4), the provisions of section 12 relating to child labor shall not apply to any employee employed in agriculture outside of school hours for the school district where such employee is living while he is so employed, if such employee—

(A) is less than twelve years of age and (i) is employed by his parent, or by a person standing in the place of his parent, on a farm owned or operated by such parent or person, or (ii) is employed, with the consent of his parent or person standing in the place of his parent, on a farm, none of the employees of which are (because of subsection 13(a)(6)(A) of this section) required to be paid at the wage rate prescribed by section 6(a)(5),

(B) is twelve years or thirteen years of age and (i) such employment is with the consent of his parent or person standing in the place of his parent, or (ii) his parent or such person is employed on the same farm as such employee, or

(C) is fourteen years of age or older.

(2) The provisions of section 12 relating to child labor shall apply to an employee below the age of sixteen employed in agriculture in an occupation that the Secretary of Labor finds and declares to be particularly hazardous for the employment of children below the age of sixteen, except where such employee is employed by his parent or by a person standing in the place of his parent on a farm owned or operated by such parent or person.

(3) The provisions of section 12 of this title relating to child labor shall not apply to any child employed as an actor or performer in motion pictures or theatrical productions, or in radio or television productions.

(4)(A) An employer or group of employers may apply to the Secretary for a waiver of the application of section 12 to the employment for not more than eight weeks in any calendar year of individuals who are less than twelve years of age, but not less than ten years of age, as hand harvest laborers in an agricultural operation which has been, and is customarily and generally recognized as being, paid on a piece rate basis in the region in which such individuals would be employed. The Secretary may not grant such a waiver unless he finds, based on objective data submitted by the applicant, that—

(i) the crop to be harvested is one with a particularly short harvesting season and the application of section 12 would cause severe economic disruption in the industry of the employer or group of employers applying for the waiver;

(ii) the employment of the individuals to whom the waiver would apply would not be deleterious to their health or well-being;

(iii) the level and type of pesticides and other chemicals used would not have an adverse effect on the health or well-being of the individuals to whom the waiver would apply;

(iv) individuals age twelve and above are not available for such employment; and

(v) the industry of such employer or group of employers has traditionally and substantially employed individuals under twelve years of age without displacing substantial job opportunities for individuals over sixteen years of age.

(B) Any waiver granted by the Secretary under subparagraph (A) shall require that—

(i) the individuals employed under such waiver be employed outside of school hours for the school district where they are living while so employed;

(ii) such individuals while so employed commute daily from their permanent residence to the farm on which they are so employed;

* * *

Sec. 215. Prohibited acts—Prima facie evidence

(a) After the expiration of one hundred and twenty days from the date of enactment of this Act, it shall be unlawful for any person—

(1) to transport, offer for transportation, ship, deliver, or sell in commerce, or to ship, deliver, or sell with knowledge that shipment or delivery or sale thereof in commerce is intended, any goods in the production of which any employee was employed in violation of section 206 or section 207, or in violation of any regulation or order of the Administrator issued under section 214; except that no provisions of this Act shall impose any liability upon any common carrier for the transportation in commerce in the regular course of its business of any goods not produced by such common carrier, and no provision of this Act shall excuse any common carrier from its obligation to accept any goods for transportation; and except that any such transportation, offer, shipment, delivery, or sale of such goods by a purchaser who acquired them in good faith in reliance on written assurance from the producer that the goods were produced in compliance with the requirements of the Act, and who acquired such goods for value without notice of any such violation, shall not be deemed unlawful;

(2) to violate any of the provisions of section 206 or section 207, or any of the provisions of any regulation or order of the Administrator issued under section 214;

(3) to discharge or in any other manner discriminate against any employee because such employee has filed any complaint or instituted or caused to be instituted any proceeding under or related to this Act, or has testified or is about to testify in any such proceeding, or has served or is about to serve on an industry committee.

(4) to violate any of the provisions of section 212;

(5) to violate any of the provisions of section 211(c) or any regulation or order made or continued in effect under the provisions of section 211(d) or to make any statement, report, or record filed or kept pursuant to the provisions of such section or of any regulation or order thereunder, knowing such statement, report, or record to be false in a material respect.

SEC. 216 Penalties

(a) Fines and imprisonment

Any person who willfully violates any of the provisions of section 15 shall upon conviction thereof be subject to a fine of not more than $10,000, or to imprisonment for not more than six months, or both. No person shall be imprisoned under this subsection except for an offense committed after the conviction of such person for a prior offense under this subsection.

(b) Damages; right of action; attorney's fees and costs; termination of right of action

Any employer who violates the provisions of section 6 or section 7 shall be liable to the employee or employees affected in the amount of their unpaid minimum wages, or their unpaid overtime compensation, as the case may be, and in an additional equal amount as liquidated damages. Any employer who violates the provisions of section 15(a)(3) of this Act shall be liable for such legal or equitable relief as may be appropriate to effectuate the purposes of section 215(a)(3) of this title, including without limitation employment, reinstatement, promotion, and the payment of wages lost and an additional equal amount as liquidated damages. An action to recover the liability prescribed in either of the preceding sentences may be maintained against any employer (including a public agency) in any Federal or State court of competent jurisdiction by any one or more employees for and in behalf of himself or themselves and other employees similarly situated. No employee shall be a party plaintiff to any such action unless he gives his consent in writing to become such a party and such consent is filed in the court in which such action is brought. The court in such action shall, in addition to any judgment awarded to the plaintiff or plaintiffs, allow a reasonable attorney's fee to be paid by the defendant, and costs of the action. The right provided by this subsection to bring an action by or on behalf of any employee, and the right of any employee to become a party plaintiff to any such action, shall terminate upon the filing of a complaint by the Secretary of Labor in an action under section 7 in which (1) restraint is sought of any further delay in the payment of unpaid minimum wages, or the amount of unpaid overtime compensation, as the case may be, owing to such employee under section 6 or section 7 by an employer liable therefor under the provisions of this subsection or (2) legal or equitable relief is sought as a result of alleged violations of section 15(a)(3).

(c) Payment of wages and compensation; waiver of claims; actions by the Secretary; limitation of actions

The Secretary is authorized to supervise the payment of the unpaid minimum wages or the unpaid overtime compensation owing to any employee or employees under section 6 or section 7, and the agreement of any employee to accept such payment shall upon payment in full constitute a waiver by such employee of any right he may have under subsection (b) of this section to such unpaid minimum wages or unpaid overtime compensation and an additional equal amount as liquidated damages. The Secretary may bring an action in any court of competent jurisdiction to recover the amount of unpaid minimum wages or overtime compensation and an equal amount as liquidated damages. The right provided by subsection (b) of this section to bring an action by or

108

on behalf of any employee to recover the liability specified in the first sentence of such subsection and of any employee to become a party plaintiff to any such action shall terminate upon the filing of a complaint by the Secretary in an action under this subsection in which a recovery is sought of unpaid minimum wages or unpaid overtime compensation under sections 6 and 7 or liquidated or other damages provided by this subsection owing to such employee by an employer liable under the provisions of subsection (b), unless such action is dismissed without prejudice on motion of the Secretary. Any sums thus recovered by the Secretary of Labor on behalf of an employee pursuant to this subsection shall be held in a special deposit account and shall be paid, on order of the Secretary of Labor, directly to the employee or employees affected. Any such sums not paid to an employee because of inability to do so within a period of three years shall be covered into the Treasury of the United States as miscellaneous receipts. * * *

* * *

(e) Civil penalties for child labor violations or section 13(c)(5)

Any person who violates the provisions of section 12, relating to child labor, or any regulation issued under that section, or any person who repeatedly or willfully violates section 6 or 7, shall be subject to a civil penalty of not to exceed $10,000 for each such violation. In determining the amount of such penalty, the appropriateness of such penalty to the size of the business of the person charged and the gravity of the violation shall be considered. * * *

SEC. 217 Injunction proceedings

The district courts, together with the United States District Court for the District of the Canal Zone, the District Court of the Virgin Islands, and the District Court of Guam shall have jurisdiction, for cause shown, to restrain violations of section 215, including in the case of violations of section 215(a)(2) the restraint of any withholding of payment of minimum wages or overtime compensation found by the court to be due to employees under this Act (except sums which employees are barred from recovering), at the time of the commencement of the action to restrain the violations, by virtue of the provisions of section 255 of the Portal-to-Portal Act of 1947.

SEC. 218 Relation to other laws

(a) No provision of this chapter or of any order thereunder shall excuse noncompliance with any Federal or State law or municipal ordinance establishing a minimum wage higher than the minimum wage established under this chapter or a maximum workweek lower than the maximum workweek established under this chapter, and no provision of this chapter relating to the employment of child labor shall justify noncompliance with any Federal or State law or municipal ordinance establishing a higher standard than the standard established under this chapter. No provision of this chapter shall justify any employer in reducing a wage paid by him which is in excess of the applicable minimum wage under this chapter, or justify any employer in increasing hours of employment maintained by him which are shorter than the maximum hours applicable under this chapter.

* * *

PORTAL TO PORTAL ACT

29 U.S.C. §§ 251–262

§ 254. Relief from liability and punishment under the Fair Labor Standards Act of 1938, the Walsh–Healy Act, and the Bacon–Davis Act for failure to pay minimum wage or overtime compensation

(a) Activities non compensable. Except as provided in subsection (b), no employer shall be subject to any liability or punishment under the Fair Labor Standards Act of 1938, as amended, the Walsh–Healey Act, or the Bacon–Davis Act, on account of the failure of such employer to pay an employee minimum wages, or to pay an employee overtime compensation, for or on account of any of the following activities of such employee engaged in on or after the date of the enactment of this Act—

(1) walking, riding, or traveling to and from the actual place of performance of the principal activity or activities which such employee is employed to perform, and

(2) activities which are preliminary to or postliminary to said principal activity or activities, which occur either prior to the time on any particular workday at which such employee commences, or subsequent to the time on any particular workday at which he ceases, such principal activity or activities. For purposes of this subsection, the use of an employer's vehicle for travel by an employee and activities performed by an employee which are incidental to the use of such vehicle for commuting shall not be considered part of the employee's principal activities if the use of such vehicle for travel is within the normal commuting area for the employer's business or establishment and the use of the employer's vehicle is subject to an agreement on the part of the employer and the employee or representative of such employee.

§ 255. Statute of limitations

Any action commenced on or after the date of the enactment of this Act to enforce any cause of action for unpaid minimum wages, unpaid overtime compensation, or liquidated damages, under the Fair Labor Standards Act of 1938, as amended, the Walsh–Healey Act, or the Bacon–Davis Act—

(a) if the cause of action accrues on or after the date of the enactment of this Act—may be commenced within two years after the cause of action accrued, and every such action shall be forever barred unless commenced within two years after the cause of action

111

accrued, except that a cause of action arising out of a willful violation may be commenced within three years after the cause of action accrued;

(b) if the cause of action accrued prior to the date of the enactment of this Act—may be commenced within whichever of the following periods is the shorter: (1) two years after the cause of action accrued, or (2) the period prescribed by the applicable State statute of limitations; and, except as provided in paragraph (c), every such action shall be forever barred unless commenced within the shorter of such two periods;

* * *

(d) with respect to any cause of action brought under section 216(b) of the Fair Labor Standards Act of 1938 against a State or a political subdivision of a State in a district court of the United States on or before April 18, 1973, the running of the statutory periods of limitation shall be deemed suspended during the period beginning with the commencement of any such action and ending one hundred and eighty days after the effective date of the Fair Labor Standards Amendments of 1974, except that such suspension shall not be applicable if in such action judgment has been entered for the defendant on the grounds other than State immunity from Federal jurisdiction.

§ 259. Reliance in future on administrative rulings

(a) In any action or proceeding based on any act or omission on or after the date of the enactment of this Act, no employer shall be subject to any liability or punishment for or on account of the failure of the employer to pay minimum wages or overtime compensation under the Fair Labor Standards Act of 1938, as amended, the Walsh–Healey Act, or the Bacon–Davis Act, if he pleads and proves that the act or omission complained of was in good faith in conformity with and in reliance on any written administrative regulation, order, ruling, approval, or interpretation, of the agency of the United States specified in subsection (b) of this section, or any administrative practice or enforcement policy of such agency with respect to the class of employers to which he belonged. Such a defense, if established, shall be a bar to the action or proceeding, notwithstanding that after such act or omission, such administrative regulation, order, ruling, approval, interpretation, practice, or enforcement policy is modified or rescinded or is determined by judicial authority to be invalid or of no legal effect.

(b) The agency referred to in subsection (a) shall be—

(1) in the case of the Fair Labor Standards Act of 1938, as amended—the Administrator of the Wage and Hour Division of the Department of Labor;

(2) in the case of the Walsh–Healey Act—the Secretary of Labor, or any Federal officer utilized by him in the administration of such Act; and

(3) in the case of the Bacon–Davis Act—the Secretary of Labor.

§ 260. Liquidated damages

In any action commenced prior to or on or after the date of the enactment of this Act to recover unpaid minimum wages, unpaid over-time compensation, or liquidated damages, under the Fair Labor Standards Act of 1938, as amended, if the employer shows to the satisfaction of the court that the act or omission giving rise to such action was in good faith and that he had reasonable grounds for believing that his act or omission was not a violation of the Fair Labor Standards Act of 1938, as amended, the court may, in its sound discretion, award no liquidated damages or award any amount thereof not to exceed the amount speci-fied in section 216 of such Act.

FAMILY AND MEDICAL LEAVE ACT

29 U.S.C. §§ 2601–2654

SEC. 2611. DEFINITIONS.

As used in this title:

(1) COMMERCE.—The terms "commerce" and "industry or activity affecting commerce" mean any activity, business, or industry in commerce or in which a labor dispute would hinder or obstruct commerce or the free flow of commerce, and include "commerce" and any "industry affecting commerce", as defined in paragraphs (1) and (3) of section 501 of the Labor Management Relations Act, 1947 (29 U.S.C. 142(1) and (3)).

(2) ELIGIBLE EMPLOYEE.—

(A) IN GENERAL.—The term "eligible employee" means an employee who has been employed—

(i) for at least 12 months by the employer with respect to whom leave is requested under section 102; and

(ii) for at least 1,250 hours of service with such employer during the previous 12–month period.

(B) EXCLUSIONS.—The term "eligible employee" does not include—

(i) any Federal officer or employee covered under subchapter V of chapter 63 of title 5, United States Code (as added by title II of this Act); or

(ii) any employee of an employer who is employed at a worksite at which such employer employs less than 50 employees if the total number of employees employed by that employer within 75 miles of that worksite is less than 50.

(C) DETERMINATION.—For purposes of determining whether an employee meets the hours of service requirement specified in subparagraph (A)(ii), the legal standards established under section 7 of the Fair Labor Standards Act of 1938 (29 U.S.C. 207) shall apply.

(3) EMPLOY; EMPLOYEE; STATE.—The terms "employ", "employee", and "State" have the same meanings given such terms in subsections (c), (e), and (g) of section 3 of the Fair Labor Standards Act of 1938 (29 U.S.C. 203(c), (e), and (g)).

(4) EMPLOYER.—

(A) IN GENERAL.—The term "employer"—

114

(i) means any person engaged in commerce or in any industry or activity affecting commerce who employs 50 or more employees for each working day during each of 20 or more calendar workweeks in the current or preceding calendar year;

(ii) includes—

(I) any person who acts, directly or indirectly, in the interest of an employer to any of the employees of such employer; and

(II) any successor in interest of an employer; and

(iii) includes any "public agency", as defined in section 3(x) of the Fair Labor Standards Act of 1938 (29 U.S.C. 203(x)); and

(iv) includes the General Accounting Office and the Library of Congress.

(B) PUBLIC AGENCY.—For purposes of subparagraph (A)(iii), a public agency shall be considered to be a person engaged in commerce or in an industry or activity affecting commerce.

(5) EMPLOYMENT BENEFITS.—The term "employment benefits" means all benefits provided or made available to employees by an employer, including group life insurance, health insurance, disability insurance, sick leave, annual leave, educational benefits, and pensions, regardless of whether such benefits are provided by a practice or written policy of an employer or through an "employee benefit plan", as defined in section 3(3) of the Employee Retirement Income Security Act of 1974 (29 U.S.C. 1002(3)).

(6) HEALTH CARE PROVIDER.—The term "health care provider" means—

(A) a doctor of medicine or osteopathy who is authorized to practice medicine or surgery (as appropriate) by the State in which the doctor practices; or

(B) any other person determined by the Secretary to be capable of providing health care services.

(7) PARENT.—The term "parent" means the biological parent of an employee or an individual who stood in loco parentis to an employee when the employee was a son or daughter.

(8) PERSON.—The term "person" has the same meaning given such term in section 3(a) of the Fair Labor Standards Act of 1938 (29 U.S.C. 203(a)).

(9) REDUCED LEAVE SCHEDULE.—The term "reduced leave schedule" means a leave schedule that reduces the usual number of hours per workweek, or hours per workday, of an employee.

(10) SECRETARY.—The term "Secretary" means the Secretary of Labor.

(11) SERIOUS HEALTH CONDITION.—The term "serious health condition" means an illness, injury, impairment, or physical or mental condition that involves—

    (A) inpatient care in a hospital, hospice, or residential medical care facility; or

    (B) continuing treatment by a health care provider.

(12) SON OR DAUGHTER.—The term "son or daughter" means a biological, adopted, or foster child, a stepchild, a legal ward, or a child of a person standing in loco parentis, who is—

    (A) under 18 years of age; or

    (B) 18 years of age or older and incapable of self-care because of a mental or physical disability.

(13) SPOUSE.—The term "spouse" means a husband or wife, as the case may be.

SEC. 2612.   LEAVE REQUIREMENT.

(a) IN GENERAL.—

(1) ENTITLEMENT TO LEAVE.—Subject to section 103, an eligible employee shall be entitled to a total of 12 workweeks of leave during any 12–month period for one or more of the following:

    (A) Because of the birth of a son or daughter of the employee and in order to care for such son or daughter.

    (B) Because of the placement of a son or daughter with the employee for adoption or foster care.

    (C) In order to care for the spouse, or a son, daughter, or parent, of the employee, if such spouse, son, daughter, or parent has a serious health condition.

    (D) Because of a serious health condition that makes the employee unable to perform the functions of the position of such employee.

(2) EXPIRATION OF ENTITLEMENT.—The entitlement to leave under subparagraphs (A) and (B) of paragraph (1) for a birth or placement of a son or daughter shall expire at the end of the 12–month period beginning on the date of such birth or placement.

(b) LEAVE TAKEN INTERMITTENTLY OR ON A REDUCED LEAVE SCHEDULE.—

(1) IN GENERAL.—Leave under subparagraph (A) or (B) of subsection (a)(1) shall not be taken by an employee intermittently or on a

reduced leave schedule unless the employee and the employer of the employee agree otherwise. Subject to paragraph (2), subsection (e)(2), and section 103(b)(5), leave under subparagraph (C) or (D) of subsection (a)(1) may be taken intermittently or on a reduced leave schedule when medically necessary. The taking of leave intermittently or on a reduced leave schedule pursuant to this paragraph shall not result in a reduction in the total amount of leave to which the employee is entitled under subsection (a) beyond the amount of leave actually taken.

(2) ALTERNATIVE POSITION.—If an employee requests intermittent leave, or leave on a reduced leave schedule, under subparagraph (C) or (D) of subsection (a)(1), that is foreseeable based on planned medical treatment, the employer may require such employee to transfer temporarily to an available alternative position offered by the employer for which the employee is qualified and that—

(A) has equivalent pay and benefits; and

(B) better accommodates recurring periods of leave than the regular employment position of the employee.

(c) UNPAID LEAVE PERMITTED.—Except as provided in subsection (d), leave granted under subsection (a) may consist of unpaid leave. Where an employee is otherwise exempt under regulations issued by the Secretary pursuant to section 13(a)(1) of the Fair Labor Standards Act of 1938 (29 U.S.C. 213(a)(1)), the compliance of an employer with this title by providing unpaid leave shall not affect the exempt status of the employee under such section.

(d) RELATIONSHIP TO PAID LEAVE.—

(1) UNPAID LEAVE.—If an employer provides paid leave for fewer than 12 workweeks, the additional weeks of leave necessary to attain the 12 workweeks of leave required under this title may be provided without compensation.

(2) SUBSTITUTION OF PAID LEAVE.—

(A) IN GENERAL.—An eligible employee may elect, or an employer may require the employee, to substitute any of the accrued paid vacation leave, personal leave, or family leave of the employee for leave provided under subparagraph (A), (B), or (C) of subsection (a)(1) for any part of the 12-week period of such leave under such subsection.

(B) SERIOUS HEALTH CONDITION.—An eligible employee may elect, or an employer may require the employee, to substitute any of the accrued paid vacation leave, personal leave, or medical or sick leave of the employee for leave provided under subparagraph (C) or (D) of subsection (a)(1) for any part of the

117

12–week period of such leave under such subsection, except that nothing in this title shall require an employer to provide paid sick leave or paid medical leave in any situation in which such employer would not normally provide any such paid leave.

(e) FORESEEABLE LEAVE.—

(1) REQUIREMENT OF NOTICE.—In any case in which the necessity for leave under subparagraph (A) or (B) of subsection (a)(1) is foreseeable based on an expected birth or placement, the employee shall provide the employer with not less than 30 days' notice, before the date the leave is to begin, of the employee's intention to take leave under such subparagraph, except that if the date of the birth or placement requires leave to begin in less than 30 days, the employee shall provide such notice as is practicable.

(2) DUTIES OF EMPLOYEE.—In any case in which the necessity for leave under subparagraph (C) or (D) of subsection (a)(1) is foreseeable based on planned medical treatment, the employee—

(A) shall make a reasonable effort to schedule the treatment so as not to disrupt unduly the operations of the employer, subject to the approval of the health care provider of the employee or the health care provider of the son, daughter, spouse, or parent of the employee, as appropriate; and

(B) shall provide the employer with not less than 30 days' notice, before the date the leave is to begin, of the employee's intention to take leave under such subparagraph, except that if the date of the treatment requires leave to begin in less than 30 days, the employee shall provide such notice as is practicable.

(f) SPOUSES EMPLOYED BY THE SAME EMPLOYER.—In any case in which a husband and wife entitled to leave under subsection (a) are employed by the same employer, the aggregate number of workweeks of leave to which both may be entitled may be limited to 12 workweeks during any 12–month period, if such leave is taken—

(1) under subparagraph (A) or (B) of subsection (a)(1); or

(2) to care for a sick parent under subparagraph (C) of such subsection.

SEC. 2613. CERTIFICATION.

(a) IN GENERAL.—An employer may require that a request for leave under subparagraph (C) or (D) of section 102(a)(1) be supported by a certification issued by the health care provider of the eligible employee or of the son, daughter, spouse, or parent of the employee, as appropriate. The employee shall provide, in a timely manner, a copy of such certification to the employer.

(b) SUFFICIENT CERTIFICATION.—Certification provided under subsection (a) shall be sufficient if it states—

(1) the date on which the serious health condition commenced;

(2) the probable duration of the condition;

(3) the appropriate medical facts within the knowledge of the health care provider regarding the condition;

(4)(A) for purposes of leave under section 102(a)(1)(C), a statement that the eligible employee is needed to care for the son, daughter, spouse, or parent and an estimate of the amount of time that such employee is needed to care for the son, daughter, spouse, or parent; and

(B) for purposes of leave under section 102(a)(1)(D), a statement that the employee is unable to perform the functions of the position of the employee;

(5) in the case of certification for intermittent leave, or leave on a reduced leave schedule, for planned medical treatment, the dates on which such treatment is expected to be given and the duration of such treatment;

(6) in the case of certification for intermittent leave, or leave on a reduced leave schedule, under section 102(a)(1)(D), a statement of the medical necessity for the intermittent leave or leave on a reduced leave schedule, and the expected duration of the intermittent leave or reduced leave schedule; and

(7) in the case of certification for intermittent leave, or leave on a reduced leave schedule, under section 102(a)(1)(C), a statement that the employee's intermittent leave or leave on a reduced leave schedule is necessary for the care of the son, daughter, parent, or spouse who has a serious health condition, or will assist in their recovery, and the expected duration and schedule of the intermittent leave or reduced leave schedule.

(c) SECOND OPINION.—

(1) IN GENERAL.—In any case in which the employer has reason to doubt the validity of the certification provided under subsection (a) for leave under subparagraph (C) or (D) of section 102(a)(1), the employer may require, at the expense of the employer, that the eligible employee obtain the opinion of a second health care provider designated or approved by the employer concerning any information certified under subsection (b) for such leave.

(2) LIMITATION.—A health care provider designated or approved under paragraph (1) shall not be employed on a regular basis by the employer.

(d) RESOLUTION OF CONFLICTING OPINIONS.—

(1) IN GENERAL.—In any case in which the second opinion described in subsection (c) differs from the opinion in the original certification provided under subsection (a), the employer may require, at the expense of the employer, that the employee obtain the opinion of a third health care provider designated or approved jointly by the employer and the employee concerning the information certified under subsection (b).

(2) FINALITY.—The opinion of the third health care provider concerning the information certified under subsection (b) shall be considered to be final and shall be binding on the employer and the employee.

(e) SUBSEQUENT RECERTIFICATION.—The employer may require that the eligible employee obtain subsequent recertifications on a reasonable basis.

SEC. 2614. EMPLOYMENT AND BENEFITS PROTECTION.

(a) RESTORATION TO POSITION.—

(1) IN GENERAL.—Except as provided in subsection (b), any eligible employee who takes leave under section 102 for the intended purpose of the leave shall be entitled, on return from such leave—

(A) to be restored by the employer to the position of employment held by the employee when the leave commenced; or

(B) to be restored to an equivalent position with equivalent employment benefits, pay, and other terms and conditions of employment.

(2) LOSS OF BENEFITS.—The taking of leave under section 102 shall not result in the loss of any employment benefit accrued prior to the date on which the leave commenced.

(3) LIMITATIONS.—Nothing in this section shall be construed to entitle any restored employee to—

(A) the accrual of any seniority or employment benefits during any period of leave; or

(B) any right, benefit, or position of employment other than any right, benefit, or position to which the employee would have been entitled had the employee not taken the leave.

(4) CERTIFICATION.—As a condition of restoration under paragraph (1) for an employee who has taken leave under section 102(a)(1)(D), the employer may have a uniformly applied practice or policy that requires each such employee to receive certification from the health care provider of the employee that the employee is able to

resume work, except that nothing in this paragraph shall supersede a valid State or local law or a collective bargaining agreement that governs the return to work of such employees.

(5) CONSTRUCTION.—Nothing in this subsection shall be construed to prohibit an employer from requiring an employee on leave under section 102 to report periodically to the employer on the status and intention of the employee to return to work.

(b) EXEMPTION CONCERNING CERTAIN HIGHLY COMPENSATED EMPLOYEES.—

(1) DENIAL OF RESTORATION.—An employer may deny restoration under subsection (a) to any eligible employee described in paragraph (2) if—

(A) such denial is necessary to prevent substantial and grievous economic injury to the operations of the employer;

(B) the employer notifies the employee of the intent of the employer to deny restoration on such basis at the time the employer determines that such injury would occur; and

(C) in any case in which the leave has commenced, the employee elects not to return to employment after receiving such notice.

(2) AFFECTED EMPLOYEES.—An eligible employee described in paragraph (1) is a salaried eligible employee who is among the highest paid 10 percent of the employees employed by the employer within 75 miles of the facility at which the employee is employed.

(c) MAINTENANCE OF HEALTH BENEFITS.—

(1) COVERAGE.—Except as provided in paragraph (2), during any period that an eligible employee takes leave under section 102, the employer shall maintain coverage under any "group health plan" (as defined in section 5000(b)(1) of the Internal Revenue Code of 1986) for the duration of such leave at the level and under the conditions coverage would have been provided if the employee had continued in employment continuously for the duration of such leave.

(2) FAILURE TO RETURN FROM LEAVE.—The employer may recover the premium that the employer paid for maintaining coverage for the employee under such group health plan during any period of unpaid leave under section 102 if—

(A) the employee fails to return from leave under section 102 after the period of leave to which the employee is entitled has expired; and

(B) the employee fails to return to work for a reason other than—

(i) the continuation, recurrence, or onset of a serious health condition that entitles the employee to leave under subparagraph (C) or (D) of section 102(a)(1); or

(ii) other circumstances beyond the control of the employee.

(3) CERTIFICATION.—

(A) ISSUANCE.—An employer may require that a claim that an employee is unable to return to work because of the continuation, recurrence, or onset of the serious health condition described in paragraph (2)(B)(i) be supported by—

(i) a certification issued by the health care provider of the son, daughter, spouse, or parent of the employee, as appropriate, in the case of an employee unable to return to work because of a condition specified in section 102(a)(1)(C); or

(ii) a certification issued by the health care provider of the eligible employee, in the case of an employee unable to return to work because of a condition specified in section 102(a)(1)(D).

(B) COPY.—The employee shall provide, in a timely manner, a copy of such certification to the employer.

(C) SUFFICIENCY OF CERTIFICATION.—

(i) LEAVE DUE TO SERIOUS HEALTH CONDITION OF EMPLOYEE.— The certification described in subparagraph (A)(ii) shall be sufficient if the certification states that a serious health condition prevented the employee from being able to perform the functions of the position of the employee on the date that the leave of the employee expired.

(ii) LEAVE DUE TO SERIOUS HEALTH CONDITION OF FAMILY MEMBER.—The certification described in subparagraph (A)(i) shall be sufficient if the certification states that the employee is needed to care for the son, daughter, spouse, or parent who has a serious health condition on the date that the leave of the employee expired.

SEC. 2615. PROHIBITED ACTS.

(a) INTERFERENCE WITH RIGHTS.—

(1) EXERCISE OF RIGHTS.—It shall be unlawful for any employer to interfere with, restrain, or deny the exercise of or the attempt to exercise, any right provided under this title.

(2) DISCRIMINATION.—It shall be unlawful for any employer to discharge or in any other manner discriminate against any individual for opposing any practice made unlawful by this title.

(b) INTERFERENCE WITH PROCEEDINGS OR INQUIRIES.—It shall be unlawful for any person to discharge or in any other manner discriminate against any individual because such individual—

(1) has filed any charge, or has instituted or caused to be instituted any proceeding, under or related to this title;

(2) has given, or is about to give, any information in connection with any inquiry or proceeding relating to any right provided under this title; or

(3) has testified, or is about to testify, in any inquiry or proceeding relating to any right provided under this title.

SEC. 2616. INVESTIGATIVE AUTHORITY.

(a) IN GENERAL.—To ensure compliance with the provisions of this title, or any regulation or order issued under this title, the Secretary shall have, subject to subsection (c), the investigative authority provided under section 11(a) of the Fair Labor Standards Act of 1938 (29 U.S.C. 211(a)).

(b) OBLIGATION TO KEEP AND PRESERVE RECORDS.—Any employer shall make, keep, and preserve records pertaining to compliance with this title in accordance with section 11(c) of the Fair Labor Standards Act of 1938 (29 U.S.C. 211(c)) and in accordance with regulations issued by the Secretary.

(c) REQUIRED SUBMISSIONS GENERALLY LIMITED TO AN ANNUAL BASIS.—The Secretary shall not under the authority of this section require any employer or any plan, fund, or program to submit to the Secretary any books or records more than once during any 12–month period, unless the Secretary has reasonable cause to believe there may exist a violation of this title or any regulation or order issued pursuant to this title, or is investigating a charge pursuant to section 107(b).

(d) SUBPOENA POWERS.—For the purposes of any investigation provided for in this section, the Secretary shall have the subpoena authority provided for under section 9 of the Fair Labor Standards Act of 1938 (29 U.S.C. 209).

SEC. 2617. ENFORCEMENT.

(a) CIVIL ACTION BY EMPLOYEES.—

(1) LIABILITY.—Any employer who violates section 105 shall be liable to any eligible employee affected—

(A) for damages equal to—

(i) the amount of—

(I) any wages, salary, employment benefits, or other compensation denied or lost to such employee by reason of the violation; or

(II) in a case in which wages, salary, employment benefits, or other compensation have not been denied or lost to the employee, any actual monetary losses sustained by the employee as a direct result of the violation, such as the cost of providing care, up to a sum equal to 12 weeks of wages or salary for the employee;

(ii) the interest on the amount described in clause (i) calculated at the prevailing rate; and

(iii) an additional amount as liquidated damages equal to the sum of the amount described in clause (i) and the interest described in clause (ii), except that if an employer who has violated section 105 proves to the satisfaction of the court that the act or omission which violated section 105 was in good faith and that the employer had reasonable grounds for believing that the act or omission was not a violation of section 105, such court may, in the discretion of the court, reduce the amount of the liability to the amount and interest determined under clauses (i) and (ii), respectively; and

(B) for such equitable relief as may be appropriate, including employment, reinstatement, and promotion.

(2) RIGHT OF ACTION.—An action to recover the damages or equitable relief prescribed in paragraph (1) may be maintained against any employer (including a public agency) in any Federal or State court of competent jurisdiction by any one or more employees for and in behalf of—

(A) the employees; or

(B) the employees and other employees similarly situated.

(3) FEES AND COSTS.—The court in such an action shall, in addition to any judgment awarded to the plaintiff, allow a reasonable attorney's fee, reasonable expert witness fees, and other costs of the action to be paid by the defendant.

(4) LIMITATIONS.—The right provided by paragraph (2) to bring an action by or on behalf of any employee shall terminate—

(A) on the filing of a complaint by the Secretary in an action under subsection (d) in which restraint is sought of any further delay in the payment of the amount described in paragraph (1)(A) to such employee by an employer responsible under paragraph (1) for the payment; or

(B) on the filing of a complaint by the Secretary in an action under subsection (b) in which a recovery is sought of the damages described in paragraph (1)(A) owing to an eligible employee by an employer liable under paragraph (1),

unless the action described in subparagraph (A) or (B) is dismissed without prejudice on motion of the Secretary.

(b) ACTION BY THE SECRETARY.—

(1) ADMINISTRATIVE ACTION.—The Secretary shall receive, investigate, and attempt to resolve complaints of violations of section 105 in the same manner that the Secretary receives, investigates, and attempts to resolve complaints of violations of sections 6 and 7 of the Fair Labor Standards Act of 1938 (29 U.S.C. 206 and 207).

(2) CIVIL ACTION.—The Secretary may bring an action in any court of competent jurisdiction to recover the damages described in subsection (a)(1)(A).

(3) SUMS RECOVERED.—Any sums recovered by the Secretary pursuant to paragraph (2) shall be held in a special deposit account and shall be paid, on order of the Secretary, directly to each employee affected. Any such sums not paid to an employee because of inability to do so within a period of 3 years shall be deposited into the Treasury of the United States as miscellaneous receipts.

(c) LIMITATION.—

(1) IN GENERAL.—Except as provided in paragraph (2), an action may be brought under this section not later than 2 years after the date of the last event constituting the alleged violation for which the action is brought.

(2) WILLFUL VIOLATION.—In the case of such action brought for a willful violation of section 105, such action may be brought within 3 years of the date of the last event constituting the alleged violation for which such action is brought.

(3) COMMENCEMENT.—In determining when an action is commenced by the Secretary under this section for the purposes of this subsection, it shall be considered to be commenced on the date when the complaint is filed.

(d) ACTION FOR INJUNCTION BY SECRETARY.—The district courts of the United States shall have jurisdiction, for cause shown, in an action brought by the Secretary—

(1) to restrain violations of section 105, including the restraint of any withholding of payment of wages, salary, employment benefits, or other compensation, plus interest, found by the court to be due to eligible employees; or

(2) to award such other equitable relief as may be appropriate, including employment, reinstatement, and promotion.

(e) SOLICITOR OF LABOR.—The Solicitor of Labor may appear for and represent the Secretary on any litigation brought under this section.

SEC. 2618.   SPECIAL RULES CONCERNING EMPLOYEES OF LOCAL EDUCATIONAL AGENCIES.

(a) APPLICATION.—

(1) IN GENERAL.—Except as otherwise provided in this section, the rights (including the rights under section 104, which shall extend throughout the period of leave of any employee under this section), remedies, and procedures under this title shall apply to—

(A) any "local educational agency" (as defined in section 9101 of the Elementary and Secondary Education Act of 1965 (20 U.S.C.S. 7801) and an eligible employee of the agency; and

(B) any private elementary or secondary school and an eligible employee of the school.

(2) DEFINITIONS.—For purposes of the application described in paragraph (1):

(A) ELIGIBLE EMPLOYEE.—The term "eligible employee" means an eligible employee of an agency or school described in paragraph (1).

(B) EMPLOYER.—The term "employer" means an agency or school described in paragraph (1).

(b) LEAVE DOES NOT VIOLATE CERTAIN OTHER FEDERAL LAWS.—A local educational agency and a private elementary or secondary school shall not be in violation of the Individuals with Disabilities Education Act (20 U.S.C. 1400 et seq.), section 504 of the Rehabilitation Act of 1973 (29 U.S.C. 794), or title VI of the Civil Rights Act of 1964 (42 U.S.C. 2000d et seq.), solely as a result of an eligible employee of such agency or school exercising the rights of such employee under this title.

(c) INTERMITTENT LEAVE OR LEAVE ON A REDUCED SCHEDULE FOR INSTRUCTIONAL EMPLOYEES.—

(1) IN GENERAL.—Subject to paragraph (2), in any case in which an eligible employee employed principally in an instructional capacity by any such educational agency or school requests leave under subparagraph (C) or (D) of section 102(a)(1) that is foreseeable based on planned medical treatment and the employee would be on leave for greater than 20 percent of the total number of working days in the period during which the leave would extend, the agency or school may require that such employee elect either—

    (A) to take leave for periods of a particular duration, not to exceed the duration of the planned medical treatment; or

    (B) to transfer temporarily to an available alternative position offered by the employer for which the employee is qualified, and that—

        (i) has equivalent pay and benefits; and

        (ii) better accommodates recurring periods of leave than the regular employment position of the employee.

(2) APPLICATION.—The elections described in subparagraphs (A) and (B) of paragraph (1) shall apply only with respect to an eligible employee who complies with section 102(e)(2).

(d) RULES APPLICABLE TO PERIODS NEAR THE CONCLUSION OF AN ACADEMIC TERM.—The following rules shall apply with respect to periods of leave near the conclusion of an academic term in the case of any eligible employee employed principally in an instructional capacity by any such educational agency or school:

(1) LEAVE MORE THAN 5 WEEKS PRIOR TO END OF TERM.—If the eligible employee begins leave under section 102 more than 5 weeks prior to the end of the academic term, the agency or school may require the employee to continue taking leave until the end of such term, if—

    (A) the leave is of at least 3 weeks duration; and

    (B) the return to employment would occur during the 3–week period before the end of such term.

(2) LEAVE LESS THAN 5 WEEKS PRIOR TO END OF TERM.—If the eligible employee begins leave under subparagraph (A), (B), or (C) of section 102(a)(1) during the period that commences 5 weeks prior to the end of the academic term, the agency or school may require the employee to continue taking leave until the end of such term, if—

    (A) the leave is of greater than 2 weeks duration; and

    (B) the return to employment would occur during the 2–week period before the end of such term.

(3) LEAVE LESS THAN 3 WEEKS PRIOR TO END OF TERM.—If the eligible employee begins leave under subparagraph (A), (B), or (C) of section 102(a)(1) during the period that commences 3 weeks prior to the end of the academic term and the duration of the leave is greater than 5 working days, the agency or school may require the employee to continue to take leave until the end of such term.

(e) RESTORATION TO EQUIVALENT EMPLOYMENT POSITION.—For purposes of determinations under section 104(a)(1)(B) (relating to the restoration of an eligible employee to an equivalent position), in the case of a local educational agency or a private elementary or secondary school, such determination shall be made on the basis of established school board policies and practices, private school policies and practices, and collective bargaining agreements.

(f) REDUCTION OF THE AMOUNT OF LIABILITY.—If a local educational agency or a private elementary or secondary school that has violated this title proves to the satisfaction of the court that the agency, school, or department had reasonable grounds for believing that the underlying act or omission was not a violation of this title, such court may, in the discretion of the court, reduce the amount of the liability provided for under section 107(a)(1)(A) to the amount and interest determined under clauses (i) and (ii), respectively, of such section.

SEC. 2619.   NOTICE.

(a) IN GENERAL.—Each employer shall post and keep posted, in conspicuous places on the premises of the employer where notices to employees and applicants for employment are customarily posted, a notice, to be prepared or approved by the Secretary, setting forth excerpts from, or summaries of, the pertinent provisions of this title and information pertaining to the filing of a charge.

(b) PENALTY.—Any employer that willfully violates this section may be assessed a civil money penalty not to exceed $100 for each separate offense.

* * *

SEC. 2651.   EFFECT ON OTHER LAWS.

(a) FEDERAL AND STATE ANTIDISCRIMINATION LAWS.—Nothing in this Act or any amendment made by this Act shall be construed to modify or affect any Federal or State law prohibiting discrimination on the basis of race, religion, color, national origin, sex, age, or disability.

(b) STATE AND LOCAL LAWS.—Nothing in this Act or any amendment made by this Act shall be construed to supersede any provision of any State or local law that provides greater family or medical leave rights than the rights established under this Act or any amendment made by this Act.

SEC. 2652. EFFECT ON EXISTING EMPLOYMENT BENEFITS.

(a) MORE PROTECTIVE.—Nothing in this Act or any amendment made by this Act shall be construed to diminish the obligation of an employer to comply with any collective bargaining agreement or any employment benefit program or plan that provides greater family or medical leave rights to employees than the rights established under this Act or any amendment made by this Act.

(b) LESS PROTECTIVE.—The rights established for employees under this Act or any amendment made by this Act shall not be diminished by any collective bargaining agreement or any employment benefit program or plan.

SEC. 2653. ENCOURAGEMENT OF MORE GENEROUS LEAVE POLICIES.

Nothing in this Act or any amendment made by this Act shall be construed to discourage employers from adopting or retaining leave policies more generous than any policies that comply with the requirements under this Act or any amendment made by this Act.

SEC. 2654. REGULATIONS.

The Secretary of Labor shall prescribe such regulations as are necessary to carry out title I and this title not later than 120 days after the date of the enactment of this Act.

SEC. 405. EFFECTIVE DATES.

(a) TITLE III.—Title III shall take effect on the date of the enactment of this Act.

(b) OTHER TITLES.—

(1) IN GENERAL.—Except as provided in paragraph (2), titles I, II, and V and this title shall take effect 6 months after the date of the enactment of this Act.

(2) COLLECTIVE BARGAINING AGREEMENTS.—In the case of a collective bargaining agreement in effect on the effective date prescribed by paragraph (1), title I shall apply on the earlier of—

(A) the date of the termination of such agreement; or

(B) the date that occurs 12 months after the date of the enactment of this Act.

* * *

HEALTH INSURANCE PORTABILITY AND ACCOUNTABILITY ACT

42 U.S.C. §§ 300gg–300gg–2

(ALSO CODIFIED IN PART AT 26 U.S.C. § 9801, AND
IN FULL AT 29 U.S.C. §§ 1181–1191c)

PART A—GROUP MARKET REFORMS

Subpart 1—Portability, Access, and Renewability Requirements

§ 300gg. Increased portability through limitation on preexisting condition exclusions

(a) Limitation on preexisting condition exclusion period; crediting for periods of previous coverage

Subject to subsection (d) of this section, a group health plan, and a health insurance issuer offering group health insurance coverage, may, with respect to a participant or beneficiary, impose a preexisting condition exclusion only if—

(1) such exclusion relates to a condition (whether physical or mental), regardless of the cause of the condition, for which medical advice, diagnosis, care, or treatment was recommended or received within the 6–month period ending on the enrollment date;

(2) such exclusion extends for a period of not more than 12 months (or 18 months in the case of a late enrollee) after the enrollment date; and

(3) the period of any such preexisting condition exclusion is reduced by the aggregate of the periods of creditable coverage (if any, as defined in subsection (c)(1) of this section) applicable to the participant or beneficiary as of the enrollment date.

(b) Definitions

For purposes of this part—

(1) Preexisting condition exclusion

(A) In general

The term "preexisting condition exclusion" means, with respect to coverage, a limitation or exclusion of benefits relating to a condition based on the fact that the condition was present before the date of enrollment for such coverage, whether or not any medical advice, diagnosis, care, or treatment was recommended or received before such date.

(B) Treatment of genetic information

Genetic information shall not be treated as a condition described in subsection (a)(1) of this section in the absence of a diagnosis of the condition related—to such information.

(2) Enrollment date

The term "enrollment date" means, with respect to an individual covered under a group health plan or health insurance coverage, the date of enrollment of the individual in the plan or coverage or, if earlier, the first day of the waiting period for such enrollment.

(3) Late enrollee

The term "late enrollee" means, with respect to coverage under a group health plan, a participant or beneficiary who enrolls under the plan other than during—

(A) the first period in which the individual is eligible to enroll under the plan, or

(B) a special enrollment period under subsection (f) of this section.

(4) Waiting period

The term "waiting period" means, with respect to a group health plan and an individual who is a potential participant or beneficiary in the plan, the period that must pass with respect to the individual before the individual is eligible to be covered for benefits under the terms of the plan.

(c) Rules relating to crediting previous coverage

(1) Creditable coverage defined

For purposes of this title, the term "creditable coverage" means, with respect to an individual, coverage of the individual under any of the following:

(A) A group health plan.

(B) Health insurance coverage.

(C) Part A or part B of title XVIII of the Social Security Act.

(D) Title XIX of the Social Security Act, other than coverage consisting solely of benefits under section 1928.

(E) Chapter 55 of Title 10.

(F) A medical care program of the Indian Health Service or of a tribal organization.

(G) A State health benefits risk pool.

(H) A health plan offered under chapter 89 of Title 5.

(I) A public health plan (as defined in regulations).

(J) A health benefit plan under section 2504(e) of Title 22.

Such term does not include coverage consisting solely of coverage of excepted benefits (as defined in section 300gg–91(c) of this title).

(2) Not counting periods before significant breaks in coverage

(A) In general

A period of creditable coverage shall not be counted, with respect to enrollment of an individual under a group health plan, if, after such period and before the enrollment date, there was a 63–day period during all of which the individual was not covered under any creditable coverage.

(B) Waiting period not treated as a break in coverage

For purposes of subparagraph (A) and subsection (d)(4) of this section, any period that an individual is in a waiting period for any coverage under a group health plan (or for group health insurance coverage) or is in an affiliation period (as defined in subsection (g)(2) of this section) shall not be taken into account in determining the continuous period under subparagraph (A).

(3) Method of crediting coverage

(A) Standard method

Except as otherwise provided under subparagraph (B), for purposes of applying subsection (a)(3) of this section, a group health plan, and a health insurance issuer offering group health insurance coverage, shall count a period of creditable coverage without regard to the specific benefits covered during the period.

(B) Election of alternative method

A group health plan, or a health insurance issuer offering group health insurance, may elect to apply subsection (a)(3) of this section based on coverage of benefits within each of several classes or categories of benefits specified in regulations rather than as provided under subparagraph (A). Such election shall be made on a uniform basis for all participants and beneficiaries. Under such election a group health plan or issuer shall count a period of creditable coverage with respect to any class or category of benefits if any level of benefits is covered within such class or category.

(C) Plan notice

In the case of an election with respect to a group health plan under subparagraph (B) (whether or not health insurance coverage is provided in connection with such plan), the plan shall—

(i) prominently state in any disclosure statements concerning the plan and state to each enrollee at the time of enrollment under the plan, that the plan has made such election, and

(ii) include in such statements a description of the effect of this election

(D) Issuer notice

In the case of an election under subparagraph (B) with respect to health insurance coverage offered by an issuer in the small or large group market, the issuer—

(i) shall prominently state in any disclosure statements concerning the coverage, and to each employer at the time of the offer or sale of the coverage, that the issuer has made such election, and

(ii) shall include in such statements a description of the effect of such election.

(4) Establishment of period

Periods of creditable coverage with respect to an individual shall be established through presentation of certifications described in subsection (e) of this section or in such other manner as may be specified in regulations.

(d) Exceptions

(1) Exclusion not applicable to certain newborns

Subject to paragraph (4), a group health plan, and a health insurance issuer offering group health insurance coverage, may not impose any preexisting condition exclusion in the case of an individual who, as of the last day of the 30–day period beginning with the date of birth, is covered under creditable coverage.

(2) Exclusion not applicable to certain adopted children

Subject to paragraph (4), a group health plan, and a health insurance issuer offering group health insurance coverage, may not impose any preexisting condition exclusion in the case of a child who is adopted or placed for adoption before attaining 18 years of age and who, as of the last day of the 30–day period beginning on the date of the adoption or placement for adoption, is covered under creditable coverage. The previous sentence shall not apply to coverage before the date of such adoption or placement for adoption.

(3) Exclusion not applicable to pregnancy

A group health plan, and health insurance issuer offering group health insurance coverage, may not impose any preexisting condition exclusion relating to pregnancy as a preexisting condition.

(4) Loss if break in coverage

Paragraphs (1) and (2) shall no longer apply to an individual after the end of the first 63–day period during all of which the individual was not covered under any creditable coverage.

* * *

(f) Special enrollment periods

(1) Individuals losing other coverage

A group health plan, and a health insurance issuer offering group health insurance coverage in connection with a group health plan, shall permit an employee who is eligible, but not enrolled, for coverage under the terms of the plan (or a dependent of such an employee if the dependent is eligible, but not enrolled, for coverage under such terms) to enroll for coverage under the terms of the plan if each of the following conditions is met:

(A) The employee or dependent was covered under a group health plan or had health insurance coverage at the time coverage was previously offered to the employee or dependent.

(B) The employee stated in writing at such time that coverage under a group health plan or health insurance coverage was the reason for declining enrollment, but only if the plan sponsor or issuer (if applicable) required such a statement at such time and provided the employee with notice of such requirement (and the consequences of such requirement) at such time.

(C) The employee's or dependent's coverage described in subparagraph (A)—

(i) was under a COBRA continuation provision and the coverage under such provision was exhausted; or

(ii) was not under such a provision and either the coverage was terminated as a result of loss of eligibility for the coverage (including as a result of legal separation, divorce, death, termination of employment, or reduction in the number of hours of employment) or employer contributions toward such coverage were terminated.

(D) Under the terms of the plan, the employee requests such enrollment not later than 30 days after the date of exhaustion of coverage described in subparagraph (C)(i) or termination of coverage or employer contribution described in subparagraph (C)(ii).

* * *

§ 300gg–1.

(a) In eligibility to enroll

(1) In general

Subject to paragraph (2), a group health plan, and a health insurance issuer offering group health insurance coverage in connection with a group health plan, may not establish rules for eligibility (including continued eligibility) of any individual to enroll under the terms of the plan based on any of the following health status-related factors in relation to the individual or a dependent of the individual:

(A) Health status.

(B) Medical condition (including both physical and mental illnesses).

(C) Claims experience.

(D) Receipt of health care.

(E) Medical history.

(F) Genetic information

(G) Evidence of insurability (including conditions arising out of acts of domestic violence).

(H) Disability.

(2) No application to benefits or exclusions

To the extent consistent with section 701, paragraph (1) shall not be construed—

(A) to require a group health plan, or group health insurance coverage, to provide particular benefits other than those provided under the terms of such plan or coverage, or

(B) to prevent such a plan or coverage from establishing limitations or restrictions on the amount, level, extent, or nature of the benefits or coverage for similarly situated individuals enrolled in the plan or coverage.

(3) Construction

For purposes of paragraph (1), rules for eligibility to enroll under a plan include rules defining any applicable waiting periods for such enrollment.

(b) In premium contributions

(1) In general

A group health plan, and a health insurance issuer offering health insurance coverage in connection with a group health plan, may not require any individual (as a condition of enrollment or continued enrollment under the plan) to pay a premium or contribution which is greater than such premium or contribution for a similarly situated individual enrolled in the plan on the basis of any health status-related factor in relation to the individual or to an individual enrolled under the plan as a dependent of the individual.

(2) Construction

Nothing in paragraph (1) shall be construed—

(A) to restrict the amount that an employer may be charged for coverage under a group health plan; or

(B) to prevent a group health plan, and a health insurance issuer offering group health insurance coverage, from establishing premium discounts or rebates or modifying otherwise applicable copayments or deductibles in return for adherence to programs of health promotion and disease prevention.

* * *

(a) Requirements for minimum hospital stay following birth

(1) In general

A group health plan, and a health insurance issuer offering group health insurance coverage, may not—

(A) except as provided in paragraph (2)—

(i) restrict benefits for any hospital length of stay in connection with childbirth for the mother or newborn child, following a normal vaginal delivery, to less than 48 hours, or

(ii) restrict benefits for any hospital length of stay in connection with childbirth for the mother or newborn child, following a cesarean section, to less than 96 hours, or

(B) require that a provider obtain authorization from the plan or the issuer for prescribing any length of stay required under subparagraph (A) (without regard to paragraph (2)).

(2) Exception

Paragraph (1)(A) shall not apply in connection with any group health plan or health insurance issuer in any case in which the decision to discharge the mother or her newborn child prior to the expiration of the minimum length of stay otherwise required under paragraph (1)(A) is made by an attending provider in consultation with the mother.

* * *

(a) In general

(1) Aggregate lifetime limits

In the case of a group health plan (or health insurance coverage offered in connection with such a plan) that provides both medical and surgical benefits and mental health benefits—

(A) No lifetime limit

If the plan or coverage does not include an aggregate lifetime limit on substantially all medical and surgical benefits, the plan or coverage may not impose any aggregate lifetime limit on mental health benefits.

(B) Lifetime limit

If the plan or coverage includes an aggregate lifetime limit on substantially all medical and surgical benefits (in this paragraph referred to as the "applicable lifetime limit"), the plan or coverage shall either—

(i) apply the applicable lifetime limit both to the medical and surgical benefits to which it otherwise would apply and to mental health benefits and not distinguish in the application of such limit between such medical and surgical benefits and mental health benefits; or

(ii) not include any aggregate lifetime limit on mental health benefits that is less than the applicable lifetime limit.

(C) Rule in case of different limits

In the case of a plan or coverage that is not described in subparagraph (A) or (B) and that includes no or different aggregate lifetime limits on different categories of medical and surgical benefits, the Secretary shall establish rules under which subparagraph (B) is applied to such plan or coverage with respect to mental health benefits by substituting for the applicable lifetime limit an average aggregate lifetime limit that is computed taking into account the weighted average of the aggregate lifetime limits applicable to such categories.

(2) Annual limits

In the case of a group health plan (or health insurance coverage offered in connection with such a plan) that provides both medical and surgical benefits and mental health benefits—

(A) No annual limit

If the plan or coverage does not include an annual limit on substantially all medical and surgical benefits, the plan or coverage may not impose any annual limit on mental health benefits.

(B) Annual limit

If the plan or coverage includes an annual limit on substantially all medical and surgical benefits (in this paragraph referred to as the "applicable annual limit"), the plan or coverage shall either—

(i) apply the applicable annual limit both to medical and surgical benefits to which it otherwise would apply and to mental health benefits and not distinguish in the application of such limit between such medical and surgical benefits and mental health benefits; or

(ii) not include any annual limit on mental health benefits that is less than the applicable annual limit.

(C) Rule in case of different limits

In the case of a plan or coverage that is not described in subparagraph (A) or (B) and that includes no or different annual limits on different categories of medical and surgical benefits, the Secretary shall establish rules under which subparagraph (B) is applied to such plan or coverage with respect to mental health benefits by substituting for the applicable annual limit an average annual limit that is computed taking into account the weighted average of the annual limits applicable to such categories.

(b) Construction

Nothing in this section shall be construed—

(1) as requiring a group health plan (or health insurance coverage offered in connection with such a plan) to provide any mental health benefits; or

(2) in the ease of a group health plan (or health insurance coverage offered in connection with such a plan) that provides mental health benefits, as affecting the terms and conditions (including cost sharing, limits on numbers of visits or days of coverage, and requirements relating to medical necessity) relating to the amount, duration, or scope of mental health benefits under the plan or coverage, except as specifically provided in subsection (a) of this section (in regard to parity in the imposition of aggregate lifetime limits and annual limits for mental health benefits).

(c) Exemptions

(1) Small employer exemption

This section shall not apply to any group health plan (and group health insurance coverage offered in connection with a group health plan) for any plan year of a small employer.

(2) Increased cost exemption

This section shall not apply with respect to a group health plan (or health insurance coverage offered in connection with a group health plan) if the application of this section to such plan (or to such coverage) results in an increase in the cost under the plan (or for such coverage) of at least 1 percent.

* * *

(a) Issuance of coverage in the small group market

(1) In general

Subject to subsections (c) through (f) of this section, each health insurance issuer that offers health insurance coverage in the small group market in a State—

    (A) must accept every small employer (as defined in section 300gg–91(e)(4) of this title) in the State that applies for such coverage; and

    (B) must accept for enrollment under such coverage every eligible individual (as defined in paragraph (2)) who applies for enrollment during the period in which the individual first becomes eligible to enroll under the terms of the group health plan and may not place any restriction which is inconsistent with section 300gg–1 of this title on an eligible individual being a participant or beneficiary.

(2) Eligible individual defined

For purposes of this section, the term "eligible individual" means, with respect to a health insurance issuer that offers health insurance coverage to a small employer in connection with a group health plan in the small group market, such an individual in relation to the employer as shall be determined—

    (A) in accordance with the terms of such plan,

    (B) as provided by the issuer under rules of the issuer which are uniformly applicable in a State to small employers in the small group market, and

    (C) in accordance with all applicable State laws governing such issuer and such market

* * *

(a) In general

Except as provided in this section, if a health insurance issuer offers health insurance coverage in the small or large group market in connection with a group health plan, the issuer must renew or continue in force such coverage at the option of the plan sponsor of the plan.

(b) General exceptions

A health insurance issuer may nonrenew or discontinue health insurance coverage offered in connection with a group health plan in the small or large group market based only on one or more of the following:

(1) Nonpayment of premiums

The plan sponsor has failed to pay premiums or contributions in accordance with the terms of the health insurance coverage or the issuer has not received timely premium payments.

(2) Fraud

The plan sponsor has performed an act or practice that constitutes fraud or made an intentional misrepresentation of material fact under the terms of the coverage.

* * *

(3) Violation of participation or contribution rules

The plan sponsor has failed to comply with a material plan provision relating to employer contribution or group participation rules, as permitted under section 300gg–11(e) of this title in the case of the small group market or pursuant to applicable State law in the case of the large group market.

(4) Termination of coverage

The issuer is ceasing to offer coverage in such market in accordance with subsection (c) of this section and applicable State law.

(5) Movement outside service area

In the case of a health insurance issuer that offers health insurance coverage in the market through a network plan, there is no longer any enrollee in connection with such plan who lives, resides, or works in the service area of the issuer (or in the area for which the issuer is authorized to do business) and, in the case of the small group market, the issuer would deny enrollment with respect to such plan under section 300gg–II(c)(I)(A) of this title.

(6) Association membership ceases

In the case of health insurance coverage that is made available in the small or large group market (as the case may be) only through one or more bona fide associations, the membership of an employer in the association (on the basis of which the coverage is provided) ceases but only if such coverage is terminated under this paragraph uniformly without regard to any health status-related factor relating to any covered individual.

* * *

(a) Continued applicability of State law with respect to health insurance issuers

(1) In general

Subject to paragraph (2) and except as provided in subsection (b) of this section, this part and part C insofar as it relates to this part shall not be construed to supersede any provision of State law which establishes, implements, or continues in effect any standard or requirement solely relating to health insurance issuers in connection with group health insurance coverage except to the extent that such standard or requirement prevents the application of a requirement of this part.

(2) Continued preemption with respect to group health plans

Nothing in this part shall be construed to affect or modify the provisions of section 1144 of Title 29 with respect to group health plans.

* * *

(a) Guaranteed availability

(1) In general

Subject to the succeeding subsections of this section and section 300gg–44 of this title, each health insurance issuer that offers health insurance coverage (as defined in section 300gg–91(b)(1) of this title) in the individual market in a State may not, with respect to an eligible individual (as defined in subsection (b) of this section) desiring to enroll in individual health insurance coverage—

(A) decline to offer such coverage to, or deny enrollment of, such individual; or

(B) impose any preexisting condition exclusion (as defined in section 300gg(b)(I)(A) of this title) with respect to such coverage.

(2) Substitution by State of acceptable alternative mechanism

The requirement of paragraph (1) shall not apply to health insurance coverage offered in the individual market in a State in which the State is implementing an acceptable alternative mechanism under section 300gg–44 of this title.

(b) Eligible individual defined

In this part, the term "eligible individual" means an individual—

(1) (A) for whom, as of the date on which the individual seeks coverage under this section, the aggregate of the periods of creditable coverage (as defined in section 300gg(c) of this title) is 18 or more months and (B) whose most recent prior creditable coverage was under a group health plan, governmental plan, or church plan (or health insurance coverage offered in connection with any such plan);

(2) who is not eligible for coverage under (A) a group health plan, (B) part A or part B of title XVIII of the Social Security Act, or (C) a State plan under title XIX of such Act (or any successor program), and does not have other health insurance coverage;

(3) with respect to whom the most recent coverage within the coverage period described in paragraph (1)(A) was not terminated based on a factor described in paragraph (1) or (2) of section 300gg–12(b) of this title (relating to nonpayment of premiums or fraud);

(4) if the individual had been offered the option of continuation coverage under a COBRA continuation provision or under a similar State program, who elected such coverage; and

(5) who, if the individual elected such continuation coverage, has exhausted such continuation coverage under such provision or program.

* * *

(f) Construction

Nothing in this section shall be construed—

(1) to restrict the amount of the premium rates that an issuer may charge an individual for health insurance coverage provided in the individual market under applicable State law; or

(2) to prevent a health insurance issuer offering health insurance coverage in the individual market from establishing premium discounts or rebates or modifying otherwise applicable copayments or deductibles in return for adherence to programs of health promotion and disease prevention.

* * *

(a) In general

Except as provided in this section, a health insurance issuer that provides individual health insurance coverage to an individual shall renew or continue in force such coverage at the option of the individual.

(b) General exceptions

A health insurance issuer may nonrenew or discontinue health insurance coverage of an individual in the individual market based only on one or more of the following:

(1) Nonpayment of premiums

The individual has failed to pay premiums or contributions in accordance with the terms of the health insurance coverage or the issuer has not received timely premium payments.

(2) Fraud

The individual has performed an act or practice that constitutes fraud or made an intentional misrepresentation of material fact under the terms of the coverage.

(3) Termination of plan

The issuer is ceasing to offer coverage in the individual market in accordance with subsection (c) of this section and applicable State law.

(4) Movement outside service area

In the case of a health insurance issuer that offers health insurance coverage in the market through a network plan, the individual no longer resides, lives, or works in the service area (or in an area for which the issuer is authorized to do business) but only if such coverage is terminated under this paragraph uniformly without regard to any health status-related factor of covered individuals.

(5) Association membership ceases

In the case of health insurance coverage that is made available in the individual market only through one or more bona fide associations, the membership of the individual in the association (on the basis of which the coverage is provided) ceases but only if such coverage is terminated under this paragraph uniformly without regard to any health status-related factor of covered individuals.

* * *

(a) Waiver of requirements where implementation of acceptable alternative mechanism

(1) In general

The requirements of section 300gg–41 of this title shall not apply with respect to health insurance coverage offered in the individual market in the State so long as a State is found to be implementing, in accordance with this section and consistent with section 300gg–62(b) of this title, an alternative mechanism (in this section referred to as an "acceptable alternative mechanism")—

(A) under which all eligible individuals are provided a choice of health insurance coverage;

(B) under which such coverage does not impose any preexisting condition exclusion with respect to such coverage;

(C) under which such choice of coverage includes at least one policy form of coverage that is comparable to comprehensive health insurance coverage offered in the individual market in such State or that is comparable to a standard option of coverage available under the group or individual health insurance laws of such State; and

(D) in a State which is implementing—

(i) a model act described in subsection (c)(1) of this title,

(ii) a qualified high risk pool described in subsection (c)(2) of this section, or

(iii) a mechanism described in subsection (c)(3) of this section.

* * *

OCCUPATIONAL SAFETY AND HEALTH ACT

29 U.S.C. §§ 651–678

DEFINITIONS

SEC. 3. (**§ 652**) For the purposes of this Act—

(1) The term "Secretary" means the Secretary of Labor.

(2) The term "Commission" means the Occupational Safety and Health Review Commission established under this Act.

(3) The term "commerce" means trade, traffic, commerce, transportation, or communication among the several States, or between a State and any place outside thereof, or within the District of Columbia, or a possession of the United States (other than the Trust Territory of the Pacific Islands), or between points in the same State but through a point outside thereof.

(4) The term "person" means one or more individuals, partnerships, associations, corporations, business trusts, legal representatives, or any organized group of persons.

(5) The term "employer" means a person engaged in a business affecting commerce who has employees, but does not include the United States or any State or political subdivision of a State.

(6) The term "employee" means an employee of an employer who is employed in a business of his employer which affects commerce.

(7) The term "State" includes a State of the United States, the District of Columbia, Puerto Rico, the Virgin Islands, American Samoa, Guam, and the Trust Territory of the Pacific Islands.

(8) The term "occupational safety and health standard" means a standard which requires conditions, or the adoption or use of one or more practices, means, methods, operations, or processes, reasonably necessary or appropriate to provide safe or healthful employment and places of employment.

(9) The term "national consensus standard" means any occupational safety and health standard or modification thereof which (1) has been adopted and promulgated by a nationally recognized standards-producing organization under procedures whereby it can be determined by the Secretary that persons interested and affected by the scope or provisions of the standard have reached substantial agreement on its adoption, (2) was formulated in a manner which afforded an opportunity for diverse views to be considered and (3) has been designated as such a standard by

146

the Secretary, after consultation with other appropriate Federal agencies.

(10) The term "established Federal standard" means any operative occupational safety and health standard established by any agency of the United States and presently in effect, or contained in any Act of Congress in force on the date of enactment of this Act.

* * *

APPLICABILITY OF THIS ACT

SEC. 4. (§ 653) (a) This Act shall apply with respect to employment performed in a workplace in a State, the District of Columbia, the Commonwealth of Puerto Rico, the Virgin Islands, American Samoa, Guam, the Trust Territory of the Pacific Islands, Wake Island, Outer Continental Shelf lands defined in the Outer Continental Shelf Lands Act, Johnston Island, and the Canal Zone. The Secretary of the Interior shall, by regulation, provide for judicial enforcement of this Act by the courts established for areas in which there are no United States district courts having jurisdiction.

(b)(1) Nothing in this Act shall apply to working conditions of employees with respect to which other Federal agencies, and State agencies acting under section 274 of the Atomic Energy Act of 1954, as amended (42 U.S.C. 2021), exercise statutory authority to prescribe or enforce standards or regulations affecting occupational safety or health.

(2) The safety and health standards promulgated under the Act of June 30, 1936, commonly known as the Walsh-Healey Act (41 U.S.C. 35 et seq.), the Service Contract Act of 1965 (41 U.S.C. 351 et seq.), Public Law 91–54, Act of August 9, 1969 (40 U.S.C. 333), Public Law 85–742, Act of August 23, 1958 (33 U.S.C. 941), and the National Foundation on Arts and Humanities Act (20 U.S.C. 951 et seq.) are superseded on the effective date of corresponding standards, promulgated under this Act, which are determined by the Secretary to be more effective. Standards issued under the laws listed in this paragraph and in effect on or after the effective date of this Act shall be deemed to be occupational safety and health standards issued under this Act, as well as under such other Acts.

(3) The Secretary shall, within three years after the effective date of this Act, report to the Congress his recommendations for legislation to avoid unnecessary duplication and to achieve coordination between this Act and other Federal laws.

(4) Nothing in this Act shall be construed to supersede or in any manner affect any workmen's compensation law or to enlarge or diminish or affect in any other manner the common law or statutory rights,

duties, or liabilities of employers and employees under any law with respect to injuries, diseases, or death of employees arising out of, or in the course of, employment.

DUTIES

SEC. 5.   (§ 654) (a) Each employer—

(1) shall furnish to each of his employees employment and a place of employment which are free from recognized hazards that are causing or are likely to cause death or serious physical harm to his employees;

(2) shall comply with occupational safety and health standards promulgated under this Act.

(b) Each employee shall comply with occupational safety and health standards and all rules, regulations, and orders issued pursuant to this Act which are applicable to his own actions and conduct.

OCCUPATIONAL SAFETY AND HEALTH STANDARDS

SEC. 6.   (§ 655) (a) Without regard to chapter 5 of title 5, United States Code, or to the other subsections of this section, the Secretary shall, as soon as practicable during the period beginning with the effective date of this Act and ending two years after such date, by rule promulgate as an occupational safety or health standard any national consensus standard, and any established Federal standard, unless he determines that the promulgation of such a standard would not result in improved safety or health for specifically designated employees. In the event of conflict among any such standards, the Secretary shall promulgate the standard which assures the greatest protection of the safety or health of the affected employees.

(b) The Secretary may by rule promulgate, modify, or revoke any occupational safety or health standard in the following manner:

(1) Whenever the Secretary, upon the basis of information submitted to him in writing by an interested person, a representative of any organization of employers or employees, a nationally recognized standards-producing organization, the Secretary of Health and Human Services, the National Institute for Occupational Safety and Health, or a State or political subdivision, or on the basis of information developed by the Secretary or otherwise available to him, determines that a rule should be promulgated in order to serve the objectives of this Act, the Secretary may request the recommendations of an advisory committee appointed under section 7 of this Act. The Secretary shall provide such an advisory committee with any proposals of his own or of the Secretary of Health and Human Services, together with all pertinent factual information developed by the Secretary or the Secretary of Health and

Human Services, or otherwise available, including the results of research, demonstrations, and experiments. An advisory committee shall submit to the Secretary its recommendations regarding the rule to be promulgated within ninety days from the date of its appointment or within such longer or shorter period as may be prescribed by the Secretary, but in no event for a period which is longer than two hundred and seventy days.

(2) The Secretary shall publish a proposed rule promulgating, modifying, or revoking an occupational safety or health standard in the Federal Register and shall afford interested persons a period of thirty days after publication to submit written data or comments. Where an advisory committee is appointed and the Secretary determines that a rule should be issued, he shall publish the proposed rule within sixty days after the submission of the advisory committee's recommendations or the expiration of the period prescribed by the Secretary for such submission.

(3) On or before the last day of the period provided for the submission of written data or comments under paragraph (2), any interested person may file with the Secretary written objections to the proposed rule, stating the grounds therefor and requesting a public hearing on such objections. Within thirty days after the last day for filing such objections, the Secretary shall publish in the Federal Register a notice specifying the occupational safety or health standard to which objections have been filed and a hearing requested, and specifying a time and place for such hearing.

(4) Within sixty days after the expiration of the period provided for the submission of written data or comments under paragraph (2), or within sixty days after the completion of any hearing held under paragraph (3), the Secretary shall issue a rule promulgating, modifying, or revoking an occupational safety or health standard or make a determination that a rule should not be issued. Such a rule may contain a provision delaying its effective date for such period (not in excess of ninety days) as the Secretary determines may be necessary to insure that affected employers and employees will be informed of the existence of the standard and of its terms and that employers affected are given an opportunity to familiarize themselves and their employees with the existence of the requirements of the standard.

(5) The Secretary, in promulgating standards dealing with toxic materials or harmful physical agents under this subsection, shall set the standard which most adequately assures, to the extent feasible, on the basis of the best available evidence, that no employee will suffer material impairment of health or functional capacity even if such employee has regular exposure to the hazard dealt with by such standard for the

period of his working life. Development of standards under this subsection shall be based upon research, demonstrations, experiments, and such other information as may be appropriate. In addition to the attainment of the highest degree of health and safety protection for the employee, other considerations shall be the latest available scientific data in the field, the feasibility of the standards, and experience gained under this and other health and safety laws. Whenever practicable, the standard promulgated shall be expressed in terms of objective criteria and of the performance desired.

(6)(A) Any employer may apply to the Secretary for a temporary order granting a variance from a standard or any provision thereof promulgated under this section. Such temporary order shall be granted only if the employer files an application which meets the requirements of clause (B) and establishes that (i) he is unable to comply with a standard by its effective date because of unavailability of professional or technical personnel or of materials and equipment needed to come into compliance with the standard or because necessary construction or alteration of facilities cannot be completed by the effective date, (ii) he is taking all available steps to safeguard his employees against the hazards covered by the standard, and (iii) he has an effective program for coming into compliance with the standard as quickly as practicable. Any temporary order issued under this paragraph shall prescribe the practices, means, methods, operations, and processes which the employer must adopt and use while the order is in effect and state in detail his program for coming into compliance with the standard. Such a temporary order may be granted only after notice to employees and an opportunity for a hearing: Provided, That the Secretary may issue one interim order to be effective until a decision is made on the basis of the hearing. No temporary order may be in effect for longer than the period needed by the employer to achieve compliance with the standard or one year, whichever is shorter, except that such an order may be renewed not more than twice (I) so long as the requirements of this paragraph are met and (II) if an application for renewal is filed at least 90 days prior to the expiration date of the order. No interim renewal of an order may remain in effect for longer than 180 days.

(B) An application for a temporary order under this paragraph (6) shall contain:

(i) a specification of the standard or portion thereof from which the employer seeks a variance,

(ii) a representation by the employer, supported by representations from qualified persons having firsthand knowledge of the facts represented, that he is unable to comply with the standard or portion thereof and a detailed statement of the reasons therefor,

(iii) a statement of the steps he has taken and will take (with specific dates) to protect employees against the hazard covered by the standard,

(iv) a statement of when he expects to be able to comply with the standard and what steps he has taken and what steps he will take (with dates specified) to come into compliance with the standard, and

(v) a certification that he has informed his employees of the application by giving a copy thereof to their authorized representative, posting a statement giving a summary of the application and specifying where a copy may be examined at the place or places where notices to employees are normally posted, and by other appropriate means.

A description of how employees have been informed shall be contained in the certification. The information to employees shall also inform them of their right to petition the Secretary for a hearing.

(C) The Secretary is authorized to grant a variance from any standard or portion thereof whenever he determines, or the Secretary of Health, Education, and Welfare certifies, that such variance is necessary to permit an employer to participate in an experiment approved by him or the Secretary of Health and Human Services designed to demonstrate or validate new and improved techniques to safeguard the health or safety of workers.

(7) Any standard promulgated under this subsection shall prescribe the use of labels or other appropriate forms of warning as are necessary to insure that employees are apprised of all hazards to which they are exposed, relevant symptoms and appropriate emergency treatment, and proper conditions and precautions of safe use or exposure. Where appropriate, such standard shall also prescribe suitable protective equipment and control or technological procedures to be used in connection with such hazards and shall provide for monitoring or measuring employee exposure at such locations and intervals, and in such manner as may be necessary for the protection of employees. In addition, where appropriate, any such standard shall prescribe the type and frequency of medical examinations or other tests which shall be made available, by the employer or at his cost, to employees exposed to such hazards in order to most effectively determine whether the health of such employees is adversely affected by such exposure. In the event such medical examinations are in the nature of research, as determined by the Secretary of Health and Human Services, such examinations may be furnished at the expense of the Secretary of Health and Human Services. The results of such examinations or tests shall be furnished only to the Secretary or the Secretary of Health and Human Services, and, at the

request of the employee, to his physician. The Secretary, in consultation with the Secretary of Health and Human Services, may by rule promulgated pursuant to section 553 of title 5, United States Code, make appropriate modifications in the foregoing requirements relating to the use of labels or other forms of warning, monitoring or measuring, and medical examinations, as may be warranted by experience, information, or medical or technological developments acquired subsequent to the promulgation of the relevant standard.

(8) Whenever a rule promulgated by the Secretary differs substantially from an existing national consensus standard, the Secretary shall, at the same time, publish in the Federal Register a statement of the reasons why the rule as adopted will better effectuate the purposes of this Act than the national consensus standard.

(c)(1) The Secretary shall provide, without regard to the requirements of chapter 5, title 5, United States Code, for an emergency temporary standard to take immediate effect upon publication in the Federal Register if he determines (A) that employees are exposed to grave danger from exposure to substances or agents determined to be toxic or physically harmful or from new hazards, and (B) that such emergency standard is necessary to protect employees from such danger.

(2) Such standard shall be effective until superseded by a standard promulgated in accordance with the procedures prescribed in paragraph (3) of this subsection.

(3) Upon publication of such standard in the Federal Register the Secretary shall commence a proceeding in accordance with section 6(b) of this Act, and the standard as published shall also serve as a proposed rule for the proceeding. The Secretary shall promulgate a standard under this paragraph no later than six months after publication of the emergency standard as provided in paragraph (2) of this subsection.

(d) Any affected employer may apply to the Secretary for a rule or order for a variance from a standard promulgated under this section. Affected employees shall be given notice of each such application and an opportunity to participate in a hearing. The Secretary shall issue such rule or order if he determines on the record, after opportunity for an inspection where appropriate and a hearing, that the proponent of the variance has demonstrated by a preponderance of the evidence that the conditions, practices, means, methods, operations, or processes used or proposed to be used by an employer will provide employment and places of employment to his employees which are as safe and healthful as those which would prevail if he complied with the standard. The rule or order so issued shall prescribe the conditions the employer must maintain, and the practices, means, methods, operations, and processes which he must adopt and utilize to the extent they differ from the standard in question.

Such a rule or order may be modified or revoked upon application by an employer, employees, or by the Secretary on his own motion, in the manner prescribed for its issuance under this subsection at any time after six months from its issuance.

(e) Whenever the Secretary promulgates any standard, makes any rule, order, or decision, grants any exemption or extension of time, or compromises, mitigates, or settles any penalty assessed under this Act, he shall include a statement of the reasons for such action, which shall be published in the Federal Register.

(f) Any person who may be adversely affected by a standard issued under this section may at any time prior to the sixtieth day after such standard is promulgated file a petition challenging the validity of such standard with the United States court of appeals for the circuit wherein such person resides or has his principal place of business, for a judicial review of such standard. A copy of the petition shall be forthwith transmitted by the clerk of the court to the Secretary. The filing of such petition shall not, unless otherwise ordered by the court, operate as a stay of the standard. The determinations of the Secretary shall be conclusive if supported by substantial evidence in the record considered as a whole.

(g) In determining the priority for establishing standards under this section, the Secretary shall give due regard to the urgency of the need for mandatory safety and health standards for particular industries, trades, crafts, occupations, businesses, workplaces or work environments. The Secretary shall also give due regard to the recommendations of the Secretary of Health and Human Services regarding the need for mandatory standards in determining the priority for establishing such standards.

* * *

INSPECTIONS, INVESTIGATIONS, AND RECORDKEEPING

SEC. 8. (§ 657) (a) In order to carry out the purposes of this Act, the Secretary, upon presenting appropriate credentials to the owner, operator, or agent in charge, is authorized—

(1) to enter without delay and at reasonable times any factory, plant, establishment, construction site, or other area, workplace or environment where work is performed by an employee of an employer; and

(2) to inspect and investigate during regular working hours and at other reasonable times, and within reasonable limits and in a reasonable manner, any such place of employment and all pertinent conditions, structures, machines, apparatus, devices, equipment, and materials

therein, and to question privately any such employer, owner, operator, agent or employee.

(b) In making his inspections and investigations under this Act the Secretary may require the attendance and testimony of witnesses and the production of evidence under oath. Witnesses shall be paid the same fees and mileage that are paid witnesses in the courts of the United States. In case of a contumacy, failure, or refusal of any person to obey such an order, any district court of the United States or the United States courts of any territory or possession, within the jurisdiction of which such person is found, or resides or transacts business, upon the application by the Secretary, shall have jurisdiction to issue to such person an order requiring such person to appear to produce evidence if, as, and when so ordered, and to give testimony relating to the matter under investigation or in question, and any failure to obey such order of the court may be punished by said court as a contempt thereof.

(c)(1) Each employer shall make, keep and preserve, and make available to the Secretary or the Secretary of Health and Human Services, such records regarding his activities relating to this Act as the Secretary, in cooperation with the Secretary of Health and Human Services, may prescribe by regulation as necessary or appropriate for the enforcement of this Act or for developing information regarding the causes and prevention of occupational accidents and illnesses. In order to carry out the provisions of this paragraph such regulations may include provisions requiring employers to conduct periodic inspections. The Secretary shall also issue regulations requiring that employers, through posting of notices or other appropriate means, keep their employees informed of their protections and obligations under this Act, including the provisions of applicable standards.

(2) The Secretary, in cooperation with the Secretary of Health and Human Services, shall prescribe regulations requiring employers to maintain accurate records of, and to make periodic reports on, work-related deaths, injuries and illnesses other than minor injuries requiring only first aid treatment and which do not involve medical treatment, loss of consciousness, restriction of work or motion, or transfer to another job.

(3) The Secretary, in cooperation with the Secretary of Health and Human Services, shall issue regulations requiring employers to maintain accurate records of employee exposures to potentially toxic materials or harmful physical agents which are required to be monitored or measured under section 6. Such regulations shall provide employees or their representatives with an opportunity to observe such monitoring or measuring, and to have access to the records thereof. Such regulations shall also make appropriate provision for each employee or former

employee to have access to such records as will indicate his own exposure to toxic materials or harmful physical agents. Each employer shall promptly notify any employee who has been or is being exposed to toxic materials or harmful physical agents in concentrations or at levels which exceed those prescribed by an applicable occupational safety and health standard promulgated under section 6, and shall inform any employee who is being thus exposed of the corrective action being taken.

(d) Any information obtained by the Secretary, the Secretary of Health and Human Services, or a State agency under this Act shall be obtained with a minimum burden upon employers, especially those operating small businesses. Unnecessary duplication of efforts in obtaining information shall be reduced to the maximum extent feasible.

(e) Subject to regulations issued by the Secretary a representative of the employer and a representative authorized by his employees shall be given an opportunity to accompany the Secretary or his authorized representative during the physical inspection of any workplace under subsection (a) for the purpose of aiding such inspection. Where there is no authorized employee representative, the Secretary or his authorized representative shall consult with a reasonable number of employees concerning matters of health and safety in the workplace.

(f)(1) Any employees or representative of employees who believe that a violation of a safety or health standard exists that threatens physical harm, or that an imminent danger exists, may request an inspection by giving notice to the Secretary or his authorized representative of such violation or danger. Any such notice shall be reduced to writing, shall set forth with reasonable particularity the grounds for the notice, and shall be signed by the employees or representative of employees, and a copy shall be provided the employer or his agent no later than at the time of inspection, except that, upon the request of the person giving such notice, his name and the names of individual employees referred to therein shall not appear in such copy or on any record published, released, or made available pursuant to subsection (g) of this section. If upon receipt of such notification the Secretary determines there are reasonable grounds to believe that such violation or danger exists, he shall make a special inspection in accordance with the provisions of this section as soon as practicable, to determine if such violation or danger exists. If the Secretary determines there are no reasonable grounds to believe that a violation or danger exists he shall notify the employees or representative of the employees in writing of such determination.

(2) Prior to or during any inspection of a workplace, any employees or representative of employees employed in such workplace may notify the Secretary or any representative of the Secretary responsible for

conducting the inspection, in writing, of any violation of this Act which they have reason to believe exists in such workplace. The Secretary shall, by regulation, establish procedures for informal review of any refusal by a representative of the Secretary to issue a citation with respect to any such alleged violation and shall furnish the employees or representative of employees requesting such review a written statement of the reasons for the Secretary's final disposition of the case.

(g)(1) The Secretary and Secretary of Health and Human Services are authorized to compile, analyze, and publish, either in summary or detailed form, all reports or information obtained under this section.

(2) The Secretary and the Secretary of Health and Human Services shall each prescribe such rules and regulations as he may deem necessary to carry out their responsibilities under this Act, including rules and regulations dealing with the inspection of an employer's establishment.

(h) The Secretary shall not use the results of enforcement activities, such as the number of citations issued or penalties assessed, to evaluate employees directly involved in enforcement activities under this Act or to impose quotas or goals with regard to the results of such activities.

CITATIONS

SEC. 9.   (§ 658) (a) If, upon inspection or investigation, the Secretary or his authorized representative believes that an employer has violated a requirement of section 5 of this Act, of any standard, rule or order promulgated pursuant to section 6 of this Act, or of any regulations prescribed pursuant to this Act, he shall with reasonable promptness issue a citation to the employer. Each citation shall be in writing and shall describe with particularity the nature of the violation, including a reference to the provision of the Act, standard, rule, regulation, or order alleged to have been violated. In addition, the citation shall fix a reasonable time for the abatement of the violation. The Secretary may prescribe procedures for the issuance of a notice in lieu of a citation with respect to de minimis violations which have no direct or immediate relationship to safety or health.

(b) Each citation issued under this section, or a copy or copies thereof, shall be prominently posted, as prescribed in regulations issued by the Secretary, at or near each place a violation referred to in the citation occurred.

(c) No citation may be issued under this section after the expiration of six months following the occurrence of any violation.

PROCEDURE FOR ENFORCEMENT

SEC. 10. (**§ 659**) (a) If, after an inspection or investigation, the Secretary issues a citation under section 9(a), he shall, within a reasonable time after the termination of such inspection or investigation, notify the employer by certified mail of the penalty, if any, proposed to be assessed under section 17 and that the employer has fifteen working days within which to notify the Secretary that he wishes to contest the citation or proposed assessment of penalty. If, within fifteen working days from the receipt of the notice issued by the Secretary the employer fails to notify the Secretary that he intends to contest the citation or proposed assessment of penalty, and no notice is filed by any employee or representative of employees under subsection (c) within such time, the citation and the assessment, as proposed, shall be deemed a final order of the Commission and not subject to review by any court or agency.

(b) If the Secretary has reason to believe that an employer has failed to correct a violation for which a citation has been issued within the period permitted for its correction (which period shall not begin to run until the entry of a final order by the Commission in the case of any review proceedings under this section initiated by the employer in good faith and not solely for delay or avoidance of penalties), the Secretary shall notify the employer by certified mail of such failure and of the penalty proposed to be assessed under section 17 by reason of such failure, and that the employer has fifteen working days within which to notify the Secretary that he wishes to contest the Secretary's notification or the proposed assessment of penalty. If, within fifteen working days from the receipt of notification issued by the Secretary, the employer fails to notify the Secretary that he intends to contest the notification or proposed assessment of penalty, the notification and assessment, as proposed, shall be deemed a final order of the Commission and not subject to review by any court or agency.

(c) If an employer notifies the Secretary that he intends to contest a citation issued under section 9(a) or notification issued under subsection (a) or (b) of this section, or if, within fifteen working days of the issuance of a citation under section 9(a), any employee or representative of employees files a notice with the Secretary alleging that the period of time fixed in the citation for the abatement of the violation is unreasonable, the Secretary shall immediately advise the Commission of such notification, and the Commission shall afford an opportunity for a hearing (in accordance with section 554 of title 5, United States Code, but without regard to subsection (a)(3) of such section). The Commission shall thereafter issue an order, based on findings of fact, affirming, modifying, or vacating the Secretary's citation or proposed penalty, or directing other appropriate relief, and such order shall become final thirty days after its issuance. Upon a showing by an employer of a good faith effort to comply with the abatement requirements of a citation, and that abatement has not been completed because of factors beyond his reasonable control, the Secretary, after an opportunity for a hearing as provided in this subsection, shall issue an order affirming or modifying the abatement requirements in such citation. The rules of procedure prescribed by the Commission shall provide affected employees or representatives of affected employees an opportunity to participate as parties to hearings under this subsection.

JUDICIAL REVIEW

SEC. 11. **(§ 660)** (a) Any person adversely affected or aggrieved by an order of the Commission issued under subsection (c) of section 10 may obtain a review of such order in any United States court of appeals for the circuit in which the violation is alleged to have occurred or where the employer has its principal office, or in the Court of Appeals for the District of Columbia Circuit, by filing in such court within sixty days following the issuance of such order a written petition praying that the order be modified or set aside. A copy of such petition shall be forthwith transmitted by the clerk of the court to the Commission and to the other parties, and thereupon the Commission shall file in the court the record in the proceeding as provided in section 2112 of title 28, United States Code. Upon such filing, the court shall have jurisdiction of the proceeding and of the question determined therein, and shall have power to grant such temporary relief or restraining order as it deems just and proper, and to make and enter upon the pleadings, testimony, and proceedings set forth in such record a decree affirming, modifying, or setting aside in whole or in part, the order of the Commission and enforcing the same to the extent that such order is affirmed or modified. The commencement of proceedings under this subsection shall not, unless ordered by the court, operate as a stay of the order of the Commission. No objection that has not been urged before the Commission shall be considered by the court, unless the failure or neglect to urge such objection shall be excused because of extraordinary circumstances. The findings of the Commission with respect to questions of fact, if supported by substantial evidence on the record considered as a whole, shall be conclusive. If any party shall apply to the court for leave to adduce additional evidence and shall show to the satisfaction of the court that such additional evidence is material and that there were reasonable grounds for the failure to adduce such evidence in the hearing before the Commission, the court may order such additional evidence to be taken before the Commission and to be made a part of the record. The Commission may modify its findings as to the facts, or make new findings, by reason of additional evidence so taken and filed, and it shall file such modified or new findings, which findings with respect to questions of fact, if supported by substantial evidence on the record considered as a whole, shall be conclusive, and its recommendations, if any, for the modification or setting aside of its original order. Upon the filing of the record with it, the jurisdiction of the court shall be exclusive and its judgment and decree shall be final, except that the same shall be subject to review by the Supreme Court of the United States, as provided in section 1254 of title 28, United States Code. Petitions filed under this subsection shall be heard expeditiously.

(b) The Secretary may also obtain review or enforcement of any final order of the Commission by filing a petition for such relief in the United States court of appeals for the circuit in which the alleged violation occurred or in which the employer has its principal office, and the provisions of subsection (a) shall govern such proceedings to the extent applicable. If no petition for review, as provided in subsection (a), is filed within sixty days after service of the Commission's order, the Commission's findings of fact and order shall be conclusive in connection with any petition for enforcement which is filed by the Secretary after the expiration of such sixty-day period. In any such case, as well as in the case of a noncontested citation or notification by the Secretary which has become a final order of the Commission under subsection (a) or (b) of section 10, the clerk of the court, unless otherwise ordered by the court, shall forthwith enter a decree enforcing the order and shall transmit a copy of such decree to the Secretary and the employer named in the petition. In any contempt proceeding brought to enforce a decree of a court of appeals entered pursuant to this subsection or subsection (a), the court of appeals may assess the penalties provided in section 17, in addition to invoking any other available remedies.

(c)(1) No person shall discharge or in any manner discriminate against any employee because such employee has filed any complaint or instituted or caused to be instituted any proceeding under or related to this Act or has testified or is about to testify in any such proceeding or because of the exercise by such employee on behalf of himself or others of any right afforded by this Act.

(2) Any employee who believes that he has been discharged or otherwise discriminated against by any person in violation of this subsection may, within thirty days after such violation occurs, file a complaint with the Secretary alleging such discrimination. Upon receipt of such complaint, the Secretary shall cause such investigation to be made as he deems appropriate. If upon such investigation, the Secretary determines that the provisions of this subsection have been violated, he shall bring an action in any appropriate United States district court against such person. In any such action the United States district courts shall have jurisdiction, for cause shown to restrain violations of paragraph (1) of

this subsection and order all appropriate relief including rehiring or reinstatement of the employee to his former position with back pay.

(3) Within 90 days of the receipt of a complaint filed under this subsection the Secretary shall notify the complainant of his determination under paragraph 2 of this subsection.

The Occupational Safety and Health Review Commission

Sec. 12. (§ 661) (a) The Occupational Safety and Health Review Commission is hereby established. The Commission shall be composed of three members who shall be appointed by the President, by and with the advice and consent of the Senate, from among persons who by reason of training, education, or experience are qualified to carry out the functions of the Commission under this Act. The President shall designate one of the members of the Commission to serve as Chairman.

(b) The terms of members of the Commission shall be six years except that (1) the members of the Commission first taking office shall serve, as designated by the President at the time of appointment, one for a term of two years, one for a term of four years, and one for a term of six years, and (2) a vacancy caused by the death, resignation, or removal of a member prior to the expiration of the term for which he was appointed shall be filled only for the remainder of such unexpired term. A member of the Commission may be removed by the President for inefficiency, neglect of duty, or malfeasance in office.

* * *

(j) An administrative law judge appointed by the Commission shall hear, and make a determination upon, any proceeding instituted before the Commission and any motion in connection therewith, assigned to such administrative law judge by the Chairman of the Commission, and shall make a report of any such determination which constitutes his final disposition of the proceedings. The report of the administrative law judge shall become the final order of the Commission within thirty days after such report by the administrative law judge unless within such period any Commission member has directed that such report shall be reviewed by the Commission.

* * *

Procedures to Counteract Imminent Dangers

Sec. 13. (§ 662) (a) The United States district courts shall have jurisdiction, upon petition of the Secretary, to restrain any conditions or practices in any place of employment which are such that a danger exists which could reasonably be expected to cause death or serious physical harm immediately or before the imminence of such danger can be eliminated through the enforcement procedures otherwise provided by this Act. Any order issued under this section may require such steps to be taken as may be necessary to avoid, correct, or remove such imminent danger and prohibit the employment or presence of any individual in locations or under conditions where such imminent danger exists, except individuals whose presence is necessary to avoid, correct, or remove such imminent danger or to maintain the capacity of a continuous process operation to resume normal operations without a complete cessation of operations, or where a cessation of operations is necessary, to permit such to be accomplished in a safe and orderly manner.

(b) Upon the filing of any such petition the district court shall have jurisdiction to grant such injunctive relief or temporary restraining order pending the outcome of an enforcement proceeding pursuant to this Act. The proceeding shall be as provided by Rule 65 of the Federal Rules, Civil Procedure, except that no temporary restraining order issued without notice shall be effective for a period longer than five days.

(c) Whenever and as soon as an inspector concludes that conditions or practices described in subsection (a) exist in any place of employment, he shall inform the affected employees and employers of the danger and that he is recommending to the Secretary that relief be sought.

(d) If the Secretary arbitrarily or capriciously fails to seek relief under this section, any employee who may be injured by reason of such failure, or the representative of such employees, might bring an action against the Secretary in the United States district court for the district in which the imminent danger is alleged to exist or the employer has its principal office, or for the District of Columbia, for a writ of mandamus to compel the Secretary to seek such an order and for such further relief as may be appropriate.

REPRESENTATION IN CIVIL LITIGATION

SEC. 14. (**§ 663**) Except as provided in section 518(a) of title 28, United States Code, relating to litigation before the Supreme Court, the Solicitor of Labor may appear for and represent the Secretary in any civil litigation brought under this Act but all such litigation shall be subject to the direction and control of the Attorney General.

CONFIDENTIALITY OF TRADE SECRETS

SEC. 15. (**§ 664**) All information reported to or otherwise obtained by the Secretary or his representative in connection with any inspection or proceeding under this Act which contains or which might reveal a trade secret referred to in section 1905 of title 18 of the United States Code shall be considered confidential for the purpose of that section, except that such information may be disclosed to other officers or employees concerned with carrying out this Act or when relevant in any proceeding under this Act. In any such proceeding the Secretary, the Commission, or the court shall issue such orders as may be appropriate to protect the confidentiality of trade secrets.

Variations, Tolerances, and Exemptions

Sec. 16. (§ 665) The Secretary, on the record, after notice and opportunity for a hearing may provide such reasonable limitations and may make such rules and regulations allowing reasonable variations, tolerances, and exemptions to and from any or all provisions of this Act as he may find necessary and proper to avoid serious impairment of the national defense. Such action shall not be in effect for more than six months without notification to affected employees and an opportunity being afforded for a hearing.

Penalties

Sec. 17. (§ 666) (a) Any employer who willfully or repeatedly violates the requirements of section 5 of this Act, any standard, rule, or order promulgated pursuant to section 6 of this Act, or regulations prescribed pursuant to this Act, may be assessed a civil penalty of not more than $70,000 for each violation, but not less than $5,000 for each willful violation.

(b) Any employer who has received a citation for a serious violation of the requirements of section 5 of this Act, of any standard, rule, or order promulgated pursuant to section 6 of this Act, or of any regulations prescribed pursuant to this Act, shall be assessed a civil penalty of up to $7,000 for each such violation.

(c) Any employer who has received a citation for a violation of the requirements of section 5 of this Act, of any standard, rule, or order promulgated pursuant to section 6 of this Act, or of regulations prescribed pursuant to this Act, and such violation is specifically determined not to be of a serious nature, may be assessed a civil penalty of up to $7,000 for each such violation.

(d) Any employer who fails to correct a violation for which a citation has been issued under section 9(a) within the period permitted for its correction (which period shall not begin to run until the date of the final order of the Commission in the case of any review proceeding under section 10 initiated by the employer in good faith and not solely for delay or avoidance of penalties), may be assessed a civil penalty of not more than $7,000 for each day during which such failure or violation continues.

(e) Any employer who willfully violates any standard, rule, or order promulgated pursuant to section 6 of this Act, or of any regulations prescribed pursuant to this Act, and that violation caused death to any employee, shall, upon conviction, be punished by a fine of not more than $10,000 or by imprisonment for not more than six months, or by both: except that if the conviction is for a violation committed after a first conviction of such person, punishment shall be by a fine of not more than $20,000 or by imprisonment for not more than one year, or by both.

(f) Any person who gives advance notice of any inspection to be conducted under this Act, without authority from the Secretary or his designees, shall, upon conviction, be punished by a fine of not more than $1,000 or by imprisonment for not more than six months, or by both.

(g) Whoever knowingly makes any false statement, representation, or certification in any application, record, report, plan, or other document filed or required to be maintained pursuant to this Act shall, upon conviction, be punished by a fine of not more than $10,000, or by imprisonment for not more than six months, or by both.

* * *

(i) Any employer who violates any of the posting requirements, as prescribed under the provisions of this Act, shall be assessed a civil penalty of up to $7,000 for each violation.

(j) The Commission shall have authority to assess all civil penalties provided in this section, giving due consideration to the appropriateness of the penalty with respect to the size of the business of the employer being charged, the gravity of the violation, the good faith of the employer, and the history of previous violations.

(k) For purposes of this section, a serious violation shall be deemed to exist in a place of employment if there is a substantial probability that death or serious physical harm could result from a condition which exists, or from one or more practices, means, methods, operations, or processes which have been adopted or are in use, in such place of employment unless the employer did not, and could not with the exercise of reasonable diligence, know of the presence of the violation.

(*l*) Civil penalties owed under this Act shall be paid to the Secretary for deposit into the Treasury of the United States and shall accrue to the United States and may be recovered in a civil action in the name of the United States brought in the United States district court for the district where the violation is alleged to have occurred or where the employer has its principal office.

STATE JURISDICTION AND STATE PLANS

SEC. 18. (§ 667) (a) Nothing in this Act shall prevent any State agency or court from asserting jurisdiction under State law over any occupational safety or health issue with respect to which no standard is in effect under section 6.

(b) Any State which, at any time, desires to assume responsibility for development and enforcement therein of occupational safety and health standards relating to any occupational safety or health issue with respect to which a Federal standard has been promulgated under section 6 shall submit a State plan for the development of such standards and their enforcement.

(c) The Secretary shall approve the plan submitted by a State under subsection (b), or any modification thereof, if such plan in his judgment—

(1) designates a State agency or agencies as the agency or agencies responsible for administering the plan throughout the State,

(2) provides for the development and enforcement of safety and health standards relating to one or more safety or health issues, which standards (and the enforcement of which standards) are or will be at least as effective in providing safe and healthful employment and places of employment as the standards promulgated under section 6 which relate to the same issues, and which standards, when applicable to products which are distributed or used in interstate commerce, are required by compelling local conditions and do not unduly burden interstate commerce,

(3) provides for a right of entry and inspection of all workplaces subject to the Act which is at least as effective as that provided in section 8, and includes a prohibition on advance notice of inspections,

(4) contains satisfactory assurances that such agency or agencies have or will have the legal authority and qualified personnel necessary for the enforcement of such standards,

(5) gives satisfactory assurances that such State will devote adequate funds to the administration and enforcement of such standards,

(6) contains satisfactory assurances that such State will, to the extent permitted by its law, establish and maintain an effective and comprehensive occupational safety and health program applicable to all employees of public agencies of the State and its political subdivisions, which program in as effective as the standards contained in an approved plan,

(7) requires employers in the State to make reports to the Secretary in the same manner and to the same extent as if the plan were not in effect, and

(8) provides that the State agency will make such reports to the Secretary in such form and containing such information, as the Secretary shall from time to time require.

(d) If the Secretary rejects a plan submitted under subsection (b), he shall afford the State submitting the plan due notice and opportunity for a hearing before so doing.

(e) After the Secretary approves a State plan submitted under subsection (b), he may, but shall not be required to, exercise his authority under sections 8, 9, 10, 13, and 17 with respect to comparable standards promulgated under section 6, for the period specified in the next sentence. The Secretary may exercise the authority referred to above until he determines, on the basis of actual operations under the State plan, that the criteria set forth in subsection (c) are being applied, but he shall not make such determination for at least three years after the plan's approval under subsection (c). Upon making the determination referred to in the preceding sentence, the provisions of sections 5(a)(2), 8 (except for the purpose of carrying out subsection (f) of this section), 9, 10, 13, and 17, and standards promulgated under section 6 of this Act, shall not apply with respect to any occupational safety or health issues covered under the plan, but the Secretary may retain jurisdiction under the above provisions in any proceeding commenced under section 9 or 10 before the date of determination.

(f) The Secretary shall, on the basis of reports submitted by the State agency and his own inspections make a continuing evaluation of the manner in which each State having a plan approved under this section is carrying out such plan. Whenever the Secretary finds, after affording due notice and opportunity for a hearing, that in the administration of the State plan there is a failure to comply substantially with any provision of the State plan (or any assurance contained therein), he shall notify the State agency of his withdrawal of approval of such plan and upon receipt of such notice such plan shall cease to be in effect, but the State may retain jurisdiction in any case commenced before the withdrawal of the plan in order to enforce standards under the plan whenever the issues involved do not relate to the reasons for the withdrawal of the plan.

(g) The State may obtain a review of a decision of the Secretary withdrawing approval of or rejecting its plan by the United States court of appeals for the circuit in which the State is located by filing in such court within thirty days following receipt of notice of such decision a petition to modify or set aside in whole or in part the action of the

Secretary. A copy of such petition shall forthwith be served upon the Secretary, and thereupon the Secretary shall certify and file in the court the record upon which the decision complained of was issued as provided in section 2112 of title 28, United States Code. Unless the court finds that the Secretary's decision in rejecting a proposed State plan or withdrawing his approval of such a plan is not supported by substantial evidence the court shall affirm the Secretary's decision. The judgment of the court shall be subject to review by the Supreme Court of the United States upon certiorari or certification as provided in section 1254 of title 28, United States Code.

(h) The Secretary may enter into an agreement with a State under which the State will be permitted to, continue to enforce one or more occupational health and safety standards in effect in such State until final action is taken by the Secretary with respect to a plan submitted by a State under subsection (b) of this section, or two years from the date of enactment of this Act, whichever is earlier.

MASSACHUSETTS WORKER'S COMPENSATION STATUTE

Mass.Gen.Laws ch. 152, §§ 1–86

SEC. 1 Definitions

The following words as used in this chapter shall, unless a different meaning is plainly required by the context or specifically prescribed, have the following meanings:

* * *

(4) "Employee", every person in the service of another under any contract of hire, express or implied, oral or written, excepting (a) masters of and seamen on vessels engaged in interstate or foreign commerce, (b) persons employed to participate in organized professional athletics, while so employed, if their contracts of hire provide for the payment of wages during the period of any disability resulting from such employment, (c) a salesperson affiliated with a real estate broker pursuant to an agreement which specifically provides for compensation only in the form of commissions earned from the sale or rental of real property, (d) a salesperson who is a direct seller of consumer products on a buy-sell or deposit-commission basis other than in a retail establishment, all of whose remuneration is directly related to sales rather than amount of time worked and whose services are performed pursuant to a written contract providing that the direct seller will not be treated as an employee for Federal tax purposes, (e) a person who operates a taxicab vehicle which is leased by such person from a taxicab company pursuant to an independent contract which specifically provides for a rental fee or other payment to the owner of such taxicab vehicle which is in no way related to the taxicab fares collected by such person; and provided, further, that such person is not treated as an employee for Federal tax purposes, (f) persons employed by an employer engaged in interstate or foreign commerce but only so far as the laws of the United States provide for compensation or liability for their injury or death, and (g) a person whose employment is not in the usual course of the trade, business, profession or occupation of his employer, but not excepting a person conclusively presumed to be an employee under section twenty-six.

Students participating in a work-based experience as part of a school-to-work program who receive personal injuries arising out of and in the course of such participation at or with particular employers, shall, for purposes of this chapter, be deemed employees of such employers.

For the purposes of this paragraph, "school to work program" shall mean workplace based education and training programs designed to improve the knowledge and skills of high school students by integrating academic and occupational learning to prepare students for gainful employment and increase their opportunities for post secondary education.

* * *

The provisions of this chapter shall remain elective as to employers of seasonal or casual or part-time domestic servants. For the purpose of this paragraph, a part-time domestic servant is one who works in the employ of the employer less than sixteen hours per week.

* * *

(7A) "Personal injury" includes infectious or contagious diseases if the nature of the employment is such that the hazard of contracting such diseases by an employee is inherent in the employment. "Personal injury" shall not include any injury resulting from an employee's purely voluntary participation in any recreational activity, including but not limited to athletic events, parties, and picnics, even though the employer pays some or all of the cost thereof. Personal injuries shall include mental or emotional disabilities only where a contributing cause of such disability is an event or series of events occurring within the employment.

* * *

Sec. 6A   Division of Administration; Notice of injury; Informational brochure rights, benefits and monitoring of benefits; Obligations; Resolution of disputes

Upon receipt of notice of injury from the employer, or any other indication of a compensable injury, the division of administration shall immediately mail, post paid, to the injured worker an informational brochure as prescribed by the division which sets forth in clear and understandable language a summary statement of the rights, benefits, and obligations of injured workers under this chapter. The division shall monitor the furnishing of benefits by the employer or insurer to ascertain that correct benefits are being provided in cases accepted as compensable injuries. In the event of controversy or dispute, the division shall attempt to resolve the dispute promptly and informally, and, upon failing to do so, shall promptly forward a claim form to the employee.

SEC. 7 Commencement of weekly benefits; time limitation; notice to contest claim; specification of grounds; failure to commence payments or give notice; calculation of compensation; penalty; waiver

(1) Within fourteen days of an insurer's receipt of an employer's first report of injury, or an initial written claim for weekly benefits on a form prescribed by the department, whichever is received first, the insurer shall either commence payment of weekly benefits under this chapter or shall notify the division of administration, the employer, and, by certified mail, the employee, of its refusal to commence payment of weekly benefits. The notice shall specify the grounds and factual basis for the refusal to commence payment of said benefits and shall state that if no claim has yet been filed, benefits will not be secured for the alleged injury unless a claim is filed with the department and insurer within any time limits provided under this chapter. Any grounds and basis for noncompensability specified by the insurer shall, unless based upon newly discovered evidence, be the sole basis of the insurer's defense on the issue of compensability in any subsequent proceeding. An insurer's inability to defend on any issue shall not relieve an employee of the burden of proving each element of any case.

(2) If an insurer fails to commence such payment or to make such notification within fourteen days, it shall pay to the employee a penalty in an amount equal to two hundred dollars. Where compensation is later ordered and interest is due the employee under section fifty, such penalty shall be considered compensation for the purpose of computing interest. If the insurer fails to commence such payment or to make such notification of denial within sixty days it shall pay an additional penalty to the department of two thousand dollars into the special fund created pursuant to section sixty-five; provided, however, that such additional penalty shall be ten thousand dollars if said payment is not commenced and said notification is not made within ninety days. Penalties under this section may be waived if an administrative judge finds that the failure to comply with the requirements herein set forth was due to events beyond the control of the insurer or its agents. No additional penalties shall be levied for continuing violations under this section, but the insurer shall be allowed no defenses against any initial claim for weekly benefits until any penalty owed under this section has been paid. No amount paid as a penalty under this section shall be included in any formula utilized to establish premium rates for workers' compensation insurance. An insurer's inability to defend on any issue shall not relieve an employee of the burden of proving each element of any case.

(3)   No individual shall receive or continue to receive benefits under this chapter if such individual has an outstanding default or arrest warrant against him. In order to determine if an individual has an

outstanding default or arrest warrant against him, the department shall transmit to the criminal history systems board a list of applicants and beneficiaries along with sufficient identifying information about such applicants and beneficiaries on at least a quarterly basis. The criminal history systems board shall send to the department a list of any applicants or beneficiaries who have a default or arrest warrant outstanding. Evidence of the outstanding default or arrest warrant appearing in the warrant management system established by section 23A of chapter 276 shall be sufficient grounds for such action by the department. The department shall notify the person against whom there is a default or arrest warrant outstanding that such person's benefits shall be denied or suspended unless such person furnishes proof within 30 days that such warrant has been recalled or that there is no such warrant outstanding for such person. Notice of potential denial or suspension shall be deemed sufficient if the notice is mailed to the most recent address furnished to the department. If proof that such warrant has been recalled or that there is no such warrant outstanding is furnished within 30 days, and if the applicant would otherwise be entitled to benefits, such benefits shall be provided from the time that they would have been provided had there not been a denial or suspension of benefits. If no such proof is furnished within 30 days, such person shall be notified that such benefits are denied or suspended subject to the opportunity for a hearing. After such notice to such person has been delivered or mailed by the department, such person may request a hearing within 90 days with respect to the existence of an outstanding warrant. If a hearing is requested within ten days from the time the notice that benefits are being denied or suspended is mailed or delivered, benefits shall not be suspended until a finding following the hearing. If a hearing is requested, the law enforcement agency responsible for the warrant shall be notified of the time, place, date of hearing and the subject of the warrant. An affidavit from the law enforcement agency responsible for the warrant or from the colonel of the state police may be introduced as prima facie evidence of the existence of a warrant without the need for members of that law enforcement agency to attend any hearings held under this section. The department shall issue a finding within 45 days of conducting the hearing as to whether there is a warrant. If there is a warrant outstanding, the benefits shall not be issued or shall be suspended. A person whose benefits have been denied or suspended due to an outstanding warrant may petition for reinstatement of such benefits at any time if such person can furnish sufficient proof as determined by the department that such warrant has been recalled. Such benefits will be provided from the time the warrant was recalled. The department shall promulgate regulations to implement this section. * * *

SEC. 7A Presumption where employee found dead at place of employment, etc., Prima Facie Evidence that claim falls within Provision of Act

In any claim for compensation where the employee has been killed, or found dead at his place of employment or is physically or mentally unable to testify, it shall be prima facie evidence that the employee was performing his regular duties on the day of injury or fatality or death or disability and that the claim comes within the provisions of this chapter, that sufficient notice of the injury has been given, and that the injury or death or disability was not occasioned by the wilful intention of the employee to injure or kill himself or another.

* * *

SEC. 7C Division of Dispute Resolution; Hearing; Representation; Compensation of Representative

Any party appearing before the division of dispute resolution may be heard in person, or may be represented by an attorney or by any other person designated by such party. No person who is not an attorney shall be compensated for representing a claimant in such a proceeding; provided, however, that nothing in this section shall bar payment by a labor organization, employee association, or insurer of any payment of regular wages or salary to a full time employee for time spent in representing a claimant. The senior judge may, for cause, deny or suspend the right of any person to practice or appear before the department. Any person denied or suspended under this provision shall have the right to appeal to the commissioner any denial or suspension within fourteen days of receipt of the notice. Upon receipt of such appeal, the commissioner shall refer the matter to the division of administrative law appeals within the executive office of administration and finance which shall have the authority to reverse, uphold or modify the removal or suspension after a hearing held pursuant to section thirteen of chapter thirty A. Any party aggrieved by said hearing shall have the right to appeal as set forth in section fourteen of said chapter thirty A.

* * *

SEC. 8 Termination or Modification of Benefits; Notice; Specification of Grounds; Filing of Complaint for Termination of Benefits; Appointment of Impartial Physician; Penalty; Extension of Payment Period

(1) An insurer who makes timely payments pursuant to subsection one of section seven may make such payments for a period of one hundred eighty calendar days from the commencement of disability without affecting its right to contest any issue arising under this

chapter. An insurer may terminate or modify payments at any time within such one hundred eighty day period without penalty if such change is based on the actual income of the employee or if it gives the employee and the division of administration at least seven days written notice of its intent to stop or modify payments and contest any claim filed. The notice shall specify the grounds and factual basis for stopping or modifying payment of benefits and the insurer's intention to contest any issue and shall state that in order to secure additional benefits the employee shall file a claim with the department and insurer within any time limits provided by this chapter.

Any grounds and basis for noncompensability specified by the insurer shall be the sole basis of the insurer's defense on the basis of compensability, unless based on newly discovered evidence; provided, however, that an insurer's inability to defend on any issue shall not relieve an employee of the burden of proving each element of any case. Any failure of an insurer to make all payments due an employee under the terms of an order, decision, arbitrator's decision, approved lump sum or other agreement, or certified letter notifying said insurer that the employee has left work after an unsuccessful attempt to return within the time frame determined pursuant to paragraph (a) of subsection (2) of this section within fourteen days of the insurer's receipt of such document, shall result in a penalty of two hundred dollars, payable to the employee to whom such payments were required to be paid by the said document; provided, however, that such penalty shall be one thousand dollars if all such payments have not been made within forty-five days, two thousand five hundred dollars if not made within sixty days, and ten thousand dollars if not made within ninety days. * * *

(2) An insurer paying weekly compensation benefits shall not modify or discontinue such payments except in the following situations:

(a) compensation has been modified or discontinued pursuant to an order or decision of an arbitrator, an administrative judge, the reviewing board or court of the commonwealth;

(b) the compensation recipient has assented thereto in writing on a form prescribed by the department and the original of such form has been filed with the department;

(c) the employee has returned to work; provided, however, that the insurer shall forthwith resume payments if, within twenty-eight calendar days of return to such employment, the employee leaves such employment and, within twenty-one calendar days thereafter, informs the employer and insurer by certified letter that the disability resulting from the injury renders him incapable of performing such work; provided, further, that if due, compensation shall be paid under section thirty-five;

(d) the insurer has possession of (i) a medical report from the treating physician, or, if an impartial medical examiner has made a report pursuant to section eleven A or subsection (4) of this section, the report of such examiner, and either of such reports indicates that the employee is capable of return to the job held at the time of injury, or other suitable job pursuant to section thirty-five D consistent with the employee's physical and mental condition as reported by said physician and (ii) a written report from the person employing said employee at the time of the injury indicating that such a suitable job is open and has been made available, and remains open to the employee; provided, however, that if due, compensation shall be paid under section thirty-five; provided, further, that if such employee accepts said employment subsequent to a modification or termination pursuant to this paragraph, compensation shall be reinstated at the prior rate if the employee should cease work in accordance with paragraph (c) of this section or should be terminated by the employer because of the employee's physical or mental incapacity to perform the duties required by the job;

(e) payments are terminated or modified pursuant to subsection (1);

(f) the insurer has received a communication from the office of education and vocational rehabilitation authorizing suspension or reduction of payment under section thirty G;

(g) the benefits payable to the employee have been exhausted pursuant to sections thirty-one, thirty-four, or thirty-five;

(h) payments are suspended or reduced pursuant to section eleven D for failure to respond to an insurer's written request to provide an earnings report, or for past overpayments;

(i) payments are suspended pursuant to section forty-five, provided that the department shall provide by rule for the manner of any such suspension, and subsequent reinstatement or forfeiture;

(j) the employee has been incarcerated pursuant to conviction for a felony or misdemeanor and has thereby forfeited any right to compensation during such period; or

(k) payments are suspended or reduced pursuant to section thirty six B; or

(*l*) the employee has died.

For purposes of clause (d) of this section, any termination of an employee within one year of resumption of work with his prior employer will be presumed to be for the reason that the employee was physically or mentally incapable of performing the duties required by the job or that the job was unsuitable for the employee, unless the insurer demonstrates the contrary by a preponderance of evidence at a subsequent proceeding.

(3) [Stricken]

(4) An insurer who makes prompt payment of benefits pursuant to section seven and continues payment for one hundred eighty days or more, without contesting liability, may, no sooner than sixty days following the referral to the industrial accident board of a complaint for termination or reduction of benefits under section thirty-four, thirty-four A or thirty five, if no conference order has been issued during such sixty day period, request the senior judge to appoint an impartial physician to examine the employee. The senior judge shall, within seven days of a request for an impartial examination, appoint a physician from the appropriate roster to conduct an examination of the employee and make a report within fourteen days. If such report contains evidence of increased capability to work, the insurer may reduce or terminate benefits in accordance with such report, pursuant to the provisions of section thirty-five D. In such instances, if the requirements of this subsection have been complied with, when an order is issued on the insurer's complaint, if such order requires that retroactive weekly benefits are due the employee, an additional payment equal to two times the average weekly wage in the commonwealth shall also be paid to the employee.

At any time subsequent to the filing of a claim or complaint solely regarding the reasonableness or necessity of a particular course of medical treatment, any party to such claim or complaint may request the senior judge to appoint a physician from the appropriate roster to conduct an examination of the employee and make a report within fourteen days. If the senior judge determines that said claim or complaint involves only the issue of reasonable and necessary medical treatment, he shall make such appointment within seven days. The impartial physician shall determine the appropriateness of any medical treatment claimed or denied by the parties, using any guidelines adopted by the health care services board or promulgated by the department. The determination by the impartial physician shall be binding upon the parties until any subsequent proceeding within the division of dispute resolution. The determination of the impartial physician shall be prima facie evidence of the appropriateness or inappropriateness of the course of medical treatment in question at any hearing at which such treatment is at issue.

(5) Except as specifically provided above, if the insurer terminates, reduces, or fails to make any payments required under this chapter, and additional compensation is later ordered, the employee shall be paid by the insurer a penalty payment equal to twenty per cent of the additional compensation due on the date of such finding. No amount paid as a penalty under this section shall be included in any formula utilized to establish premium rates for workers' compensation insurance. No termi-

nation or modification of benefits not based on actual earnings or an order of the board shall be allowed without seven days written notice to the employee and the department.

(6) Any one hundred eighty day payment without prejudice period herein provided may be extended to a period not to exceed one year by agreement of the parties provided that:

(a) the agreement sets out the last day of such extension; and

(b) a conciliator, administrative judge, or administrative law judge approves such agreement as not detrimental to the employee's case.

All the provisions of subsection (1) of this section shall apply to any period of payment without prejudice extended as provided in this subsection. Any payment without prejudice under this section shall toll the statute of limitations pursuant to section forty-one.

* * *

SEC. 11B Promulgation of Rules for Depositions and Interrogatories; Notice of Proceeding; Powers of Member of Board; Witness Fee; Jurisdiction of Superior Court; Witnesses Outside Jurisdiction; Payment of Expenses; Manner of Taking Evidence; Transcripts; Decision of Members

Procedures within the division of dispute resolution shall be as simple and summary as reasonable. The commissioner shall promulgate rules providing for the use of depositions and interrogatories. In any proceeding under this chapter, the division shall give notice of the date, time, and place of the proceeding to all parties in interest. Any member of the board may subpoena witnesses, administer oaths, and examine such parts of the books and records of the parties to a proceeding as relate to questions before such member. The fee for attending as witness before the department or a member of the board shall be that provided for witnesses before the superior court department of the trial court. The superior court shall have jurisdiction to enforce the provisions of this section relating to the attendance and testimony of witnesses and the examination of books and records.

A member may upon the filing of a written request of any party appearing before him, together with interrogatories and cross-interrogatories, if any, request officers in other jurisdictions, having power and duties similar to those of a member of the board, to take depositions or testimony of persons or witnesses residing in such jurisdictions. On the return of any such deposition to the division it shall be forwarded to the appropriate member. A reasonable fee for services in connection with the taking of such depositions and the expenses thereof shall be assessed upon the requesting party.

The expenses for services in connection with the taking of depositions shall be paid by the party requesting that such witness be deposed or whose witness is ordered to be deposed; provided, however, that if the decision of the member or reviewing board is in favor of the employee, the cost of such proceeding shall be added to the amount awarded to the employee and be paid by the insurer under the provisions of this chapter.

The evidence at the hearing shall be taken by an employee of the department sworn to record the entire proceeding. The record of the hearing shall be transcribed verbatim or electronically recorded. Upon the request of a member or the reviewing board, or at the request of a party, a transcript or recording or both, whichever such party requests shall be forwarded to such party without charge. The original recording shall remain in the control of the department. Verbatim transcripts shall be made manually from the stenographic notes only if a certified copy of the proceedings is required by the reviewing board or a court of the commonwealth. Decisions of members of the board shall set forth the issues in controversy the decision on each and a brief statement of the grounds for each such decision. Decisions shall issue no more than twenty-eight days following the close of testimony, unless further extension is authorized in writing by the director of dispute resolution.

Sec. 11C Appeal to reviewing board; fee; waiver; standard for reversal; submission of briefs; written decisions

Any party aggrieved by a decision of an administrative judge after a hearing held pursuant to section eleven shall have thirty days from the filing date of such decision within which to file an appeal from said decision to the reviewing board. A party who has by mistake, accident, or other reasonable cause failed to appeal from a decision within the time limited herein may within one year of the filing of said decision petition the commissioner of the department who may permit such appeal if justice and equity require it, notwithstanding that a decree has previously been rendered on any decision filed, pursuant to section twelve. Appeals to the reviewing board must be accompanied by a fee of thirty per cent of the average weekly wage in the commonwealth, which shall be paid into the special fund pursuant to section sixty-five. Such fee may be waived by the reviewing board for indigent claimants. The reviewing board shall reverse the decision of an administrative judge only if it determines that such administrative judge's decision is beyond the scope of his authority, arbitrary or capricious, or contrary to law. The reviewing board may, when appropriate, recommit a case before it to an administrative judge for further findings of fact. Where the reviewing board affirms the decision of an administrative judge, it may do so in summary fashion and without discussion of the issues raised on appeal.

* * *

SEC. 12 Enforcement of order by Superior Court; Appellate procedure

(1) Whenever any party in interest presents a certified copy of an order or decision of a board member or of the reviewing board and any papers in connection therewith to the superior court department of the trial court for the county in which the injury occurred or for the county of Suffolk, the court shall enforce the order or decision, notwithstanding whether the matters at issue have been appealed and a decision on the merits of the appeal is pending. In the event that the order or decision is reversed on appeal, the enforcement order shall be deemed vacated and unenforceable from the date of such reversal. If the request for an enforcement order is presented to the superior court for the county of Suffolk, the court may, on motion of any party in interest, order the case removed to the superior court for the county in which the injury occurred.

* * *

SEC. 12A Award of attorneys' fees and costs of appeal to claimant

If on appeal to the appeals court or the supreme judicial court pursuant to section twelve the claimant prevails, the court shall allow the claimant, in addition to the award in the judgement, an amount equal to the reasonable cost of his attorney's fees, briefs and other necessary expenses that result from the appeal. When any party in interest obtains an enforcement order from the superior court department of the trial court pursuant to said section twelve, the court shall also allow the party the reasonable cost of attorney's fees, briefs and other expenses provided for by this section.

SEC. 13 Establishment of rate of payment for health care services; Procedures for determining excessive charge; Review of clinical health care providers; Hiring medical consultant; Monitoring treatment; Creation of health care services board

(1) The rate of payment by insurers for health care services adjudged compensable under this chapter shall be established by the division of health care finance and policy under the provisions of chapter one hundred and eighteen G; provided, however, that a different rate for services may be agreed upon by the insurer, the employer and the health care service provider.

Except as provided above, no insurer shall be liable for hospitalization expenses adjudged compensable under this chapter at a rate in excess of the rate set by the said division, or for other health services in excess of the rate established for that service by the said division, regardless of the setting in which the service is administered: provided, however, that the amount required to be reimbursed by insurers to hospitals for outpatient physical, occupational and speech therapy services only (codes 178010 through 178013, 178050 through 178053, and 178090 through 178093, inclusive) shall be the higher of:

(a) the amount required by the said division to be reimbursed by insurers to non-hospitals for the above-mentioned outpatient physical, occupational and speech therapy services; and

(b) either the amount which can be derived from the ratio of total costs to total charges calculated for the hospital requesting reimbursements, in accordance with methods utilized by the said division to determine payment on account factors for hospitals subject to chapter one hundred and eighteen G, or ninety-five percent of the rates payable to such hospital for such services on May fifteenth, nineteen hundred and ninety-five, whichever is the lower amount.

Requests for reimbursement for health services under this chapter shall be signed by the person performing such service and shall be accompanied by a detailed description of the service rendered as well as the name and licensure number of the person performing such service. All health services provided under this chapter shall be subject to the provisions of section three of chapter one hundred and seventy-five H and 42 CFR 1001.951–1001.953, the so-called "safe harbor regulations" as adopted by the federal government on July twenty-ninth, nineteen hundred and ninety-one. No employee shall be liable for health care services adjudged compensable under this chapter.

Except with respect to rates to be paid for health care services, as defined in said chapter one hundred and eighteen G, which shall be reviewable under said chapter one hundred and eighteen G, the commissioner shall by rule establish procedures for determining whether or not the charge for a health service is excessive. In order to accomplish this purpose, the commissioner shall consult with insurers, associations and organizations representing the medical and other providers of treatment services, and other appropriate groups. The charges for such health services shall be reasonable.

(2) The department shall review the clinical health care providers who render services to injured employees. This review shall be achieved by establishing a quality control system within the department. The commissioner may hire a medical consultant or consultants, full or part-time, to assist in the administration of this section. Any medical consultant shall be a physician licensed under the laws of the commonwealth.

Such medical consultant shall perform all duties assigned by the commissioner relating to the supervision of the total range of care of injured employees and shall also advise the department on matters on which the commissioner requests the consultant's advice.

The commissioner shall monitor the medical and surgical treatment provided to injured employees and the services of other health care providers, and shall also monitor hospital utilization as it relates to the treatment of injured employees. The monitoring shall include determinations concerning the appropriateness of the service, whether the treatment is necessary and effective, the proper costs of services, and the quality of treatment. The commissioner with the advice of the health care service board may penalize, disqualify, or suspend a provider from receiving payment for services rendered under this chapter if the commissioner or his designee determines that the provider has violated any part of this chapter or rule adopted under this chapter.

The commissioner shall have the sole authority to make determinations under this section; provided, however, that aggrieved parties shall have a right to appeal to the superior court.

(3) There is hereby created a health care services board composed of the commissioner or his designee as an ex officio member and chairman, one person representing chiropractors, one person representing dentists, one person representing hospital administrators, one person representing physical therapists, and six physicians representing different health care specialties which the commissioner determines are the most frequently utilized by injured employees. The board shall also have one person representing employees, one person representing employers, and one person representing the public. Members shall be appointed by the commissioner for two-year terms. The health care services board shall receive and investigate complaints from employees, employers and insurers regarding health care providers who provide services under this chapter who are alleged to have engaged in patterns of (i) discrimination against compensation complaints, (ii) overutilization of procedures, (iii) unnecessary surgery or other procedures, or (iv) other inappropriate treatment of compensation recipients. Where such board finds a pattern of abuse, it shall refer its findings to the appropriate board of registration. No member of the health care services board shall be liable for damages resulting from any investigation under this paragraph in any action brought by any party against such board or any individual member thereof, provided that the performance of the duties of such member were undertaken in good faith. The health care services board shall develop itself or the commissioner may contract with one or more organizations with demonstrated expertise in the treatment of work-related injuries and illnesses to develop written guidelines for appropriate and necessary treatment based on diagnosis of injuries and illnesses. Said guidelines shall include appropriate mechanisms for deviation of treatment. The board shall no later than July first, nineteen hundred

and ninety-two, distribute said guidelines in draft form for public comment and no later than January first, nineteen hundred and ninety-three, endorse the first version of said guidelines for use by health care providers in the treatment of injuries and illnesses under this chapter. The board shall at least annually review and where appropriate revise said guidelines. The cost of any contract for development, review, revision or dissemination of said guidelines shall be paid out of the Workers' Compensation Special Fund pursuant to section sixty-five.

The health care services board shall develop criteria in order to select and maintain a roster of qualified impartial physicians to provide objective medical opinions pursuant to sections eight and eleven A of this chapter. Said criteria shall further be used, when necessary, to remove any impartial physicians from the roster when a medical provider fails to comply with the criteria. Upon the establishment of criteria, the health care services board shall refer said criteria to the senior administrative judge who shall develop a roster of impartial physicians.

The commissioner shall have the authority to hire the personnel necessary to carry out the duties of the board pursuant to this section.

SEC. 13A   Contest of claim by insurer; acceptance of liability; reasonable attorney' fee awarded; settlement; determination of fee

(1) Whenever an insurer contests an initial liability claim for benefits submitted on a form prescribed by the department, by failing to commence the compensation requested within twenty-one days of receipt of such claim, and then, at any time prior to a conference held under section ten A, the insurer agrees to pay, with or without prejudice, the compensation claimed to be due, said insurer shall pay an attorney's fee to the employee's counsel in the amount of seven hundred dollars, plus necessary expenses; provided, however, that only one such fee shall be paid with respect to any such written claim under this paragraph. An insurer shall reduce such a fee to three hundred fifty dollars when pursuant to a conciliator's finding said attorney failed to appear at a scheduled conciliation and such failure was not beyond the control of said attorney. Only one fee under this paragraph shall be paid with respect to any written claim. A conciliator shall have the authority to extend the twenty-one day period within which no attorney's fee is due to no more than thirty-five days, if in the opinion of the conciliator such extension increases the likelihood of the payment of the claim prior to referral to the industrial accident board. Such extensions shall be granted after consultation with the parties and a written indication shall be appended to the case file.

(2) Whenever an insurer contests an initial liability claim for benefits as provided by subsection (1), and then is ordered to pay such

benefits by an administrative judge pursuant to a conference held under section ten A, said insurer shall pay an attorney's fee to the employee's counsel in the amount of one thousand dollars, plus necessary expenses; provided, however, that an administrative judge may increase or decrease such fee based on the complexity of the dispute or the effort expended by the attorney; provided, further, that only one such fee under this paragraph shall be paid with respect to any such written claim. An insurer shall reduce such a fee to five hundred dollars when, pursuant to a conciliator's finding said attorney failed to appear at a scheduled conciliation and such failure was not beyond the control of said attorney.

(3) Whenever an insurer contests a claim for benefits on a form prescribed by the department other than an initial liability claim as provided by subsection (1), by failing to commence the compensation requested within twenty-one days of receipt of such claim and then, at any time prior to a conference pursuant to section ten A the insurer agrees to pay the compensation claimed to be due, said insurer shall pay an attorney's fee to the employee's counsel in the amount of five hundred dollars, plus necessary expenses; provided, however, that only one such fee shall be paid with respect to any such written claim under this paragraph. An insurer shall reduce such a fee to two hundred fifty dollars when, pursuant to a conciliator's finding, said attorney failed to appear at a scheduled conciliation and such failure was not beyond the control of said attorney. For purposes of this subsection, the filing of a subsequent written request on a prescribed form shall be deemed an additional written claim for benefits. A conciliator shall have the authority to extend the twenty-one day period within which no attorney's fee is due to no more than thirty-five days, if, in the opinion of the conciliator, such extension increases the likelihood of the payment of the claim prior to referral to the industrial accident board. Such extensions shall be granted after consultation with the parties and a written indication shall be appended to the case file.

(4) Whenever an insurer files a complaint to reduce or discontinue an employee's benefits or whenever an insurer contests a claim for benefits on a form prescribed by the department other than an initial liability claim as provided by subsection (1), by failing to commence the compensation requested within twenty-one days of receipt of such claim, if the order of the administrative judge pursuant to a conference held under section ten A, reflects the written offer submitted by the claimant or by a conciliator on the claimant's behalf, pursuant to section ten or section ten A, said insurer shall pay an attorney's fee to the employee's counsel in the amount of seven hundred dollars, plus necessary expenses. If the order of the administrative judge reflects the written offer submitted by the insurer or by a conciliator on the insurer's behalf, pursuant to

section ten or section ten A, no attorney's fee shall be payable to the employee's counsel. If the order reflects an amount different from both submissions, the fee shall be in the amount of three hundred fifty dollars, plus necessary expenses. Any fee payable under this paragraph shall be reduced by half when the attorney failed to appear at a scheduled conciliation, and such failure was not beyond the control of said attorney. Only one such fee shall be paid with respect to any particular written claim under this paragraph.

(5) Whenever an insurer files a complaint or contests a claim for benefits and then either (i) accepts the employee's claim or withdraws its own complaint within five days of the date set for a hearing pursuant to section eleven; or (ii) the employee prevails at such hearing the insurer shall pay a fee to the employee's attorney in an amount equal to three thousand five hundred dollars plus necessary expenses. An administrative judge may increase or decrease such fee based on the complexity of the dispute or the effort expended by the attorney.

(6) Whenever an insurer appeals a decision of an administrative judge and the employee prevails in the decision of the reviewing board, the insurer shall pay a fee to the employee's attorney in the amount of one thousand dollars, plus necessary expenses. An administrative judge may increase or decrease such fee based on the complexity of the dispute or the effort expended by the attorney.

(7) Whenever an employee appeals a decision of an administrative judge and the employee prevails in the decision of the reviewing board, the employee shall pay an attorney's fee sufficient to defray the reasonable costs of counsel retained by said employee. Subject to the approval of the reviewing board, such fee shall be an amount agreed to by the employee and his attorney.

(8) Whenever an insurer and an employee agree to a settlement under section forty-eight, the attorney's fee shall be paid from the settlement in accordance with the following provisions:

(a) when the insurer and the employee reach such settlement prior to insurer acceptance of liability or prior to a decision of an administrative judge, the reviewing board, or the appeals court of the commonwealth finding insurer liability, such fee shall be no more than fifteen percent of the amount of such settlement;

(b) when the insurer and the employee reach such settlement subsequent to insurer acceptance of liability or subsequent to a decision of an administrative judge, the reviewing board, or the appeals court of the commonwealth finding insurer liability which is in effect at the time such agreement is entered into, such fee shall be no more than twenty percent of amount of such settlement.

(9) In any hearing or review requested by an insurer aggrieved by an order or decision with respect to an injury occurring prior to November first, nineteen hundred and eighty-six or in a proceeding brought by an insurer or self-insurer as to the continuance of compensation being paid under this chapter for an injury occurring prior to November first, nineteen hundred and eighty-six, there shall be awarded an amount sufficient to compensate the employee for the reasonable costs of such hearing review or proceeding including reasonable counsel fees and expenses, provided that the employee prevails at such hearing review or proceeding. Such amounts shall be paid by the insurer. Any other attorneys' fees for services provided claimants for injuries prior to November first, nineteen hundred and eighty-six, shall be of an amount agreed upon between the employee and the attorney.

(10) The attorneys' fees specified in this section shall be the only fees payable for any services provided to employees under this chapter unless otherwise provided by an arbitration agreement pursuant to section ten B. In any instance in which an attorney's fee under subsection (1) to (6), inclusive, is due as a result of a cash award being made to the employee either voluntarily, or pursuant to an order or decision, the insurer may reduce the amount payable to the employee within the first month from the date of the voluntary payment order or decision, by the amount owed the claimant's attorney; provided, however, that the amount paid to the employee shall not be reduced to a sum less than seventy-eight percent of what the employee would have received within that month if no attorney's fee were payable. The dollar amounts specified in said subsections (1) to (6), inclusive, of this section shall be changed October first of each year by the percentage change in adjusted benefits from the preceding year as calculated and limited in paragraph (a) of section thirty-four B. The department shall provide by rule the necessary expenses that are reimbursable under this section. No fees shall be payable under subsection (1), (2), (3) or (4) unless the claim subject to the dispute was filed according to the provisions of section ten.

(11) In any proceeding at which a penalty pursuant to section seven or section eight is awarded an employee by an administrative judge, the attorney's fee payable for such proceeding shall not be included in any formula utilized to establish premium rates for workers' compensation.

SEC. 15 Legal liabilities for injuries; election, etc.

Where the injury for which compensation is payable was caused under circumstances creating a legal liability in some person other than the insured to pay damages in respect thereof, the employee shall be entitled, without election, to the compensation and other benefits provided under this chapter. Either the employee or insurer may proceed to enforce the liability of such person, but the insurer may not do so unless compensation has been paid in accordance with sections seven, eight, ten A, eleven C, twelve, or nineteen nor until seven months following the date of such injury. The sum recovered shall be for the benefit of the insurer, unless such sum is greater than that paid by it to the employee, in which even the excess shall be retained by or paid to the employee. For the purposes of this section, "excess" shall mean the amount by which the total sum received in payment for the injury, exclusive of interest and costs exceeds the compensation paid under this chapter. The party bringing the action shall be entitled to retain any costs recovered by him. Any interest received in such action shall be apportioned between the insurer and the employee in proportion to the amounts received by them respectively, exclusive of interest and costs. The expense of any attorney's fees shall be divided between the insurer and the employee in proportion to the amounts received by them respectively under this section. Except in the case of a settlement by agreement by the parties to, and during a trial of, such an action at law, no settlement by agreement shall be made with such other person without the approval of either the board, the reviewing board, or the court in which the action has been commenced after an opportunity has been afforded both the insurer and the employee to be heard on the merits of the settlement and on the amount, if any, to which the insurer is entitled out of such settlement by way of reimbursement, which amount shall be determined at the time of such approval. In the case of a settlement by agreement by the parties to and during a trial of such an action at law, only the justice presiding at the trial shall have and exercise, relative to the approval of such settlement by agreement and to the protection of the rights and interests of the employee, the powers granted in the preceding sentence. Nothing in this section, or in section eighteen or twenty-four shall be construed to bar an action at law for damages for personal injuries or wrongful death by an employee against any person other than the insured person employing such employee and liable for payment of the compensation provided by this chapter for the employee's personal injury or wrongful death and said insured person's employees.

* * *

Sec. 23   Acceptance of compensation; release

If an employee files any claim or accepts payment of compensation on account of personal injury under this chapter, or submits to a proceeding before the department under sections ten to twelve, inclusive, such action shall constitute a release to the insurer of all claims or demands at common law, if any, arising from the injury. If an employee accepts payment of compensation under this chapter on account of personal injury or makes an agreement under section forty-eight, such action shall constitute a release to the insured of all claims or demands at common law, if any, arising from the injury.

Sec. 24 Notice by employee to retain rights at common law

An employee shall be held to have waived his right of action at common law or under the law of any other jurisdiction in respect to an injury that is compensable under this chapter, to recover damages for personal injuries, if he shall not have given his employer, at the time of his contract of hire, written notice that he claimed such right, or, if the contract of hire was made before the employer became an insured person or self-insurer, if the employee shall not have given the said notice within thirty days of the time said employer became an insured person or self-insurer. An employee who has given notice to his employer that he claimed his right of action as aforesaid may waive such claim by a written notice, which shall take effect five days after it is delivered to the employer or his agent. The notices required by this section shall be given in such manner as the department may approve. If an employee has not given notice to his employer that he preserves his right of action at common law as provided by this section, the employee's spouse, children, parents and any other member of the employee's family or next of kin who is wholly or partly dependent upon the earnings of such employee at the time of injury or death, shall also be held to have waived any right created by statute, at common law, or under the law of any other jurisdiction against such employer, including, but not limited to claims for damages due to emotional distress, loss of consortium, parental guidance, companionship or the like, when such loss is a result of any injury to the employee that is compensable under this chapter.

Sec. 25A Compensation compulsory, provision for self-insurance; optional deductible

In order to promote the health, safety and welfare of employees, every employer shall provide for the payment to his employees of the compensation provided for by this chapter in the following manner:

(1) By insurance with an insurer or by membership in a workers' compensation self-insurance group, established pursuant to the provisions of sections twenty-five E to twenty-five U, inclusive, or

(2) Subject to the rules of the department, by obtaining from the department annually a license as a self-insurer by conforming to the provisions of one of the two following subparagraphs and also to the provisions of subparagraph (c) if required. Every employer desiring to be licensed as a self-insurer shall make application for such license on a form provided by the department. The application shall contain: (1) a sworn itemized statement of the assets and liabilities of the applicant; (2) a payroll report for the preceding fiscal year of the applicant; (3) a detailed description of the nature and kind of business carried on.

(a) By keeping on deposit with the state treasurer in trust for the benefit and security of employees such amount of securities, not less in market value than twenty thousand dollars, as may be required by the department, said securities to be in the form of cash, bonds, stocks or other evidences of indebtedness as the department may require, and to be used, liquidated and disbursed only upon order of the department for the purposes of paying the benefits provided for by this chapter. The department shall, at least semiannually, determine the liabilities of a self-insurer both incurred or to be incurred because of personal injuries to employees under this chapter. The department shall require an additional deposit or further security when the sum of the self-insurer's liability both incurred or to be incurred exceeds the deposit or any required reinsurance, or permit a decrease of said deposit provided the value of said deposit in no case shall be less than twenty thousand dollars.

* * *

(b) By furnishing annually a bond running to the commonwealth, with some surety company authorized to transact business in the commonwealth as surety, in such form as may be approved by the department and in such amount not less than twenty thousand dollars as may be required by the department. . . .

* * *

(c) As a further guarantee of a self-insurer's ability to pay the benefits provided for by this chapter to injured employees, every self-insurer shall make arrangements satisfactory to the department, by reinsurance, to protect it from extraordinary losses or losses caused by one disaster. * * *

Sec. 26A   Suicide by employee

Dependents shall not be precluded from recovery under this chapter, nor shall the insurance company be relieved from making payment to the commonwealth under section sixty-five, for death by suicide of the employee, if it be shown by the weight of the evidence that, due to the injury, the employee was of such unsoundness of mind as to make him irresponsible for his act of suicide.

Sec. 27   Wilful misconduct of employee bars compensation

If the employee is injured by reason of his serious and wilful misconduct, he shall not receive compensation; but this provision shall not bar compensation to his dependents if the injury results in death.

SEC. 29 Waiting period; mental or emotional disability arising from personnel action as personal injury

No compensation pursuant to section thirty-four or thirty-five shall be paid for any injury which does not incapacitate the employee from earning full wages for a period of five or more calendar days. If incapacity extends for a period of twenty-one days or more, compensation shall be paid from the date of onset of incapacity. If incapacity extends for a period of at least five but less than twenty-one days, compensation shall be paid from the sixth day of incapacity. Except as otherwise provided in this chapter, no compensation shall be paid for any period for which any wages were earned. No mental or emotional disability arising principally out of a bona fide, personnel action including a transfer, promotion, demotion, or termination except such action which is the intentional infliction of emotional harm shall be deemed to be a personal injury within the meaning of this chapter.

SEC. 30 Medical services, etc.

The insurer shall furnish to an injured employee adequate and reasonable health care services, and medicines if needed, together with the expenses necessarily incidental to such services, and in the case of an injured employee, a physical examination shall be given at least once a year while the employee is hospitalized. Except for the employee's first scheduled appointment, which, pursuant to the terms of a preferred provider arrangement entered into under this section may be required to be with a health care provider within the plan, the employee may select a treating health care professional other than any provided or agreed to by the insurer and may switch to another such professional once. When referred by the treating health care professional to another provider in a particular specialty, the employee may also change once to a different provider in such specialty. In cases of emergency or where the insurer or administrative judge agrees, the employee may seek treatment from additional providers. Where services are provided to employees under this section, the reasonable and necessary cost of such services shall be paid by the insurer.

On or before July first, nineteen hundred and ninety-three, the commissioner shall promulgate regulations regarding the provision of adequate and reasonable health care services. In doing so, he shall utilize the treatment guidelines developed and endorsed under the provisions of section thirteen. Any provision of health care services in material compliance with such regulations shall be presumed to be adequate and reasonable. Any material departure from said regulations shall be presumed to be either an inadequate or unreasonable provision of health care services.

An employee receiving benefits from the Workers' Compensation Trust Fund may be required to choose a treating physician from a health maintenance organization which has been chosen by the fund. In any instance in which the fund requires such a choice of an employee, the fund shall pay all co-payments, deductibles, or other costs required by the health maintenance organization for necessary and reasonable medical and hospital services under this chapter.

In any case where an administrative judge, the reviewing board, the office of education and vocational rehabilitation or the health care services board is of the opinion that the fitting of an employee eligible for compensation with an artificial eye or limb, or other mechanical appliance, will promote his restoration to or continue him in industry, it may be ordered that such employee be provided with such item, at the expense of the insurer. The provisions of this section shall be applicable so long as such services are necessary, notwithstanding the fact that maximum compensation under other sections of this chapter may have been received by the injured employee.

Any insurer may enter into a preferred provider arrangement in compliance with the requirements of chapter one hundred and seventy-six I of the General Laws and the regulations thereunder. Notwithstanding any other provision of this chapter, if an insurer enters into a preferred provider arrangement for health care services required under this chapter, those employees who are subject to the arrangement shall receive such care in the manner prescribed by the arrangement; provided, however, that a worker may receive immediate emergency treatment from a health care provider who is not a member of the managed care organization, and the insurer shall pay the reasonable and necessary costs of such treatment. Notwithstanding the provisions of this section, if an employee requests the services of a health care provider licensed or certified under the provisions of chapter one hundred and twelve and such specialty is not represented within the preferred provider organization with whom the employer has contracted, and the employee utilizes the services of such provider, the insurer or preferred provider organization shall pay the reasonable and necessary costs of such service. Said employee shall be allowed to choose any such health care provider.

Any insurer, with the written consent of the insured employer may, except as provided by the terms of a collective bargaining agreement, if any, approved under this chapter enter into a preferred provider arrangement for the employees of such employers in compliance with the requirements of chapter one hundred and seventy-six I and the regulations thereunder. If an insurer enters into a preferred provider arrangement for health care services required under this chapter, those employees who are subject to the arrangement shall receive such care in the manner prescribed by the arrangement consistent with this section.

Notwithstanding the provisions of this section if an employee requests, for his first scheduled appointment, the services of a health care provider licensed or certified under the provisions of chapter one hundred twelve and the specialty of said health care provider is not represented within the preferred provider organization with which the employer has contracted, and the employee utilizes the services of such provider, the insurer or preferred provider organization shall pay the reasonable and necessary costs of such service as provided under this chapter. In no instance shall employees be required to make copayments or pay deductibles. * * *

SEC. 30A Furnishing of medical reports; failure to comply; civil fine

Any medical report pertaining to an injury which appears to be compensable shall be furnished by the physician or other medical provider to the employee, the insurer, and the department within fourteen days of completion of the examination of the employee. Each failure to comply with such reporting requirement shall be punishable by a civil fine to be determined by the director of administration, of not less than twenty-five nor greater than one thousand dollars. A schedule of incremental increases relative to violations shall be determined by the commissioner.

SEC. 31 Death payments

If death results from the injury, the insurer shall pay the following dependents of the employee, including his or her children by a former spouse, wholly dependent upon his or her earnings for support at the time of his or her injury, or at the time of his or her death, compensation as follows, payable, except as hereinafter provided, in the manner set forth in section thirty-two.

To the widow or widower so long as he or she remains unmarried, a weekly compensation equal to two-thirds of the average weekly wages of the deceased employee, but not more than the average weekly wage in the commonwealth, as determined according to the provisions of subsection (*a*) of section twenty-nine of chapter one hundred and fifty-one A, and promulgated by the director of the division of employment security on or before October first preceding the deceased employee's injury or death; provided, however, that in no instance shall said widow or widower, receive less than one hundred and ten dollars per week, to the widow or widower six dollars more a week for each child of the deceased employee under the age of eighteen or over said age and physically or mentally incapacitated from earning, or over said age and a full time student qualified for exemption as a dependent under section one hundred and fifty-one (*e*) of the Internal Revenue Code, except that no additional compensation for the benefits of the children of the employee shall be payable when combined with the compensation due the spouse of the deceased employee as hereinbefore provided in this section would allow the widow or widower an amount in excess of one hundred and fifty dollars per week; provided that in case any child of the deceased employee is a child by a former wife or husband, the death benefit shall be divided between the surviving wife or husband and all dependent children of the deceased employee in equal shares, the surviving wife or husband taking the same share as a child. If the widow or widower dies or if there is no surviving wife or husband of the deceased employee, such amount or amounts as would have been payable to or for his or her own use and for the benefit of all children of the employee shall be paid in equal shares to all the surviving children of the employee.

If the widow or widower remarries, all payments under the foregoing provisions shall terminate and the insurer shall pay each week to each of such children sixty dollars but in no event shall the payments exceed the amount which would have been payable to the surviving spouse.

The total payments due under this section shall not be more than the average weekly wage in effect in the commonwealth at the time of the injury as determined according to the provisions of subsection (*a*) of section twenty-nine of chapter one hundred and fifty-one A, and promulgated by the director of the division of employment security on or before the October first prior to the date of the injury multiplied by two hundred and fifty plus any costs of living increases provided by this section except that payment to or for the benefit of children of the deceased employee under the age of eighteen shall not be discontinued prior to the age of eighteen, and except that after a dependent unremarried widow or widower or physically or mentally incapacitated child over the age of eighteen has received the maximum payments, he or she shall continue to receive further payments but only during such periods as he or she is in fact not fully self-supporting. Either party may request hearings at reasonable intervals before a board member on the question of granting such payments, or on the question of restoration of such payments or on the question of discontinuance of such payments. A member of the board may set a case for hearing on his or her initiative, after due notice to both parties.

In all other cases of total dependency, the insurer shall pay each person, wholly dependent upon the earnings of the deceased employee, for support at the time of the injury, or at the time of the employee's death a weekly payment equal to the weekly amount of that support but not more than two-thirds of the average weekly wage of the deceased employee or more than eighty dollars a week; provided, however, that if there is more than one such dependent, the total amount payable shall not exceed the weekly amount which is, or would be payable to a surviving spouse of the deceased employee. If at the time of the employee's injury or death the deceased employee leaves dependents only partially dependent upon the deceased employee's earnings or dependent's next of kin to whom the deceased has made contributions for support, independent of gifts and gratuities, the insurer shall pay such dependents a weekly compensation equal to the amount that they received from the deceased employee but individually or in combination, no more than would be paid to a surviving spouse.

When weekly payments have been made to an injured employee before the employee's death, compensation under this section to dependents shall begin from the date of death of the employee.

SEC. 33 Funeral expenses

In all cases, the insurer shall pay the reasonable expenses of burial not exceeding four thousand dollars.

SEC. 34 Total incapacity

While the incapacity for work resulting from the injury is total, during each week of incapacity the insurer shall pay the injured employee compensation equal to sixty percent of his or her average weekly wage before the injury, but not more than the maximum weekly compensation rate, unless the average weekly wage of the employee is less than the minimum weekly compensation rate, in which case said weekly compensation shall be equal to his average weekly wage.

The total number of weeks of compensation due the employee under this section shall not exceed one hundred fifty-six.

SEC. 34A Total and permanent incapacity

While the incapacity for work resulting from the injury is both permanent and total, the insurer shall pay to the injured employee, following payment of compensation provided in sections thirty four and thirty-five, a weekly compensation equal to two-thirds of his average weekly wage before the injury, but not more than the maximum weekly compensation rate nor less than the minimum weekly compensation rate.

SEC. 34B Review date; supplemental benefits to sections 31 or 34A

October first of each year shall be the review date for the purposes of this section.

Any person receiving or entitled to receive the benefits under the provisions of section thirty-one or section thirty-four A whose benefits are based on a date of personal injury at least twenty-four months prior to the review date shall be paid, without application, a supplement to weekly compensation to the extent such supplement shall not reduce any benefits such person is receiving pursuant to federal social security law. The supplemental benefits shall be paid in accordance with the following provisions:—

(a) The director of administration shall determine the percentage change between the average weekly wage in the commonwealth on the date of the injury and the average weekly wage in the Commonwealth on the review date. For purposes of this section, no increase in the average weekly wage in the commonwealth shall exceed the lesser of the following: (i) the percentage change in the most recent annual consumer price index calculated by the Bureau of Labor Statistics of the United States Department of Labor for the Northeast region for all urban consumers; (ii) five percent.

(b) The death benefit under section thirty-one or the permanent and total disability benefit under section thirty-four A that was being paid prior to any adjustments under this section shall be the base benefit. The base benefit shall be increased on each review date by the percentage increase in the average weekly wage in the commonwealth as calculated in the paragraph (a); the resulting amount shall be termed the adjusted benefit and is the amount of benefit to be paid on and after the review date. If the adjusted benefit is larger than the base benefit, the difference shall be termed the supplemental benefit. In no instance shall the adjusted benefit under the section be greater than three times the base benefit.

(c) The supplemental benefits under this section shall be paid by the insurer concurrent with the base benefit. Insurers shall be entitled to quarterly reimbursements for supplemental benefits, pursuant to section sixty-five, for cases involving injuries that occurred on or before October first, nineteen hundred and eighty-six, and for those cases occurring thereafter, to the extent such supplemental benefits are due to the increase of greater than five per cent in the average weekly wage in the commonwealth in any single year. * * *

Sec. 35E   Old age benefits; effect on entitlement to workers' compensation benefits

Any employee who is at least sixty-five years of age and has been out of the labor force for a period of at least two years and is eligible for old age benefits pursuant to the federal social security act or eligible for benefits from a public or private pension which is paid in part or entirely by an employer shall not be entitled to benefits under sections thirty-four or thirty-five unless such employee can establish that but for the injury, he or she would have remained active in the labor market. The presumption of non-entitlement to benefits created by this section shall not be overcome by the employee's uncorroborated testimony, or that corroborated only by any of his family members, that but for the injury, such employee would have remained active in the labor market. Claims for compensation, or complaint for modification, or discontinuance of benefits based on this section shall not be filed more often than once every twelve months.

Sec. 36 Payments for certain specific injuries

(1) In addition to all other compensation to the employee shall be paid the sums hereafter designated for the following specific injuries; provided, however, that the employee has not died from any cause within thirty days of such injury:

(a) For the loss by enucleation or otherwise or the total loss of use of one eye, or for injury to one eye which produces an inability which is not correctible to use both eyes together for single binocular vision, or the reduction to twenty-seventieths of normal vision in one eye, with glasses, a sum equal to the average weekly wage in the commonwealth at the date of the injury multiplied by thirty-nine.

(b) For the loss by enucleation or otherwise, or the total loss of use of both eyes, or the reduction to twenty-seventieths of normal vision in both eyes, with glasses, a sum equal to the average weekly wage in the commonwealth at the date of the injury multiplied by ninety-six.

(c) For any correctible permanent but partial reduction in either the acuity or field of vision of one or both eyes, such sum in proportion to the amount applicable in the event of total loss, total loss of use, or the reduction to twenty-seventieths of normal vision of one or both eyes as the correctible partial reduction bears to such total loss, total loss of use or reduction to twenty-seventieths of normal vision; provided that, for any permanent but partial reduction in either acuity of field of vision of either eye which requires the use of corrective device, such as glasses or contact lens, to produce normal vision, a sum equal to the average weekly wage in the commonwealth at the date of the injury multiplied by seven.

(d) For the loss of hearing of one ear, a sum equal to the average weekly wage in the commonwealth at the date of the injury multiplied by twenty-nine; for the loss of hearing of both ears, a sum equal to the average weekly wage in the commonwealth at the date of the injury multiplied by seventy-seven.

(e) For the amputation or permanent, total loss of use of the major arm, a sum equal to the average weekly wage in the commonwealth at the date of the injury multiplied by forty-three; for the amputation or permanent total loss of use of the minor arm, a sum equal to the average weekly wage in the commonwealth at the date of the injury multiplied by thirty-nine; for the amputation or permanent total loss of use of both arms, a sum equal to the average weekly wage in the commonwealth at the date of the injury multiplied by ninety-six.

(f) For the amputation or permanent, total loss of use of the major hand at the wrist, a sum equal to the average weekly wage in the commonwealth at the date of the injury multiplied by thirty-four; for the amputation or permanent, total loss of use of the minor hand at the wrist, a sum equal to the average weekly wage in the commonwealth at the date of injury multiplied by twenty-nine; for the amputation or permanent, total loss of use of both hands at the wrist, a sum equal to the average weekly wage in the commonwealth at the date of injury multiplied by seventy-seven.

(g) For the amputation or permanent, total loss of use of either leg, a sum equal to the average weekly wage in the commonwealth at the date of the injury multiplied by thirty-nine; for the amputation or permanent, total loss of use of both legs, a sum equal to the average weekly wage in the commonwealth on the date of injury multiplied by ninety-six.

(h) For the amputation or permanent, total loss of use of either foot at any point above the ankle joint, a sum equal to the average weekly wage in the commonwealth at the date of injury multiplied by twenty-nine; for the amputation or permanent, total loss of use of both feet at any point above the ankle joints, a sum equal to the average weekly wage in the commonwealth at the date of injury multiplied by sixty-eight.

(i) For any permanent but partial loss of use of a member, whether leg, foot, arm, or hand, such sum in proportion to the amount applicable in the event of amputation or permanent, total loss of use of said member as the said partial loss bears to the total loss of use of said member.

(j) For each loss of bodily function or sense, other than those specified in preceding paragraphs of this section, the amount which, according to the determination of the member or reviewing board, is a proper and equitable compensation, not to exceed the average weekly wage in the commonwealth at the date of injury multiplied by thirty-two; provided, however, that the total amount payable under this paragraph shall not exceed the average weekly wage in the commonwealth at the date of injury multiplied by eighty.

(k) For bodily disfigurement, an amount which, according to the determination of the member or reviewing board, is a proper and equitable compensation, not to exceed fifteen thousand dollars; which sum shall be payable in addition to all other sums due under this section. No amount shall be payable under this section for disfigurement that is purely scar-based, unless such disfigurement is on the face, neck or hands.

(2) Where applicable, losses under this section shall be determined in accordance with standards set forth in the American Medical Association Guides to the Evaluation of Permanent Impairments. Nothing in this section shall adversely affect the employee's rights to any compensation which is or may become due under the provisions of any other section.

Sec. 36B Unemployment compensation benefits; effect on entitlement to workers' compensation benefits

(1) No benefits shall be payable under section thirty-four or section thirty-four A for any week in which the employee has received or is receiving unemployment compensation benefits.

(2) Any employee claiming or receiving benefits under section thirty-five who may be entitled to unemployment compensation benefits shall upon written request from the insurer apply for such benefits. Failure to do so within sixty days after written request shall constitute grounds for suspension of benefits under said section thirty-five. Any unemployment compensation benefits received shall be credited against partial disability benefits payable for the same time period, or, if for a period of time for which partial disability benefits have already been paid, shall be credited against any future partial disability benefits which are or may become payable.

§ 37. Reimbursement to Employer or Insurer for Payments for Injuries to Employee Having a Previous Physical Impairment, etc.

Whenever an employee who has a known physical impairment which is due to any previous accident, disease or any congenital condition and is, or is likely to be, a hindrance or obstacle to his employment, and who, in the course of and arising out of his employment, receives a personal injury for which compensation is required by this chapter and which results in a disability that is substantially greater by reason of the combined effects of such impairment and subsequent personal injury than that disability which would have resulted from the subsequent personal injury alone, the insurer or self-insurer shall pay all compensation provided by this chapter. If said subsequent injury is caused by the preexisting impairment or if said subsequent personal injury of such an employee shall result in the death of the employee, and it shall be determined that the death would not have occurred except for such pre existing physical impairment, the insurer shall pay all compensation provided by this chapter.

Insurers making payments under this section shall be reimbursed by the state treasurer from the trust fund created by section sixty-five in an amount not to exceed seventy-five percent of all compensation due under sections thirty-one, thirty-two, thirty-three, thirty-four A, thirty-six A, and, where benefits are due under any of such sections, section thirty; provided, however, that the insurer is not a self-insurer, a group self insurer or municipality that has chosen not to be subject to the assessments which fund said reimbursements; and, provided, further, that no reimbursement shall be made for any amounts paid during the first one hundred and four weeks from the onset of disability or death.

There shall be no reimbursement under this section unless the employer had personal knowledge of the existence of such pre-existing physical impairment within thirty days of the date of employment or retention of the employee by such employer from either a physical examination, employment application questionnaire, or statement from the employee. Proof of the pre-existence of such impairment shall be established only by the production of medical records existing prior to the date of employment or retention in employment of the employee. Nothing in this paragraph shall be construed to allow employers to compel an employee or job applicant to disclose any information regarding physical impairments in violation of any applicable law.

The office of legal counsel shall in all instances have the authority to defend claims against the fund. Such office shall have the right to contest any amount accredited to the above named sections which has been redeemed by an insurer by payment of a lump sum settlement pursuant to section forty-eight, but reimbursement shall not require the approval of the lump sum by said office or by the state treasurer. No reimbursement shall be made for payments due during the first one hundred and four weeks from the date of onset of disability or death, whether paid under an agreement, decision, or lump sum settlement. Any petition for reimbursement under this section shall be filed no later than two years from the date on which the benefit payment for which the reimbursement request is being filed was made.

SEC. 48 Lump sum payments; subsequent claim for medical benefits; factors reviewed by office of education and vocational rehabilitation; releases; effect on other actions or proceedings

(1) Under the conditions and limitations specified in this chapter, the insurer and employee may, with the written consent of the employer if such employer is an experience modified insured, by an agreement pursuant to section nineteen, redeem any liability for compensation, in whole or in part, by the payment by the insurer of a lump sum amount. Where the employee is not represented by counsel, where the parties seek determination by an administrative judge or administrative law

196

judge of the fair and reasonable amount to be paid out of the lump sum to discharge a lien cognizable under section forty-six A, or where any party requests that such agreement be approved by an administrative judge or administrative law judge prior to the filing of such agreement with the department, a lump sum agreement shall not have been perfected until and unless approved by an administrative judge or administrative law judge as being in the claimant's best interest. In all other cases the agreement shall not have been perfected until reviewed and approved as complete by a conciliator, administrative judge or administrative law judge as appropriate. A conciliator shall be made available in each regional office to review settlements without appointment.

(2) When the insurer and the employee reach such agreement subsequent to insurer acceptance of liability or subsequent to a decision of an administrative judge, the reviewing board, or an appeals court of the commonwealth finding insurer liability which decision is in effect at the time such agreement is entered into, said agreement shall not redeem liability for the payment of medical benefits or vocational rehabilitation benefits with respect to such injury.

No lump sum agreement made prior to the establishment of liability for compensation shall prohibit an employee from subsequently filing a claim for medical benefits only, in any instance in which such employee has suffered a substantial deterioration of his medical condition which (i) could not reasonably have been foreseen at the time said agreement was entered into, and (ii) is the result of an injury for which the insurer would have been liable under this chapter, absent the lump sum settlement. Claims under this paragraph shall be considered only if brought within one year of the date the employee first became aware of the causal relationship between the substantial deterioration and the employment. Claims shall be consistent with the procedures set forth in sections ten, ten A, and eleven. No liability for such claims shall be redeemed by any additional lump sum settlement; provided, however, that no employee shall be entitled to vocational rehabilitation benefits for any injury, unless such employee shall have requested such benefits within two years of the perfection of any settlement under this section of benefits due for said injury.

(3) No lump sum agreement shall contain as part of a settlement a general or specific release that would serve as a bar to (i) employment with any employer, (ii) the receipt by the employee of any pay or benefits due him by an employer, (iii) the bringing of any future workers' compensation claim or (iv) the bringing of any claims of wrongful discharge or breach of contract. All such general or specific releases shall be null and void. Any employer, insurer, employer or attorney attempting to obtain such release from an employee shall be punished by

a fine of ten thousand dollars. Where the employee has been found suitable for vocational rehabilitation services pursuant to section thirty G, lump sum agreements shall be valid only where the employee returned to continuous employment for a period of six or more months; or completed an approved rehabilitation plan; or received express written consent from the office of education and vocational rehabilitation; or an order or decision from an administrative judge or administrative law judge authorizing such agreement. Any employee who receives an amount in violation of this paragraph shall have the right to re-open his or her claim for compensation. Any employee who accepts a lump sum settlement for benefits claimed under section 34A shall be precluded from any further lump sum settlements for said benefits.

(4) Whenever a lump sum agreement has been perfected in accordance with the terms of this section, such agreement shall affect only the insurer and the employee who are parties to such lump sum agreement and shall not affect any other action or proceeding arising out of a separate and distinct injury under this chapter, whether the injury precedes or arises subsequent to the date of settlement, and whether or not the same insurer is claimed to be liable for such separate and distinct injury.

Notwithstanding any provision of this section or of sections seventy-five A or seventy-five B, the acceptance of any amount in return for the right to claim future weekly benefits shall create a presumption that the employee is physically incapable of returning to work with the employer where the alleged injury occurred. Such presumption shall continue for a period of one month for each fifteen hundred dollar amount included in the settlement for future weekly benefits. No re-employment rights shall inure to such employee under this chapter during any period of presumption of incapacity as herein provided.

(5) Whenever a lump sum agreement or payment has been approved by the reviewing board in accordance with the terms of this section, such agreement shall affect only the insurer and employee who are parties to such lump sum agreement and shall not affect any other action or proceeding arising out of a separate and distinct injury resulting in an incapacity whether the injury precedes or arises subsequent to the date of settlement.

MISCELLANEOUS PROVISIONS

SEC. 66 Modification of liability

Actions brought against employers to recover damages for personal injuries or consequential damages sustained within or without the commonwealth by an employee in the course of his employment or for death resulting from personal injury so sustained shall be commenced within twenty years from the date the employee first became aware of the causal relationship between the disability and his employment. In such actions brought by said employees or by the Workers' Compensation Trust Fund pursuant to the provisions of subsection (8) of section sixty-five, it shall not be a defense:

1.   That the employee was negligent;

2.   That the injury was caused by the negligence of a fellow employee;

3.   That the employee had assumed voluntarily or contractually the risk of the injury;

4.   That the employee's injury did not result from negligence or other fault of the employer, if such injury arose out of and in the course of employment.

SEC. 75A   Insured persons; preferences in hiring; violation by employee

Any person who has lost a job as a result of an injury compensable under this chapter shall be given preference in hiring by the employer for whom he worked at the time of compensable injury over any persons not at the time of application for reemployment employed by such employer; provided, however, that a suitable job is available. Actions may be filed under this section with the superior court department of the trial court for the county in which the alleged violation occurred. An employer found to have violated this section shall be exclusively liable to pay to the employee lost wages, shall grant the employee a suitable job, and shall reimburse such reasonable attorney fees incurred in the protection of rights granted by this section as shall be determined by the court.

In the event that any right set forth in this section is inconsistent with an applicable collective bargaining agreement or chapter thirty-one, the collective bargaining agreement or said chapter thirty-one shall prevail.

SEC. 75B   Qualified handicapped persons; discrimination prohibited; violation by employer; disclosure of data maintained by department

(1) Any employee who has sustained a work-related injury and is capable of performing the essential functions of a particular job, or who would be capable of performing the essential functions of such job with reasonable accommodations, shall be deemed to be a qualified handicapped person under the provisions of chapter one hundred and fifty-one B.

(2) No employer or duly authorized agent of an employer shall discharge, refuse to hire or in any other manner discriminate against an employee because the employee has exercised a right afforded by this chapter, or who has testified or in any manner cooperated with an inquiry or proceeding pursuant to this chapter, unless the employee knowingly participated in a fraudulent proceeding. Any person claiming to be aggrieved by a violation of this section may initiate proceedings in the superior court department of the trial court for the county in which the alleged violation occurred. An employer found to have violated this paragraph shall be exclusively liable to pay to the employee lost wages, shall grant the employee suitable employment, and shall reimburse such reasonable attorney fees incurred in the protection of rights granted as shall be determined by the court. The court may grant whatever equitable relief it deems necessary to protect rights granted by this section.

(3) In the event that any right set forth in this section is inconsistent with an applicable collective bargaining agreement, such agreement shall prevail. An employee may not otherwise waive rights granted by this section.

(4) Upon a determination by the commissioner that a request for data maintained by the department is intended to be used in such a manner as to violate the purposes of this section, the commissioner may find that the disclosure of such data constitutes an unwarranted invasion of personal privacy pursuant to chapter four and deny said request. Nothing in this section shall be construed to prohibit an insurer's right to obtain any information held by the department regarding any employee who has filed a claim against such insurer.

FEDERAL OLD–AGE, SURVIVORS, AND DISABILITY INSURANCE BENEFITS ACT (SOCIAL SECURITY ACT)

42 U.S.C. §§ 401–433

SEC. 402 Old-age and survivors insurance benefit payments

(a) Old-age insurance benefits

Every individual who—

(1) is a fully insured individual (as defined in section 214(a) of this title),

(2) has attained age 62, and

(3) has filed application for old-age insurance benefits or was entitled to disability insurance benefits for the month preceding the month in which he attained the retirement age (as defined in section 216(*l*) of this title),

shall be entitled to an old-age insurance benefit for each month, * * *

* * *

SEC. 414 Insured status for purposes of old-age and survivors insurance benefits

For the purposes of this subchapter—

(a) Fully insured individual

The term "fully insured individual" means any individual who had not less than—

(1) one quarter of coverage (whenever acquired) for each calendar year elapsing after 1950 (or, if later, the year in which he attained age 21) and before the year in which he died or (if earlier) the year in which he attained age 62, except that in no case shall an individual be a fully insured individual unless he has at least 6 quarters of coverage; or

(2) 40 quarters of coverage; or

(3) in the case of an individual who died before 1951, 6 quarters of coverage;

not counting as an elapsed year for purposes of paragraph (1) any year any part of which was included in a period of disability (as defined in section 216(i) of this title).

(b) Currently insured individual

The term "currently insured individual" means any individual who had not less than six quarters of coverage during the thirteen-quarter period ending with (1) the quarter in which he died, (2) the quarter in which he became entitled to old-age insurance benefits, (3) the quarter in which he became entitled to primary insurance benefits under this subchapter as in effect prior to August 28, 1950, or (4) in the case of any individual entitled to disability insurance benefits, the quarter in which he most recently became entitled to disability insurance benefits, not counting as part of such thirteen-quarter period any quarter any part of which was included in a period of disability unless such quarter was a quarter of coverage.

Sec. 416   Additional definitions

* * *

(*l*) Retirement age

(1) The term "retirement age" means—

(A) with respect to an individual who attains early retirement age (as defined in paragraph (2)) before January 1, 2000, 65 years of age;

(B) with respect to an individual who attains early retirement age after December 31, 1999, and before January 1, 2005, 65 years of age plus the number of months in the age increase factor (as determined under paragraph (3)) for the calendar year in which such individual attains early retirement age;

(C) with respect to an individual who attains early retirement age after December 31, 2004, and before January 1, 2017, 66 years of age;

(D) with respect to an individual who attains early retirement age after December 31, 2016, and before January 1, 2022, 66 years of age plus the number of months in the age increase factor (as determined under paragraph (3)) for the calendar year in which such individual attains early retirement age; and

(E) with respect to an individual who attains early retirement age after December 31, 2021, 67 years of age.

(2) The term "early retirement age" means age 62 in the case of an old-age, wife's, or husband's insurance benefit, and age 60 in the case of a widow's or widower's insurance benefit.

(3) The age increase factor for any individual who attains early retirement age in a calendar year within the period to which subparagraph (B) or (D) of paragraph (1) applies shall be determined as follows:

(A) With respect to an individual who attains early retirement age in the 5–year period consisting of the calendar years 2000 through 2004, the age increase factor shall be equal to two-twelfths of the number of months in the period beginning with January 2000 and ending with December of the year in which the individual attains early retirement age.

(B) With respect to an individual who attains early retirement age in the 5–year period consisting of the calendar years 2017 through 2021, the age increase factor shall be equal to two-twelfths of the number of months in the period beginning with January 2017 and ending with December of the year in which the individual attains early retirement age.

SEC. 423 Disability insurance benefit payments

* * *

(c) Definitions; insured status; waiting period

For purposes of this section—

(1) An individual shall be insured for disability insurance benefits in any month if—

(A) he would have been a fully insured individual * * * had he attained age 62 and filed application for [old age] benefits * * *, and

(B)(i) he had not less than 20 quarters of coverage during the 40–quarter period which ends with the quarter in which such month occurred, or

(ii) if such month ends before the quarter in which he attains (or would attain) age 31, not less than one-half (and not less than 6) of the quarters during the period ending with the quarter in which such month occurred and beginning after he attained the age of 21 were quarters of coverage, or (if the number of quarters in such period is less than 12) not less than 6 of the quarters in the 12–quarter period ending with such quarter were quarters of coverage, or

(iii) in the case of an individual (not otherwise insured under clause (i)) who, by reason of section 216(i)(3)(B)(ii), had a prior period of disability that began during a period before the quarter in which he or she attained age 31, not less than one-half of the quarters beginning after such individual attained age 21 and ending with the quarter in which such month occurs are quarters of coverage, or (if the number of quarters in such period is less than 12) not less than 6 of the quarters in the 12–

quarter period ending with such quarter are quarters of coverage;

except that the provisions of subparagraph (B) of this paragraph shall not apply in the case of an individual who is blind (within the meaning of "blindness" as defined in section 216(i)(1)).　＊ ＊ ＊

＊ ＊ ＊

(d) Disability defined

(1) The term "disability" means—

(A) inability to engage in any substantial gainful activity by reason of any medically determinable physical or mental impairment which can be expected to result in death or which has lasted or can be expected to last for a continuous period of not less than 12 months; or

(B) in the case of an individual who has attained the age of 55 and is blind ＊ ＊ ＊ inability by reason of such blindness to engage in substantial gainful activity requiring skills or abilities comparable to those of any gainful activity in which he has previously engaged with some regularity and over a substantial period of time.

(2) For purposes of paragraph (1)(A)—

(A) an individual shall be determined to be under a disability only if his physical or mental impairment or impairments are of such severity that he is not only unable to do his previous work but cannot, considering his age, education, and work experience, engage in any other kind of substantial gainful work which exists in the national economy, regardless of whether such work exists in the immediate area in which he lives, or whether a specific job vacancy exists for him, or whether he would be hired if he applied for work. For purposes of the preceding sentence (with respect to any individual), "work which exists in the national economy" means work which exists in significant numbers either in the region where such individual lives or in several regions of the country.

(B) In determining whether an individual's physical or mental impairment or impairments are of a sufficient medical severity that such impairment or impairments could be the basis of eligibility under this section, the Commissioner of Social Security shall consider the combined effect of all of the individual's impairments without regard to whether any such impairment, if considered separately, would be of such severity. If the Commissioner of Social Security does find a medically severe combination of impairments, the combined impact of the impairments shall be considered throughout the disability determination process.

(C) An individual shall not be considered to be disabled for purposes of this title if alcoholism or drug addiction would (but for this subparagraph) be a contributing factor material to the Commissioner's determination that the individual is disabled.

(3) For purposes of this subsection, a "physical or mental impairment" is an impairment that results from anatomical, physiological, or psychological abnormalities which are demonstrable by medically acceptable clinical and laboratory diagnostic techniques.

* * *

(5)(A) An individual shall not be considered to be under a disability unless he furnishes such medical and other evidence of the existence thereof as the Commissioner of Social Security may require. An individual's statement as to pain or other symptoms shall not alone be conclusive evidence of disability as defined in this section; there must be medical signs and findings, established by medically acceptable clinical or laboratory diagnostic techniques, which show the existence of a medical impairment that results from anatomical, physiological, or psychological abnormalities which could reasonably be expected to produce the pain or other symptoms alleged and which, when considered with all evidence required to be furnished under this paragraph (including statements of the individual or his physician as to the intensity and persistence of such pain or other symptoms which may reasonably be accepted as consistent with the medical signs and findings), would lead to a conclusion that the individual is under a disability. Objective medical evidence of pain or other symptoms established by medically acceptable clinical or laboratory techniques (for example, deteriorating nerve or muscle tissue) must be considered in reaching a conclusion as to whether the individual is under a disability. Any non-Federal hospital, clinic, laboratory, or other provider of medical services, or physician not in the employ of the Federal Government, which supplies medical evidence required and requested by the Commissioner of Social Security under this paragraph shall be entitled to payment from the Commissioner of Social Security for the reasonable cost of providing such evidence.

* * *

(f) Standard of review for termination of disability benefits

A recipient of benefits * * * based on the disability of any individual may be determined not to be entitled to such benefits on the basis of a finding that the physical or mental impairment on the basis of which such benefits are provided has ceased, does not exist, or is not disabling only if such finding is supported by—

(1) substantial evidence which demonstrates that—

(A) there has been any medical improvement in the individual's impairment or combination of impairments (other than medical improvement which is not related to the individual's ability to work), and

(B) the individual is now able to engage in substantial gainful activity, or

(2) substantial evidence which—

(A) consists of new medical evidence and a new assessment of the individual's residual functional capacity, and demonstrates that—

(i) although the individual has not improved medically, he or she is nonetheless a beneficiary of advances in medical or vocational therapy or technology (related to the individual's ability to work), and

(ii) the individual is now able to engage in substantial gainful activity, or

* * *

(3) substantial evidence which demonstrates that, as determined on the basis of new or improved diagnostic techniques or evaluations, the individual's impairment or combination of impairments is not as disabling as it was considered to be at the time of the most recent prior decision that he or she was under a disability or continued to be under a disability, and that therefore the individual is able to engage in substantial gainful activity; or

(4) substantial evidence (which may be evidence on the record at the time any prior determination of the entitlement to benefits based on disability was made, or newly obtained evidence which relates to that determination) which demonstrates that a prior determination was in error.

MONTANA WRONGFUL DISCHARGE
FROM EMPLOYMENT ACT

Mont.Code Ann. § 39–2–901 (1987)

Sec. 1. Short Title. [Sections 1 through 9] may be cited as the "Wrongful Discharge From Employment Act".

Sec. 2. Purpose. [Sections 1 through 9] set forth certain rights and remedies with respect to wrongful discharge. Except as provided in [section 7], [sections 1 through 9] provide the exclusive remedy for a wrongful discharge from employment.

Sec. 3. Definitions. [Sections 1 through 9], the following definitions apply:

(1) "Constructive discharge" means the voluntary termination of employment by an employee because of a situation created by an act or omission of the employer which an objective, reasonable person would find so intolerable that voluntary termination is the only reasonable alternative. Constructive discharge does not mean voluntary termination because of an employer's refusal to promote the employee or improve wages, responsibilities, or other terms and conditions of employment.

(2) "Discharge" includes a constructive discharge as defined in subsection (1) and any other termination of employment including resignation, elimination of the job, layoff for lack of work, failure to recall or rehire, and any other cutback in the number of employees for a legitimate business reason.

(3) "Employee" means a person who works for another for hire. The term does not include a person who is an independent contractor.

(4) "Fringe benefits" means the value of any employer-paid vacation leave, sick leave, medical insurance plan, disability insurance plan, life insurance plan, and pension benefit plan in force on the date of the termination.

(5) "Good cause" means reasonable, job-related grounds for dismissal based on a failure to satisfactorily perform job duties, disruption of the employer's operation, or other legitimate business reason. The legal use of a lawful product off the employer's premises during nonworking hours is not a legitimate business reason, unless the employer acts within the provisions of 39–2–313(3) or (4).

207

(6) "Lost wages" means the gross amount of wages that would have been reported to the internal revenue service as gross income on Form W–2 and includes additional compensation deferred at the option of the employee.

(7) "Public policy" means a policy in effect at the time of the discharge concerning the public health, safety, or welfare established by constitutional provision, statute, or administrative rule.

Sec. 4. Elements of wrongful discharge. (1) A discharge is wrongful only if:

(a) it was in retaliation for the employee's refusal to violate public policy or for reporting a violation of public policy;

(b) the discharge was not for good cause and the employee had completed the employer's probationary period of employment; or

(c) the employer violated the express provisions of its own written personnel policy.

(2)(a) During a probationary period of employment, the employment may be terminated at the will of either the employer or the employee on notice to the other for any reason or for no reason.

(b) If an employer does not establish a specific probationary period or provide that there is no probationary period prior to or at the time of hire, there is a probationary period of 6 months from the date of hire.

Sec. 5. Remedies. (1) If an employer has committed a wrongful discharge the employee may be awarded lost wages and fringe benefits for a period not to exceed 4 years from the date of discharge, together with interest on the lost wages and fringe benefits. Interim earnings, including amounts the employee could have earned with reasonable diligence, must be deducted from the amount awarded for lost wages. Before interim earnings are deducted from lost wages, there must be deducted from the interim earnings any reasonable amounts expended by the employee in searching for, obtaining, or relocating to new employment.

(2) The employee may recover punitive damages otherwise allowed by law if it is established by clear and convincing evidence that the employer engaged in actual fraud or actual malice in the discharge of the employee in violation of [39–2–904(1)(a)].

(3) There is no right under any legal theory to damages for wrongful discharge under [sections 1 through 9] for pain and suffering,

emotional distress, compensatory damages, punitive damages, or any other form of damage except as provided for in subsections (1) and (2).

Sec. 6. Limitation of actions. (1) An action under [sections 1 through 9] must be filed within 1 year after the date of discharge.

(2) If an employer maintains written internal procedures, other than those specified in [section 7], under which an employee may appeal a discharge within the organizational structure of the employer, the employee shall first exhaust those procedures prior to filing an action under [sections 1 through 9]. The employee's failure to initiate or exhaust available internal procedures is a defense to an action brought under [sections 1 through 9]. If the employer's internal procedures are not completed within 90 days from the date the employee initiates the internal procedures, the employee may file an action under [sections 1 through 9] and for purposes of this subsection the employer's internal procedures are considered exhausted. The limitation period in subsection (1) is tolled until the procedures are exhausted. In no case may the provisions of the employer's internal procedures extend the limitation period in subsection (1) more than 120 days.

(3) If the employer maintains written internal procedures under which an employee may appeal a discharge within the organizational structure of the employer, the employer shall within 7 days of the date of the discharge notify the discharged employee of the existence of such procedures and shall supply the discharged employee with a copy of them. If the employer fails to comply with this subsection, the discharged employee need not comply with subsection (2).

Sec. 12. Exemptions. This part does not apply to a discharge:

(1) that is subject to any other state or federal statute that provides a procedure or remedy for contesting the dispute. The statutes include those that prohibit discharge for filing complaints, charges, or claims with administrative bodies or that prohibit unlawful discrimination based on race, national origin, sex, age, disability, creed, religion, political belief, color, marital status, and other similar grounds.

(2) of an employee covered by a written collective bargaining agreement or a written contract of employment for a specific term.

Sec. 13. Preemption of commonlaw remedies. Except as provided in [sections 1 through 9], no claim for discharge may arise from tort or express or implied contract.

Sec. 14. Arbitration. (1) A party may make a written offer to arbitrate a dispute that otherwise could be adjudicated under this part.

(2) An offer to arbitrate must be in writing and contain the following provisions:

(a) A neutral arbitrator must be selected by mutual agreement or, in the absence of agreement, as provided in 27–5–211.

(b) The arbitration must be governed by the Uniform Arbitration Act, Title 27, chapter 5. If there is a conflict between the Uniform Arbitration Act and this part, this part applies.

(c) The arbitrator is bound by this part.

(3) If a complaint is filed under this part, the offer to arbitrate must be made within 60 days after service of the complaint and must be accepted in writing within 30 days after the date the offer is made.

(4) A discharged employee who makes a valid offer to arbitrate that is accepted by the employer and who prevails in such arbitration is entitled to have the arbitrator's fee and all costs of arbitration paid by the employer.

(5) If a valid offer to arbitrate is made and accepted, arbitration is the exclusive remedy for the wrongful discharge dispute and there is no right to bring or continue a lawsuit under this part. The arbitrator's award is final and binding, subject to review of the arbitrator's decision under the provisions of the Uniform Arbitration Act.

Sec. 15. Effect of rejection of offer to arbitrate. A party who makes a valid offer to arbitrate that is not accepted by the other party and who prevails in an action under this part is entitled as an element of costs to reasonable attorney fees incurred subsequent to the date of the offer.

MODEL EMPLOYMENT TERMINATION ACT

National Conference of Commissioners of Uniform State Laws
(August 1991)

(Note: Brackets indicate possible additions,
deletions, or changes in language.)

SECTION 1. DEFINITIONS. In this [Act]:

(1) "Employee" means an individual who works for hire, including an individual employed in a supervisory, managerial, or confidential position, but not an independent contractor.

(2) "Employer" means a person [, excluding this State, a political subdivision, a municipal corporation, or any other governmental subdivision, agency, or instrumentality,] that has employed [five] or more employees for each working day in each of 20 or more calendar weeks in the two-year period next preceding a termination or an employer's filing of a complaint pursuant to Section 5(c), excluding a parent, spouse, child, or other member of the employer's immediate family or of the immediate family of an individual having a controlling interest in the employer.

(3) "Fringe benefit" means vacation leave, sick leave, medical insurance plan, disability insurance plan, life insurance plan, pension benefit plan, or other benefit of economic value, to the extent the leave, plan, or benefit is paid for by the employer.

(4) "Good cause" means (i) a reasonable basis related to an individual employee for termination of the employee's employment in view of relevant factors and circumstances, which may include the employee's duties, responsibilities, conduct on the job or otherwise, job performance, and employment record, or (ii) the exercise of business judgment in good faith by the employer, including setting its economic or institutional goals and determining methods to achieve those goals, organizing or reorganizing operations, discontinuing, consolidating, or divesting operations or positions or parts of operations or positions, determining the size of its work force and the nature of the positions filled by its work force, and determining and changing standards of performance for positions.

(5) "Good faith" means honesty in fact.

(6) "Pay," as a noun, means hourly wages or periodic salary, including tips, regularly paid and nondiscretionary commissions and bonuses, and regularly paid overtime, but not fringe benefits.

(7) "Person" means an individual, corporation, business trust, estate, trust, partnership, association, joint venture, or any other legal or

211

commercial entity [, excluding government or a governmental subdivision, agency, or instrumentality].

(8) "Termination" means:

(i) a dismissal, including that resulting from the elimination of a position, of an employee by an employer;

(ii) a layoff or suspension of an employee by an employer for more than two consecutive months; or

(iii) a quitting of employment or a retirement by an employee induced by an act or omission of the employer, after notice to the employer of the act or omission without appropriate relief by the employer, so intolerable that under the circumstances a reasonable individual would quit or retire.

SECTION 2.   SCOPE

(a) This [Act] applies only to a termination that occurs after the effective date of this [Act].

(b) This [Act] does not apply to a termination at the expiration of an express oral or written agreement of employment for a specified duration, which was valid, subsisting, and in effect on the [effective] date of this [Act].

(c) Except as provided in subsection (e), this [Act] displaces and extinguishes all common-law rights and claims of a terminated employee against the employer, its officers, directors, and employees, which are based on the termination or on acts taken or statements made that are reasonably necessary to initiate or effect the termination if the employee's termination requires good cause under Section 3(a), is subject to an agreement for severance pay under Section 4(c), or is permitted by the expiration of an agreement for a specified duration under Section 4(d).

(d) An employee whose termination is not subject to Section 3(a) or 4(d) and who is not a party to an agreement under Section 4(c) retains all common-law rights and claims.

(e) This [Act] does not displace or extinguish rights or claims of a terminated employee against an employer arising under state or federal statutes or administrative rules or regulations having the force of law [or local ordinances valid under state law], a collective-bargaining agreement between an employer and a labor organization, or an express oral or written agreement relating to employment which does not violate this [Act].   Those rights and claims may not be asserted under this [Act], except as otherwise provided in this [Act].   The existence or adjudication of those rights or claims does not limit the employee's rights or claims under this [Act], except as stated in Section 7(d).

SECTION 3. PROHIBITED TERMINATIONS

(a) Unless otherwise provided in an agreement for severance pay under Section 4(c) or for a specified duration under Section 4(d), an employer may not terminate the employment of an employee without good cause.

(b) Subsection (a) applies only to an employee who has been employed by the same employer for a total period of one year or more and has worked for the employer for at least 520 hours during the 26 weeks next preceding the termination. A layoff or other break in service is not counted in determining whether an employee's period of employment totals one year, but the employee is considered to be employed during paid vacations and other authorized leaves. If an employee is rehired after a break in service exceeding one year, not counting absences due to labor disputes or authorized leaves, the employee is considered to be newly hired. The 26–week period for purposes of this subsection does not include any week during which the employee was absent because of layoffs of one year or less, paid vacations, authorized leaves, or labor disputes.

SECTION 4. AGREEMENTS BETWEEN EMPLOYER AND EMPLOYEE

(a) A right of an employee under this [Act] may not be waived by agreement except as provided in this section.

(b) By express written agreement, an employer and an employee may provide that the employee's failure to meet specified business-related standards of performance or the employee's commission or omission of specified business-related acts will constitute good cause for termination in proceedings under this [Act]. Those standards or prohibitions are effective only if they have been consistently enforced and they have not been applied to a particular employee in a disparate manner without justification. If the agreement authorizes changes by the employer in the standards or prohibitions, the changes must be clearly communicated to the employee.

(c) By express written agreement, an employer and an employee may mutually waive the requirement of good cause for termination, if the employer agrees that upon the termination of the employee for any reason other than willful misconduct of the employee, the employer will provide severance pay in an amount equal to at least one month's pay for each period of employment totaling one year, up to a maximum total payment equal to 30 months' pay at the employee's rate of pay in effect immediately before the termination. The employer shall make the payment in a lump sum or in a series of monthly installments, none of which may be less than one month's pay plus interest on the principal balance. The lump-sum payment must be made or payment of the

213

monthly installments must begin within 30 days after the employee's termination. An agreement under this subsection constitutes a waiver by the employer and the employee of the right to civil trial, including jury trial, concerning disputes over the nature of the termination and the employee's entitlement to severance pay, and constitutes a stipulation by the parties that those disputes will be subject to the procedures and remedies of this [Act].

(d) The requirement of good cause for termination does not apply to the termination of an employee at the expiration of an express oral or written agreement of employment for a specified duration related to the completion of a specified task, project, undertaking, or assignment. If the employment continues after the expiration of the agreement, Section 3 applies to its termination unless the parties enter into a new express oral or written agreement under this subsection. The period of employment under an agreement described in this subsection counts toward the minimum periods of employment required by Section 3(b).

(e) An employer may provide substantive and procedural rights in addition to those provided by this [Act], either to one or more specific employees by express oral or written agreement, or to employees generally by a written personnel policy or statement, and may provide that those rights are enforceable under the procedures of this [Act].

(f) An employing person and an employee not otherwise subject to this [Act] may become subject to its provisions to the extent provided by express written agreement, in which case the employing person is deemed to be an employer.

(g) An agreement between an employer and an employee subject to this [Act] imposes a duty of good faith in its formation, performance, and enforcement.

(h) By express written agreement, an employer and an employee may settle at any time a claim arising under this [Act].

(i) By express written agreement before or after a dispute or claim arises under this [Act], an employer and an employee may agree to private arbitration or other alternative dispute-resolution procedure for resolving the dispute or claim.

(j) By express written agreement after a dispute or claim arises under this [Act], an employer and an employee may agree to judicial resolution of the dispute or claim.

(k) The substantive provisions of this [Act] apply under an agreement authorized by subsections (i) and (j).

SECTION 5. PROCEDURE AND LIMITATIONS

(a) An employee whose employment is terminated may file a complaint and demand for arbitration under this [Act] with the [Commission; Department; Service] not later than 180 days after the effective date of the termination, the date of the breach of an agreement for severance pay under Section 4(c), or the date the employee learns or should have learned of the facts forming the basis of the claim, whichever is latest. The time for filing is suspended while the employee is pursuing the employer's internal remedies and has not been notified in writing by the employer that the internal procedures have been concluded. Resort to an employer's internal procedures is not a condition for filing a complaint under this [Act].

(b) Except when an employee quits, an employer, within 10 business days after a termination, shall mail or deliver to the terminated employee a written statement of the reasons for the termination and a copy of this [Act] or a summary approved by the [Commission; Department; Service].

(c) An employer may file a complaint and demand for arbitration under this [Act] with the [Commission; Department; Service] to determine whether there is good cause for the termination of a named employee. At least 15 business days before filing, the employer shall mail or deliver to the employee a written statement of the employer's intention to file and the factors alleged to constitute good cause for a termination.

(d) The [Commission; Department; Service] shall promptly mail or deliver to the respondent a copy of the complaint and demand for arbitration. Within 21 days after receipt of a complaint, the respondent must file an answer with the [Commission; Department; Service] and mail a copy of the answer to the complainant. The answer of a respondent employer must include a copy of the statement of the reasons for the termination furnished the employee.

[(e) When a complaint is filed, a complainant employee or employer shall pay a filing fee to the [Commission; Department; Service] in [the amount of $_____] [an amount not exceeding the maximum filing fee for a civil action in the courts of general jurisdiction of this State]. The [Commission; Department; Service] may waive or defer payment of the filing fee upon a showing of the complainant employee's indigency.]

SECTION 6. ARBITRATION; SELECTION AND POWERS OF ARBITRATOR; HEARINGS; BURDEN OF PROOF

(a) Except as otherwise provided in this [Act], the [Uniform Arbitration Act] [_____ arbitration act of this State] applies to proceedings under this [Act] as if the parties had agreed to arbitrate under that statute. The [Commission; Department; Service] shall adopt procedural rules to regulate arbitration under this [Act]. The [Administrative Procedure Act and other] statutes of this State applicable to the procedures of state agencies do not apply to arbitration under this [Act].

(b) The [Commission; Department; Service] shall adopt rules specifying the qualifications, method of selection, and appointment of arbitrators. An arbitrator serving under this [Act] exercises the authority of the state.

(c) Subject to rules adopted by the [Commission; Department; Service], all forms of discovery [provided by applicable state statute, rule, or regulation] are available in the discretion of the arbitrator, who shall ensure there is no undue delay, expense, or inconvenience. Upon request, the employer shall provide the complainant or respondent employee a complete copy of the employee's personnel file.

(d) A party may be represented in arbitration by an attorney or other person authorized under the laws of this State to represent an individual in arbitration.

(e) A complainant employee has the burden of proving that a termination was without good cause or that an employer breached an agreement for severance pay under Section 4(c). A complainant employer has the burden of proving that there is good cause for a termination. In all arbitrations, the employer shall present its case first unless the employee alleges that a quitting or retirement was a termination within the meaning of Section 1(8)(iii).

(f) If an employee establishes that a termination was motivated in part by impermissible grounds, the employer, to avoid liability, must establish by a preponderance of the evidence that it would have terminated the employment even in the absence of the impermissible grounds.

SECTION 7. AWARDS

(a) Within 30 days after the close of an arbitration hearing or at a later time agreeable to the parties, the arbitrator shall mail or deliver to the parties a written award sustaining or dismissing the complaint, in whole or in part, and specifying appropriate remedies, if any.

(b) An arbitrator may make one or more of the following awards for a termination in violation of this [Act]:

(1) reinstatement to the position of employment the employee held when employment was terminated or, if that is impractical, to a comparable position;

(2) full or partial backpay and reimbursement for lost fringe benefits, with interest, reduced by interim earnings from employ-

ment elsewhere, benefits received, and amounts that could have been received with reasonable diligence;

(3) if reinstatement is not awarded, a lump-sum severance payment at the employee's rate of pay in effect before the termination, for a period not exceeding [36 months] after the date of the award, together with the value of fringe benefits lost during that period, reduced by likely earnings and benefits from employment elsewhere, and taking into account such equitable considerations as the employee's length of service with the employer and the reasons for the termination; and

(4) reasonable attorney's fees and costs.

(c) An arbitrator may make either or both of the following awards for a violation of an agreement for severance pay under Section 4(c):

(1) enforcement of the severance pay and other applicable provisions of the agreement, with interest; and

(2) reasonable attorney's fees and costs.

(d) An arbitrator may not make an award except as provided in subsections (b) and (c). The arbitrator may not award damages for pain and suffering, emotional distress, defamation, fraud, or other injury under the common law; punitive damages; compensatory damages; or any other monetary award. In making a monetary award under this section, the arbitrator shall reduce the award by the amount of any monetary award to the employee in another forum for the same conduct of the employer. In making an award, the arbitrator is subject to the rules of issue, fact, and judgment preclusion applicable in courts of record in this State.

(e) If an arbitrator dismisses an employee's complaint and finds it frivolous, unreasonable, or without foundation, the arbitrator may award reasonable attorney's fees and costs to the prevailing employer.

(f) An arbitrator may sustain an employer's complaint and make an award declaring that there is good cause for the termination of a named employee. If the arbitrator dismisses the employer's complaint, the arbitrator may award reasonable attorney's fees and costs to the prevailing employee.

SECTION 8. JUDICIAL REVIEW AND ENFORCEMENT

(a) Either party to an arbitration may seek vacation, modification, or enforcement of the arbitrator's award in the [court of general jurisdiction] for the [county] in which the termination occurred or in which the employee resides.

(b) An application for vacation or modification must be filed within [90] days after issuance of the arbitrator's award. An application for enforcement may be filed at any time after issuance of the arbitrator's award.

(c) The court may vacate or modify an arbitrator's award only if the court finds that:

(1) the award was procured by corruption, fraud, or other improper means;

(2) there was evident partiality by the arbitrator or misconduct prejudicing the rights of a party;

(3) the arbitrator exceeded the powers of an arbitrator;

(4) the arbitrator committed a prejudicial error of law; or

(5) another ground exists for vacating the award under the [Uniform Arbitration Act] [_____ arbitration act of this State].

(d) In an application for vacation, modification, or enforcement of an arbitrator's award, the court may award a prevailing employee reasonable attorney's fees and costs. In an application by an employee for vacation of an arbitrator's award, the court may award a prevailing employer reasonable attorney's fees and costs if the court finds the employee's application is frivolous, unreasonable, or without foundation.

SECTION 9. POSTING

An employer shall post a copy of this [Act] or a summary approved by the [Commission; Department; Service] in a prominent place in the work area. An employer who violates this section is subject to a civil penalty not exceeding [$_____]. The [Attorney General] may bring a civil action, on behalf of this State, to impose and collect any civil penalty arising under this section.

SECTION 10. RETALIATION PROHIBITED AND CIVIL ACTION CREATED

An employer or other employing person may not directly or indirectly take adverse action in retaliation against an individual for filing a complaint, giving testimony, or otherwise lawfully participating in proceedings under this [Act], whether or not the individual is an employee having rights under this [Act]. An employer or other employing person who violates this section is liable to the individual subjected to the adverse action in retaliation for damage caused by the action, punitive damages when appropriate, and reasonable attorney's fees. A separate civil action may be brought to enforce this liability. The employer is also subject to applicable procedures and remedies provided by Sections 5 through 8.

SECTION 11.   SEVERABILITY CLAUSE

If any provision of this [Act] or its application to any person or circumstance is held invalid, the invalidity does not affect other provisions or applications of this [Act] which can be given effect without the invalid provision or application, and to this end the provisions of this [Act] are severable.

SECTION 12.   EFFECTIVE DATE

This [Act] takes effect _____.

SECTION 13.   REPEALS

The following acts and parts of acts are repealed:

(1) ....

(2) ....

(3) ....

SECTION 14.   SAVINGS AND TRANSITIONAL PROVISIONS

This [Act] does not apply to the termination of an employee within six months after the effective date of this [Act] based upon the employee's refusal to enter into an agreement meeting the minimum standards of Section 4(c), which the employer, in the exercise of good faith business judgment, may impose as a condition of continued employment.

APPENDIX

Note: Instead of the arbitration system provided by Sections 5 through 8 of the preceding text, states may select the following Alternative A or Alternative B as the means of enforcement.

ALTERNATIVE A

SECTION 5. ADMINISTRATIVE PROCEEDINGS

[Insert provisions consigning enforcement of the [Act] to a new or existing administrative agency, staffed by civil service or other governmental personnel, operating under applicable state statutes. Delete Sections 5 through 8 of the preceding text and renumber the remaining sections and any cross references accordingly.]

SECTION 6. REMEDIES

(a) The [Commission; Department; Service] may provide one or more of the following remedies for a termination in violation of this [Act]:

(1) reinstatement to the position of employment the employee held when employment was terminated or, if that is impractical, to a comparable position;

(2) full or partial backpay and reimbursement for lost fringe benefits, with interest, reduced by interim earnings from employment elsewhere, benefits received, and amounts that could have been received with reasonable diligence;

(3) if reinstatement is not ordered, a lump-sum severance payment at the employee's rate of pay in effect before the termination, for a period not exceeding [36 months] from the date of the order, together with the value of fringe benefits lost during that period, reduced by likely earnings and benefits from employment elsewhere, and taking into account such equitable considerations as the employee's length of service with the employer and the reasons for the termination; and

(4) reasonable attorney's fees and costs.

(b) The [Commission; Department; Service] may grant either or both of the following remedies for a violation of an agreement for severance pay under Section 4(c):

(1) enforcement of the severance pay and other applicable provisions of the agreement, with interest; and

(2) reasonable attorney's fees and costs.

(c) The [Commission; Department; Service] may not make an award except as provided in subsections (a) and (b). The [Commission; Department; Service] may not award damages for pain and suffering, emotional distress, defamation, fraud, or other injury under the common law; punitive damages; compensatory damages; or any other monetary award under this [Act]. In making a monetary award under this section, the [Commission; Department; Service] shall reduce the award by the amount of any monetary award to the employee in another forum for the same conduct of the employer. In making an award, the [Commission; Department; Service] is subject to the rules of issue, fact, and judgment preclusion applicable in courts of record in this State.

(d) If the [Commission; Department; Service] dismisses an employee's complaint and finds it frivolous, unreasonable, or without foundation, the [Commission; Department; Service] may award reasonable attorney's fees and costs to the prevailing employer.

(e) Upon the complaint of an employer, the [Commission; Department; Service] may issue an order declaring whether there is good cause for the termination of a named employee. If the [Commission; Department; Service] dismisses the employer's complaint, the [Commission; Department; Service] may award reasonable attorney's fees and costs to the prevailing employee.

ALTERNATIVE B

[Alternative B would leave the enforcement of the statute to the civil courts. Delete Sections 5 through 8 of the preceding text and renumber the remaining sections and any cross references accordingly.]

[SECTION 5.   JUDICIAL REMEDIES

(a) The court may grant one or more of the following remedies for a termination in violation of this [Act]:

(1) reinstatement to the position of employment the employee held when employment was terminated or, if that is impractical, to a comparable position;

(2) full or partial backpay and reimbursement for lost fringe benefits, with interest, reduced by interim earnings from employment elsewhere, benefits received, and amounts that could have been received with reasonable diligence;

(3) if reinstatement is not awarded, a lump-sum severance payment at the employee's rate of pay in effect before the termination, for a period not exceeding [36 months] from the date of the award, together with the value of fringe benefits lost during that period, reduced by likely earnings and benefits from employment elsewhere, and taking into account such equitable considerations as the employee's length of service with the employer and the reasons for the termination; and

(4) reasonable attorney's fees and costs.

(b) The court may grant either or both of the following remedies for a violation of an agreement for severance pay under Section 4(c):

(1) enforcement of the severance pay and other applicable provisions of the agreement, with interest; and

(2) reasonable attorney's fees and costs.

(c) The court may not make an award except as provided in subsections (a) and (b). The court may not award damages for pain and suffering, emotional distress, defamation, fraud, or other injury under the common law; punitive damages; compensatory damages; or any other monetary award under this [Act]. In making a monetary award under this section, the court shall reduce the award by the amount of any monetary award to the employee in another forum for the same conduct of the employer. In making an award, the court is subject to the rules of issue, fact, and judgment preclusion applicable in courts of record in this State.

(d) If the court dismisses an employee's complaint and finds it frivolous, unreasonable, or without foundation, the court may award reasonable attorney's fees and costs to the prevailing employer.

(e) Upon the complaint of an employer, the court may enter a judgment declaring whether there is good cause for the termination of a named employee. If the court dismisses the employer's complaint, the court may award reasonable attorney's fees and costs to the prevailing employee.

FEDERAL UNEMPLOYMENT TAX ACT

26 U.S.C. §§ 3301–3311

Sec. 3301 Rate of tax

There is hereby imposed on every employer (as defined in section 3306(a)) for each calendar year an excise tax, with respect to having individuals in his employ, equal to—

(1) 6.2 percent in the case of calendar years 1988 through 2007; or

(2) 6.0 percent in the calendar year 2008, and each calendar year thereafter;

* * *

Sec. 3302 Credits against tax

(a) Contributions to state unemployment funds.—

(1) The taxpayer may, to the extent provided in this subsection and subsection (c), credit against the tax imposed by section 3301 the amount of contributions paid by him into an unemployment fund maintained during the taxable year under the unemployment compensation law of a State which is certified as provided in section 3304 for the 12–month period ending on October 31 of such year.

* * *

(c) Limit on total credits.—

(1) The total credits allowed to a taxpayer under this section shall not exceed 90 percent of the tax against which such credits are allowable.

* * *

Sec. 3304 Approval of State laws

(a) Requirements.—The Secretary of Labor shall approve any State law submitted to him, within 30 days of such submission, which he finds provides that—

* * *

(5) compensation shall not be denied in such State to any otherwise eligible individual for refusing to accept new work under any of the following conditions:

(A) if the position offered is vacant due directly to a strike, lockout, or other labor dispute;

(B) if the wages, hours, or other conditions of the work offered are substantially less favorable to the individual than those prevailing for similar work in the locality;

(C) if as a condition of being employed the individual would be required to join a company union or to resign from or refrain from joining any bona fide labor organization;

(6)(A) compensation is payable on the basis of service to which section 3309(a)(1) applies, in the same amount, on the same terms, and subject to the same conditions as compensation payable on the basis of other service subject to such law; except that—

(i) with respect to services in an instructional, research, or principal administrative capacity for an educational institution to which section 3309(a)(1) applies, compensation shall not be payable based on such services for any week commencing during the period between two successive academic years or terms (or, when an agreement provides instead for a similar period between two regular but not successive terms, during such period) to any individual if such individual performs such services in the first of such academic years (or terms) and if there is a contract or reasonable assurance that such individual will perform services in any such capacity for any educational institution in the second of such academic years or terms,

* * *

(12) no person shall be denied compensation under such State law solely on the basis of pregnancy or termination of pregnancy;

(13) compensation shall not be payable to any individual on the basis of any services, substantially all of which consist of participating in sports or athletic events or training or preparing to so participate, for any week which commences during the period between two successive sport seasons (or similar periods) if such individual performed such services in the first of such seasons (or similar periods) and there is a reasonable assurance that such individual will perform such services in the later of such seasons (or similar periods);

(14)(A) compensation shall not be payable on the basis of services performed by an alien unless such alien is an individual who was lawfully admitted for permanent residence at the time such services were performed, was lawfully present for purposes of performing such services, or was permanently residing in the United

States under color of law at the time such services were performed (including an alien who was lawfully present in the United States as a result of the application of the provisions of section 212(d)(5) of the Immigration and Nationality Act),

* * *

Sec. 3306 Definitions

(a) Employer. For purposes of this chapter—

(1) In general.—The term "employer" means, with respect to any calendar year, any person who—

(A) during any calendar quarter in the calendar year or the preceding calendar year paid wages of $1,500 or more, or

(B) on each of some 20 days during the calendar year or during the preceding calendar year, each day being in a different calendar week, employed at least one individual in employment for some portion of the day.

For purposes of this paragraph, there shall not be taken into account any wages paid to, or employment of, an employee performing domestic services referred to in paragraph (3).

* * *

CALIFORNIA UNEMPLOYMENT INSURANCE CODE

Cal. Unemp. Ins. Code §§ 1–15078

SEC. 100 Declaration of policy

As a guide to the interpretation and application of this division the public policy of this State is declared as follows:

Experience has shown that large numbers of the population of California do not enjoy permanent employment by reason of which their purchasing power is unstable. This is detrimental to the interests of the people of California as a whole.

The benefit to all persons resulting from public and private enterprise is realized in the final consumption of goods and services. It is contrary to public policy to permit the supply of consumption goods and services at prices which do not provide against that harm to the population consequent upon periods of unemployment of those who contribute to the production and distribution of such goods and services.

Experience has shown that private charity and local relief cannot alone prevent the effects of unemployment. Experience has shown that if the State awaits the coming of excessive unemployment it can neither create immediately the organization necessary to orderly, economical and effective relief nor bear the financial burden of relief without disrupting its whole system of ordinary revenues and without jeopardizing its credit.

The Legislature therefore declares that in its considered judgment the public good and the general welfare of the citizens of the State require the enactment of this measure under the police power of the State, for the compulsory setting aside of funds to be used for a system of unemployment insurance providing benefits for persons unemployed through no fault of their own, and to reduce involuntary unemployment and the suffering caused thereby to a minimum.

It is the intent of the Legislature that unemployed persons claiming unemployment insurance benefits shall be required to make all reasonable effort to secure employment on their own behalf.

SEC. 101 Statute as part of national plan; effect of repeal or amendment of federal legislation

This part is a part of a national plan of unemployment reserves and social security, and is enacted for the purpose of assisting in the stabilization of employment conditions. The imposition of the tax herein imposed upon California industry alone, without a corresponding tax being imposed upon all industry in the United States, would, by the corresponding penalty upon California industry, defeat the very purposes of this law as set forth in this article. Therefore when existing federal legislation which provides for a tax upon the payment of wages by employers in this State, against which all or any part of the employer contributions required under this part may be credited is repealed, amended, interpreted, affected or otherwise changed in such manner that no portion of such contributions may be thus credited, then upon the date of such change, the provisions of this part requiring employer contributions and providing for payment of unemployment compensation benefits shall cease to be operative and any assets in the Unemployment Fund or Unemployment Administration Fund shall in the discretion of the State Treasurer be held in the then existing depositaries or otherwise in the State Treasury. In the case of the Unemployment Administration Fund, such money may thereafter be dealt with by the State Treasurer pursuant to the conditions of the grant thereof to the State by the United States Government or agency thereof.

SEC. 601 "Employment"; services included

"Employment" means service, including service in interstate commerce, performed by an employee for wages or under any contract of hire, written or oral, express or implied.

SEC. 621 "Employee"; persons included

"Employee" means all of the following:

(a) Any officer of a corporation.

(b) Any individual who, under the usual common law rules applicable in determining the employer-employee relationship, has the status of an employee.

(c)(1) Any individual, other than an individual who is an employee under subdivision (a) or (b), who performs services for remuneration for any employing unit if the contract of service contemplates that substantially all of such services are to be performed personally by such individual either:

(A) As an agent-driver or commission-driver engaged in distributing meat products, vegetable products, fruit products, bakery products, beverages (other than milk), or laundry or drycleaning services, for his or her principal.

(B) As a traveling or city salesperson, other than as an agent-driver or commission-driver, engaged upon a full-time basis in the solicitation on behalf of, and the transmission to, his or her principal (except for sideline sales activities on behalf of some other person) of orders from wholesalers, retailers, contractors, or operators of hotels, restaurants, or other similar establishments for merchandise for resale or supplies for use in their business operations.

(C) As a home worker performing work, according to specifications furnished by the person for whom the services are performed, on materials or goods furnished by such person which are required to be returned to such person or a person designated by him or her.

(2) An individual shall not be included in the term "employee" under the provisions of this subdivision if such individual has a substantial investment in facilities used in connection with the performance of such services, other than in facilities for transportation, or if the services are in the nature of a single transaction not part of a continuing relationship with the employing unit for whom the services are performed.

* * *

SEC. 629   Domestic service in private home

(a) "Employment" does not include domestic service in a private home, except that "employment" includes domestic service in a private home if performed for an employing unit or a person who paid in cash remuneration of one thousand dollars ($1,000) or more to individuals employed in the domestic service in any calendar quarter in the calendar year or the preceding calendar year.

(b) For purposes of subdivision (a), "employment" does not include work performed by a domestic worker for whom an employment agency, as defined in paragraph (3) of subdivision (a) or subdivision (h) of Section 1812.501 of the Civil Code, procures, offers, refers, provides, or attempts to provide domestic work in a private home, if all of the factors set forth in Section 687.2 characterize the nature of the relationship between the employment agency and the domestic worker for whom the agency procures, offers, refers, provides, or attempts to provide domestic work.

SEC. 642   Service by student or student's spouse in employ of school, college, or university

"Employment" does not include service performed in the employ of a school, college, or university, if such service is performed:

(a) By a student who is enrolled and is regularly attending classes at such school, college, or university, or

(b) By the spouse of such a student, if such spouse is advised, at the time such spouse commences to perform such service, that:

(1) The employment of such spouse to perform such service is provided under a program to provide financial assistance to such student by such school, college, or university, and

(2) Such employment will not be covered by any program of unemployment insurance or disability compensation.

SEC. 649 Service by minor in delivery or distribution of newspapers and magazines

"Employment" does not include service performed by an individual if:

(a) Such service is performed by an individual under the age of 18 in the delivery or distribution of newspapers, shopping news, or magazines, not including delivery or distribution to any point for subsequent delivery or distribution, unless such service is performed by an individual under the age of 18 whose principal occupation is regular full-time work and whose attendance at school is incidental to full-time employment.

(b) Such service is performed by an individual in, and at the time of, the sale of newspapers or magazines to ultimate consumers, under an arrangement under which the newspapers or magazines are to be sold by him at a fixed price, his compensation being based on the retention of the excess of such price over the amount at which the newspapers or magazines are charged to him whether or not he is guaranteed a minimum amount of compensation for such service, or is entitled to be credited with the unsold newspapers or magazines turned back.

SEC. 651 Services performed as golf caddy

"Employment" does not include services performed by an individual as a golf caddy in caddying or carrying a golf player's clubs.

SEC. 653 Services performed by baseball player on other than salary basis

"Employment" does not include services performed in the employ of a baseball club pursuant to a contract or agreement under which the baseball player agrees to perform for expenses and a share of the profits of the club, rather than for a fixed salary.

SEC. 926 "Wages"

Except as otherwise provided in this article "wages" means all remuneration payable to an employee for personal services, whether by private agreement or consent or by force of statute, including commissions and bonuses, and the reasonable cash value of all remuneration payable to an employee in any medium other than cash.

SEC. 976 Accrual and payment of contributions

Employer contributions to the Unemployment Fund shall accrue and become payable by every employer, * * * for each calendar year with respect to wages paid for employment. The contributions are due and shall be paid to the department for the Unemployment Fund by each employer in accordance with this division and shall not be deducted in whole or in part from the wages of individuals in his employ.

SEC. 977   Contribution rate; schedules

(a) If, as of the computation date, the employer's net balance of reserve equals or exceeds that percentage of his or her average base payroll which appears on any line in column 1 of the following table, but is less than that percentage of his or her average base payroll which appears on the same line in column 2 of that table, his or her contribution rate shall be the figure appearing on that same line in the appropriate schedule, as defined in subdivision (b), which shall be a percentage of the wages specified in Section 930.

| | Reserve Ratio | | Contribution Rate | | | | | | |
| | Column 1 | Column 2 | Schedules | | | | | | |
Line			AA	A	B	C	D	E	F
01	less than	− 20	5.4	5.4	5.4	5.4	5.4	5.4	5.4
02	− 20 to	− 18	5.2	5.3	5.4	5.4	5.4	5.4	5.4
03	− 18 to	− 16	5.1	5.2	5.4	5.4	5.4	5.4	5.4
04	− 16 to	− 14	5.0	5.1	5.3	5.4	5.4	5.4	5.4
05	− 14 to	− 12	4.9	5.0	5.3	5.4	5.4	5.4	5.4
06	− 12 to	− 11	4.8	4.9	5.2	5.4	5.4	5.4	5.4
07	− 11 to	− 10	4.7	4.8	5.1	5.3	5.4	5.4	5.4
08	− 10 to	− 09	4.6	4.7	5.1	5.3	5.4	5.4	5.4
09	− 09 to	− 08	4.5	4.6	4.9	5.2	5.4	5.4	5.4
10	− 08 to	− 07	4.4	4.5	4.8	5.1	5.3	5.4	5.4
11	− 07 to	− 06	4.3	4.4	4.7	5.0	5.3	5.4	5.4
12	− 06 to	− 05	4.2	4.3	4.6	4.9	5.2	5.4	5.4
13	− 05 to	− 04	4.1	4.2	4.5	4.8	5.1	5.3	5.4
14	− 04 to	− 03	4.0	4.1	4.4	4.7	5.0	5.3	5.4
15	− 03 to	− 02	3.9	4.0	4.3	4.6	4.9	5.2	5.4
16	− 02 to	− 01	3.8	3.9	4.2	4.5	4.8	5.1	5.4
17	− 01 to	00	3.7	3.8	4.1	4.4	4.7	5.0	5.4
18	00 to	01	3.4	3.6	3.9	4.2	4.5	4.8	5.1
19	01 to	02	3.2	3.4	3.7	4.0	4.3	4.6	4.9
20	02 to	03	3.0	3.2	3.5	3.8	4.1	4.4	4.7
21	03 to	04	2.8	3.0	3.3	3.6	3.9	4.2	4.5
22	04 to	05	2.6	2.8	3.1	3.4	3.7	4.0	4.3
23	05 to	06	2.4	2.6	2.9	3.2	3.5	3.8	4.1
24	06 to	07	2.2	2.4	2.7	3.0	3.3	3.6	3.9
25	07 to	08	2.0	2.2	2.5	2.8	3.1	3.4	3.7
26	08 to	09	1.8	2.0	2.3	2.6	2.9	3.2	3.5
27	09 to	10	1.6	1.8	2.1	2.4	2.7	3.0	3.3
28	10 to	11	1.4	1.6	1.9	2.2	2.5	2.8	3.1
29	11 to	12	1.2	1.4	1.7	2.0	2.3	2.6	2.9
30	12 to	13	1.0	1.2	1.5	1.8	2.1	2.4	2.7
31	13 to	14	0.8	1.0	1.3	1.6	1.9	2.2	2.5
32	14 to	15	0.7	0.9	1.1	1.4	1.7	2.0	2.3
33	15 to	16	0.6	0.8	1.0	1.2	1.5	1.8	2.1
34	16 to	17	0.5	0.7	0.9	1.1	1.3	1.6	1.9
35	17 to	18	0.4	0.6	0.8	1.0	1.2	1.4	1.7

36	18 to	19	0.3	0.5	0.7	0.9	1.1	1.3	1.5
37	19 to	20	0.2	0.4	0.6	0.8	1.0	1.2	1.4
38	20 or	more	0.1	0.3	0.5	0.7	0.9	1.1	1.3

(b)(1) Whenever the balance in the Unemployment Fund on September 30 of any calendar year is greater than 1.8 percent of the wages (as defined by Section 940) in employment subject to this part paid during the 12–month period ending upon the computation date, employers shall pay into the Unemployment Fund contributions for the succeeding calendar year upon all wages with respect to employment at the rates specified in Schedule AA.

(2) Whenever the balance in the Unemployment Fund on September 30 of any calendar year is equal to or less than 1.8 percent and greater than 1.6 percent of the wages (as defined by Section 940) in employment subject to this part paid during the 12–month period ending upon the computation date, employers shall pay into the Unemployment Fund contributions for the succeeding calendar year upon all wages with respect to employment at the rates specified in Schedule A.

(3) Whenever the balance in the Unemployment Fund on September 30 of any calendar year is equal to or less than 1.6 percent and greater than 1.4 percent of the wages (as defined by Section 940) in employment subject to this part paid during the 12–month period ending upon the computation date, employers shall pay into the Unemployment Fund contributions for the succeeding calendar year upon all wages with respect to employment at the rates specified in Schedule B.

(4) Whenever the balance in the Unemployment Fund on September 30 of any calendar year is equal to or less than 1.4 percent and greater than 1.2 percent of the wages (as defined by Section 940) in employment subject to this part paid during the 12–month period ending upon the computation date, employers shall pay into the Unemployment Fund contributions for the succeeding calendar year upon all wages with respect to employment at the rates specified in Schedule C.

(5) Whenever the balance in the Unemployment Fund on September 30 of any calendar year is equal to or less than 1.2 percent and greater than 1.0 percent of the wages (as defined by Section 940) in employment subject to this part paid during the 12–month period ending upon the computation date, employers shall pay into the Unemployment Fund contributions for the succeeding calendar year upon all wages with respect to employment at the rates specified in Schedule D.

(6) Whenever the balance in the Unemployment Fund on September 30 of any calendar year is equal to or less than 1.0 percent and greater than or equal to 0.8 percent of the wages (as defined by Section 940) in employment subject to this part paid during the 12–month period ending

upon the computation date, employers shall pay into the Unemployment Fund contributions for the succeeding calendar year upon all wages with respect to employment at the rates specified in Schedule E.

(7) Whenever the balance in the Unemployment Fund on September 30 of any calendar year is equal to or less than 0.8 percent and greater than or equal to 0.6 percent of the wages (as defined by Section 940) in employment subject to this part paid during the 12-month period ending upon the computation date, employers shall pay into the Unemployment Fund contributions for the succeeding calendar year upon all wages with respect to employment at the rates specified in Schedule F.

Sec. 984 Worker contributions; amount; rate changes by director

(a)(1) Each worker shall pay worker contributions at the rate determined by the director pursuant to this section with respect to wages, as defined by Sections 926, 927, and 985. On or before October 31 of each calendar year, the director shall prepare a statement, which shall be a public record, declaring the rate of worker contributions for the calendar year and shall notify promptly all employers of employees covered for disability insurance of the rate.

(2)(A) Except as provided in paragraph (3), the rate of worker contributions for calendar year 1987 and for each subsequent calendar year shall be 1.45 times the amount disbursed from the Disability Fund during the 12–month period ending September 30 and immediately preceding the calendar year for which the rate is to be effective, less the amount in the Disability Fund on that September 30, with the resulting figure divided by total wages paid pursuant to Sections 926, 927, and 985 during the same 12–month period, and then rounded to the nearest one-tenth of 1 percent.

(3) The rate of worker contributions shall not exceed 1.3 percent or be less than 0.1 percent. The rate of worker contributions shall not decrease from the rate in the previous year by more than two-tenths of 1 percent.

(b) Worker contributions required under Sections 708 and 708.5 shall be at a rate determined by the director to reimburse the Disability Fund for unemployment compensation disability benefits paid and estimated to be paid to all employers and self-employed individuals covered by those sections. On or before November 30th of each calendar year, the director shall prepare a statement, which shall be a public record, declaring the rate of contributions for the succeeding calendar year for all employers and self-employed individuals covered under Sections 708 and 708.5 and shall notify promptly all employers and self-employed individuals of the rate. The rate shall be determined by dividing the estimated benefits and administrative costs paid in the prior year by the product of the annual remuneration deemed to have been received under Sections 708 and 708.5 and the estimated number of persons who were covered at any time in the prior year. The resulting rate shall be rounded to the next higher one-hundredth percentage point. The rate may also be reduced or increased by a factor estimated to maintain as nearly as practicable a cumulative zero balance in the funds contributed pursuant to Sections 708 and 708.5. Estimates made pursuant to this subdivision may be made on the basis of statistical sampling, or another method determined by the director.

(c) The director's action in determining a rate under this section shall not constitute an authorized regulation.

* * *

Sec. 986 Contributions by workers; withholding by employer; transmission of contribution

(a) Notwithstanding any provision of law in this state to the contrary, each employer shall:

(1) Except as provided in subdivision (a)(2) of this section, withhold in trust the amount of his workers' contributions from their wages at the time the wages are paid, shall show the deduction on his payroll records, and shall furnish each worker with a statement in writing showing the amount which has been deducted, in such form and at such times as may be prescribed.

(2) Hold in trust the amount of his workers' contributions, at the time their wages are paid, where he undertakes or agrees to pay without deduction from the wages of his workers the amount of worker contributions required of his workers under this division.

Sec. 1026 Maintaining accounts; Credits and charges

(a) The director shall maintain a separate account for each employer, and shall credit each account with all the contributions paid on his or her behalf.

(b) Unemployment compensation benefits paid to an unemployed individual during any benefit year shall be charged against the account of his or her employer during his or her base period, but if the individual performed services in employment for more than one employer during his or her base period, unemployment compensation benefits paid to him or her shall be charged against the respective accounts of the employers in the proportion that the total wages paid to the individual in employment for each employer bears to the total wages paid to the individual in employment for all employers during the base period.

* * *

SEC. 1030 Employer's submission of facts concerning termination of claimant's employment; Ruling by department; Presumption as to leaving without good cause; Appeal

(a) Any employer who is entitled under Section 1327 to receive notice of the filing of a new or additional claim may, within 10 days after mailing of the notice, submit to the department any facts within its possession disclosing whether the claimant left the employer's employ voluntarily and without good cause or left under one of the following circumstances:

(1) The claimant was discharged from the employment for misconduct connected with his or her work.

(2) The claimant's discharge or quitting from his or her most recent employer was the result of an irresistible compulsion to use or consume intoxicants including alcoholic beverages.

(3) The claimant was a student employed on a temporary basis and whose employment began within, and ended with his or her leaving to return to school at the close of, his or her vacation period.

(4) The claimant left the employer's employ to accompany his or her spouse to or join her or him at a place from which it is impractical to commute to the employment, to which a transfer of the claimant by the employer is not available.

(5) The claimant left the employer's employ to protect his or her children or himself or herself from domestic violence abuse.

The period during which the employer may submit these facts may be extended by the director for good cause.

(b) Any base period employer that is not entitled under Section 1327 to receive notice of the filing of a new or additional claim and is entitled under Section 1329 to receive notice of computation may, within 15 days after mailing of the notice of computation, submit to the department any facts within its possession disclosing whether the claimant left the employer's employ voluntarily and without good cause or left under one of the following circumstances:

(1) The claimant was discharged from the employment for misconduct connected with his or her work.

(2) The claimant was a student employed on a temporary basis and whose employment began within, and ended with his or her leaving to return to school at the close of, his or her vacation period.

(3) The claimant left the employer's employ to accompany his or her spouse to or join her or him at a place from which it is impractical to commute to the employment, to which a transfer of the claimant by the employer is not available.

(4) The claimant left the employer's employ to protect his or her children or himself or herself from domestic violence abuse.

The period during which the employer may submit these facts may be extended by the director for good cause.

(c) The department shall consider these facts together with any information in its possession. If the employer is entitled to a ruling under subdivision (b) or to a determination under Section 1328, the department shall promptly notify the employer of its ruling as to the cause of the termination of the claimant's employment. The employer may appeal from a ruling or reconsidered ruling to an administrative law judge within 20 days after mailing or personal service of notice of the ruling or reconsidered ruling. The 20–day period may be extended for good cause, which includes, but is not limited to, mistake, inadvertence, surprise, or excusable neglect. The director is an interested party to any appeal. The department may for good cause reconsider any ruling or reconsidered ruling within either five days after the date an appeal to an administrative law judge is filed or, if no appeal is filed, within 20 days after mailing or personal service of notice of the ruling or reconsidered ruling. However, a ruling or reconsidered ruling that relates to a determination that is reconsidered pursuant to subdivision (a) of Section 1332 may also be reconsidered by the department within the time provided for reconsideration of that determination.

(d) For purposes of this section only, if the claimant voluntarily leaves the employer's employ without notification to the employer of the reasons for the leaving, and if the employer submits all of the facts within its possession concerning the leaving within the applicable time period referred to in this section, the leaving is presumed to be without good cause.

(e) An individual whose employment is terminated under the compulsory retirement provisions of a collective bargaining agreement to which the employer is a party shall not be deemed to have voluntarily left his or her employment without good cause.

SEC. 1032 When benefits paid to claimant not chargeable to account of employer; "Spouse"

If it is ruled under Section 1030 or 1328 that the claimant left the employer's employ voluntarily and without good cause, or left under one of the following circumstances, benefits paid to the claimant subsequent to the termination of employment that are based upon wages earned from the employer prior to the date of the termination of employment shall not be charged to the account of the employer, except as provided by Section 1026, unless the employer failed to furnish the information specified in Section 1030 within the time limit prescribed in that section or unless that ruling is reversed by a reconsidered ruling:

(a) The claimant was discharged by reason of misconduct connected with his or her work.

(b) The claimant was a student employed on a temporary basis and whose employment began within, and ended with his or her leaving to return to school at the close of, his or her vacation period.

(c) The claimant left the employer's employ to accompany his or her spouse to or join her or him at a place from which it is impractical to commute to the employment, to which a transfer of the claimant by the employer is not available.

(d) The claimant left the employer's employ to protect his or her children or himself or herself from domestic violence abuse.

(e) The claimant left the employer's employ to take a substantially better job.

(f) The claimant's discharge or quitting from his or her most recent employer was the result of an irresistible compulsion to use or consume intoxicants including alcoholic beverages.

For purposes of this section and Section 1030 "spouse" includes a person to whom marriage is imminent.

* * *

SEC. 1252   When individual deemed "unemployed"

(a) An individual is "unemployed" in any week in which he or she meets any of the following conditions:

(1) Any week during which he or she performs no services and with respect to which no wages are payable to him or her.

(2) Any week of less than full-time work, if the wages payable to him or her with respect to the week, when reduced by twenty-five dollars ($25) or 25 percent of the wages payable, whichever is greater, do not equal or exceed his or her weekly benefit amount.

(3) Any week for which, except for the requirements of subdivision (d) of Section 1253, he or she would be eligible for benefits under Section 1253.5.

(4) Any week during which he or she performs full-time work for five days as a juror, or as a witness under subpoena.

(b) Authorized regulations shall be prescribed making such distinctions as may be necessary in the procedures applicable to unemployed individuals as to total unemployment, part-total employment, partial unemployment of individuals attached to their regular jobs, and other forms of short-time work.

(c) For the purpose of this section only "wages" includes any and all compensation for personal services whether performed as an employee or as an independent contractor or as a juror or as a witness, but does not include any payment received by a member of the National Guard or reserve component of the armed forces for inactive duty training, annual training, or emergency state active duty.

SEC. 1253.4 Eligibility of individual participating in sporting events

Unemployment compensation benefits, extended duration benefits, and federal-state extended benefits shall not be payable to any individual on the basis of any services, substantially all of which consist of participating in sports or athletic events or training or preparing to so participate, for any week which commences during the period between two successive sport seasons, or similar periods, if such individual performed such services in the first of such seasons, or similar periods, and there is a reasonable assurance that such individual will perform such services in the later of such seasons, or similar periods.

SEC. 1253.9 Student qualification for benefits

An unemployed individual may not be disqualified for unemployment compensation benefits solely on the basis that he or she is a student. An unemployed individual may be considered to be able and available for work pursuant to subdivision (c) of Section 1253, if the school attendance does not eliminate a substantial portion of the individual's full-time labor market availability. If an unemployed individual restricts his or her availability to part-time work due to school attendance, he or she may be considered to be able to work and available for work if he or she meets the criteria set forth in Section 1253.8.

SEC. 1255.5 Eligibility of individual during period in which benefits are allowed or received under workers' compensation or employers' liability laws

(a) An individual is not eligible for unemployment compensation benefits or extended duration benefits for the same day or days of unemployment for which he is allowed by the Workmen's Compensation Appeals Board, or for which he receives, benefits in the form of cash payments for temporary total disability indemnity, under a workmen's compensation law, or employer's liability law of this state, or of any other state, or of the federal government, except that if such cash

237

payments are less than the amount he would otherwise receive as unemployment compensation benefits or extended duration benefits under this division, he shall be entitled to receive for such day or days, if otherwise eligible, unemployment compensation benefits or extended duration benefits reduced by the amount of such cash payments.

(b) Notwithstanding any other provision of this division, an individual who is ineligible to receive unemployment compensation benefits or extended duration benefits under subdivision (a) of this section for one or more days of a week of unemployment and who is eligible to receive unemployment compensation benefits or extended duration benefits for the other days of that week is, with respect to that week, entitled to an amount of unemployment compensation benefits or extended duration benefits computed by reducing his weekly benefit amount by the amount of temporary total disability indemnity received for that week.

* * *

SEC. 1256 Disqualification by voluntary termination of employment without good cause or discharge for misconduct

An individual is disqualified for unemployment compensation benefits if the director finds that he or she left his or her most recent work voluntarily without good cause or that he or she has been discharged for misconduct connected with his or her most recent work.

An individual is presumed to have been discharged for reasons other than misconduct in connection with his or her work and not to have voluntarily left his or her work without good cause unless his or her employer has given written notice to the contrary to the department as provided in Section 1327, setting forth facts sufficient to overcome the presumption. The presumption provided by this section is rebuttable.

An individual whose employment is terminated under the compulsory retirement provisions of a collective bargaining agreement to which the employer is a party, shall not be deemed to have left his or her work without good cause.

An individual may be deemed to have left his or her most recent work with good cause if he or she leaves employment to accompany his or her spouse to a place from which it is impractical to commute to the employment. For purposes of this section, "spouse" includes a person to whom marriage is imminent.

An individual may be deemed to have left his or her most recent work with good cause if he or she leaves employment to protect his or her children, or himself or herself, from domestic violence abuse.

An individual shall be deemed to have left his or her most recent work with good cause if he or she elects to be laid off in place of an employee with less seniority pursuant to a provision in a collective bargaining agreement that provides that an employee with more seniority may elect to be laid off in place of an employee with less seniority when the employer has decided to lay off employees.

SEC. 1256.5   Disqualification based on use of intoxicants

(a) An individual is disqualified for unemployment compensation benefits if either of the following occur:

(1) The director finds that he or she was discharged from his or her most recent work for chronic absenteeism due to intoxication or reporting to work while intoxicated or using intoxicants on the job, or gross neglect of duty while intoxicated, when any of these incidents is caused by an irresistible compulsion to use or consume intoxicants, including alcoholic beverages.

(2) He or she otherwise left his or her most recent employment for reasons caused by an irresistible compulsion to use or consume intoxicants, including alcoholic beverages.

(b) An individual disqualified under this section, under a determination transmitted to him or her by the department, is ineligible to receive unemployment compensation benefits under this part for the week in which the separation occurs, and continuing until he or she has performed service in bona fide employment for which remuneration is received equal to or in excess of five times his or her weekly benefit amount, or until a physician or authorized treatment program administrator certifies that the individual has entered into and is continuing in, or has completed, a treatment program for his or her condition and is able to return to employment.

(c) The department shall advise each individual disqualified under this section of the benefits available under Part 2 (commencing with Section 2601), and, if assistance in locating an appropriate treatment program is requested, refer the individual to the appropriate county drug or alcohol program administrator.

SEC. 1256.7   Sexual harassment as good cause for leaving employment

An individual shall be deemed to have left his or her most recent work with good cause if the director finds that he or she leaves employment because of sexual harassment, provided the individual has taken reasonable steps to preserve the working relationship. No steps shall be required if the director finds it would have been futile. For purposes of this subdivision, unwelcome sexual advances, requests for sexual favors, and other verbal, visual, or physical conduct of a sexual nature constitutes sexual harassment when any of the following occur:

(1) Submission to the conduct is made either explicitly or implicitly a term or condition of an individual's employment.

(2) Submission to or rejection of the conduct by an individual is used as the basis for employment decisions affecting the individual.

(3) The conduct has the purpose or effect of unreasonably interfering with an individual's work performance or creating an intimidating, hostile, or offensive working environment.

Findings of fact and law by the director shall not collaterally estop adjudication of the issue of sexual harassment in another forum.

SEC. 1257   Disqualification by making false statement; withholding of material fact; failure or refusal to apply for or accept suitable employment

An individual is also disqualified for unemployment compensation benefits if:

(a) He or she willfully, for the purpose of obtaining unemployment compensation benefits, either made a false statement or representation, including, but not limited to, using a false name, false social security number, or other false identification, with actual knowledge of the falsity thereof, or withheld a material fact in order to obtain any unemployment compensation benefits under this division.

(b) He or she, without good cause, refused to accept suitable employment when offered to him or her, or failed to apply for suitable employment when notified by a public employment office.

SEC. 1258   What constitutes suitable employment; matters considered

"Suitable employment" means work in the individual's usual occupation or for which he is reasonably fitted, regardless of whether or not it is subject to this division.

In determining whether the work is work for which the individual is reasonably fitted, the director shall consider the degree of risk involved to the individual's health, safety, and morals, his physical fitness and prior training, his experience and prior earnings, his length of unemployment and prospects for securing local work in his customary occupation, and the distance of the available work from his residence, and such other factors as would influence a reasonably prudent person in the individual's circumstances.

SEC. 1258.5   Classes of employments deemed not suitable

"Suitable employment" does not include employment with an employer who does not:

(a) Possess an appropriate state license to engage in his business, trade, or profession; or

(b) Withhold or hold in trust the employee contributions required by Part 2 (commencing with Section 2601) of this division for unemployment compensation disability benefits and does not transmit all such employee contributions to the department for the Disability Fund as required by Section 986; or

(c) Carry either workers' compensation insurance or possess a certificate of self-insurance as required by Division 4 (commencing with Section 3201) of the Labor Code.

SEC. 1260 Period of ineligibility of statutorily disqualified persons

(a) An individual disqualified under Section 1256, under a determination transmitted to him by the department, is ineligible to receive unemployment compensation benefits for the week in which the act that causes his disqualification occurs and continuing until he has, subsequent to the act that causes disqualification and his registration for work, performed service in bona fide employment for which remuneration is received equal to or in excess of five times his weekly benefit amount.

(b) An individual disqualified under subdivision (b) of Section 1257, under a determination transmitted to him by the department, is ineligible to receive unemployment compensation benefits for not less than 2 nor more than 10 consecutive weeks beginning with:

(1) The week in which the cause of his disqualification occurs, if he registers for work in that week.

(2) The week subsequent to the occurrence of the cause of his disqualification in which he first registers for work, if he does not register for work in the week in which the cause of his disqualification occurs.

(c) An individual disqualified under subdivision (a) of Section 1257, under a determination transmitted to him or her by the department, and who was not paid any benefit amount as a result of his or her false statement or representation, is ineligible to receive unemployment compensation benefits for two weeks commencing with the week in which the determination is mailed to or personally served upon him or her, or any subsequent week, for which he or she is first otherwise in all respects eligible for unemployment compensation benefits and for not more than 13 subsequent weeks for which he or she is otherwise in all respects eligible for unemployment compensation benefits. No disqualification under this subdivision shall be applied to any week if all or any portion of the week is beyond the three-year period next succeeding the date of the mailing or personal service of the determination. This subdivision shall not apply to an individual convicted under Section 2101.

(d) An individual disqualified under subdivision (a) of Section 1257, under a determination transmitted to him or her by the department, and who was paid any benefit amount as a result of his or her false statement or representation, is ineligible to receive unemployment compensation benefits for five weeks commencing with the week in which the determination is mailed to or personally served upon him or her, or any subsequent week, for which he or she is first otherwise in all respects eligible for unemployment compensation benefits and for not more than 10 subsequent weeks for which he or she is otherwise in all respects eligible for unemployment compensation benefits. No disqualification under this subdivision shall be applied to any week if all or any portion of the week is beyond the three-year period next succeeding the date of the mailing or personal service of the determination. This subdivision shall not apply to an individual convicted under Section 2101.

(e) Notwithstanding subdivision (c) or (d), an individual who is subject to a disqualification that is imposed under subdivision (b) of Section 1257 may, if he or she is otherwise in all respects eligible for unemployment compensation benefits, concurrently serve a disqualification imposed under subdivision (a) of Section 1257.

SEC. 1260.1   Limitation as to denial of benefits cancellation of credits, or reduction of rights

Notwithstanding any other provision of this division, benefits shall not be denied to any individual by reason of cancellation of wage credits or total reduction of his benefit rights for any cause other than discharge for misconduct connected with his work, fraud in connection with a claim for benefits, or receipt of disqualifying income. This section shall not be construed to authorize cancellation of wage credits or total reduction of benefit rights for any cause whatsoever, nor shall it limit or affect any other section that provides for cancellation of wage credits or total reduction of benefit rights for any cause permitted under this section.

SEC. 1262   Eligibility of person leaving work because of trade dispute

An individual is not eligible for unemployment compensation benefits, and no such benefit shall be payable to him, if he left his work because of a trade dispute. Such individual shall remain ineligible for the period during which he continues out of work by reason of the fact that the trade dispute is still in active progress in the establishment in which he was employed.

Sec. 1279 Deduction of "wages" from benefit payments

(a) Each individual eligible under this chapter who is unemployed in any week shall be paid with respect to that week an unemployment compensation benefit in an amount equal to his or her weekly benefit amount less the smaller of the following:

(1) The amount of wages in excess of twenty-five dollars ($25) payable to him or her for services rendered during that week.

(2) The amount of wages in excess of 25 percent of the amount of wages payable to him or her for services rendered during that week.

(b) The benefit payment, if not a multiple of one dollar ($1), shall be computed to the next higher multiple of one dollar ($1).

(c) For the purpose of this section only "wages" includes any and all compensation for personal services whether performed as an employee or as an independent contractor or as a juror or as a witness, but does not include any payments, regardless of their designation, made by a city of this state to an elected official thereof as an incident to public office, nor any payment received by a member of the National Guard or reserve component of the armed forces for inactive duty training, annual training, or emergency state active duty.

WORKER ADJUSTMENT AND RETRAINING NOTIFICATION ACT

29 U.S.C. §§ 2101–2109

§ 2101. Definitions; exclusions from definition of loss of employment

(a) Definitions

As used in this Act—

(1) the term "employer" means any business enterprise that employs—

> **(A)** 100 or more employees, excluding part-time employees; or

> **(B)** 100 or more employees who in the aggregate work at least 4,000 hours per week (exclusive of hours of overtime);

(2) the term "plant closing" means the permanent or temporary shutdown of a single site of employment, or one or more facilities or operating units within a single site of employment, if the shutdown results in an employment loss at the single site of employment during any 30-day period for 50 or more employees excluding any part-time employees;

(3) the term "mass layoff" means a reduction in force which—

> **(A)** is not the result of a plant closing; and

> **(B)** results in an employment loss at the single site of employment during any 30-day period for—

>> **(i)(I)** at least 33 percent of the employees (excluding any part-time employees); and

>> **(II)** at least 50 employees (excluding any part-time employees); or

>> **(ii)** at least 500 employees (excluding any part-time employees);

(4) the term "representative" means an exclusive representative of employees within the meaning of section 9(a) or 8(f) of the National Labor Relations Act, section 152(f) or section 2 of the Railway Labor Act.

(5) the term "affected employees" means employees who may reasonably be expected to experience an employment loss as a consequence of a proposed plant closing or mass layoff by their employer;

(6) subject to subsection (b) of this section, the term "employment loss" means (A) an employment termination, other than a discharge for

244

cause, voluntary departure, or retirement, (B) a layoff exceeding 6 months, or (C) a reduction in hours of work of more than 50 percent during each month of any 6-month period;

(7) the term "unit of local government" means any general purpose political subdivision of a State which has the power to levy taxes and spend funds, as well as general corporate and police powers; and

(8) the term "part-time employee" means an employee who is employed for an average of fewer than 20 hours per week or who has been employed for fewer than 6 of the 12 months preceding the date on which notice is required.

(b) Exclusions from definition of employment loss

(1) In the case of a sale of part or all of an employer's business, the seller shall be responsible for providing notice for any plant closing or mass layoff in accordance with section 3 of the Act, up to and including the effective date of the sale. After the effective date of the sale of part or all of an employer's business, the purchaser shall be responsible for providing notice for any plant closing or mass layoff in accordance with section 3 of this Act. Notwithstanding any other provision of this Act, any person who is an employee of the seller (other than a part-time employee) as of the effective date of the sale shall be considered an employee of the purchaser immediately after the effective date of the sale.

(2) Notwithstanding subsection (a)(6) of this section, an employee may not be considered to have experienced an employment loss if the closing or layoff is the result of the relocation or consolidation of part or all of the employer's business and, prior to the closing or layoff—

(A) the employer offers to transfer the employee to a different site of employment within a reasonable commuting distance with no more than a 6-month break in employment; or

(B) the employer offers to transfer the employee to any other site of employment regardless of distance with no more than a 6-month break in employment, and the employee accepts within 30 days of the offer or of the closing or layoff, whichever is later.

§ 2102. Notice required before plant closings and mass layoffs

(a) Notice to employees, state dislocated worker units, and local governments

An employer shall not order a plant closing or mass layoff until the end of a 60-day period after the employer serves written notice of such an order—

(1) to each representative of the affected employees as of the time of the notice or, if there is no such representative at that time, to each affected employee; and

(2) to the State or entity designated by the State to carry out rapid response activities under section 134(a)(2)(A) of the Workforce Investment Act of 1998, and the chief elected official of the unit of local government within which such closing or layoff is to occur.

If there is more than one such unit, the unit of local government which the employer shall notify is the unit of local government to which the employer pays the highest taxes for the year preceding the year for which the determination is made.

(b) Reduction of notification period

(1) An employer may order the shutdown of a single site of employment before the conclusion of the 60-day period if as of the time that notice would have been required the employer was actively seeking capital or business which, if obtained, would have enabled the employer to avoid or postpone the shutdown and the employer reasonably and in good faith believed that giving the notice required would have precluded the employer from obtaining the needed capital or business.

(2)(A) An employer may order a plant closing or mass layoff before the conclusion of the 60-day period if the closing or mass layoff is caused by business circumstances that were not reasonably foreseeable as of the time that notice would have been required.

(B) No notice under this Act shall be required if the plant closing or mass layoff is due to any form of natural disaster, such as a flood, earthquake, or the drought currently ravaging the farmlands of the United States.

(3) An employer relying on this subsection shall give as much notice as is practicable and at that time shall give a brief statement of the basis for reducing the notification period.

(c) Extension of layoff period

A layoff of more than 6 months which, at its outset, was announced to be a layoff of 6 months or less, shall be treated as an employment loss under this Act unless—

(1) the extension beyond 6 months is caused by business circumstances (including unforeseeable changes in price or cost) not reasonably foreseeable at the time of the initial layoff; and

(2) notice is given at the time it becomes reasonably foreseeable that the extension beyond 6 months will be required.

(d) Determinations with respect to employment loss

For purposes of this section, in determining whether a plant closing or mass layoff has occurred or will occur, employment losses for 2 or more groups at a single site of employment, each of which is less than the minimum number of employees specified in section 2(a)(2) or (3) but which in the aggregate exceed that minimum number, and which occur within any 90-day period shall be considered to be a plant closing or mass layoff unless the employer demonstrates that the employment losses are the result of separate and distinct actions and causes and are not an attempt by the employer to evade the requirements of the Act.

§ 2103. Exemptions

This Act shall not apply to a plant closing or mass layoff if—

(1) the closing is of a temporary facility or the closing or layoff is the result of the completion of a particular project or undertaking, and the affected employees were hired with the understanding that their employment was limited to the duration of the facility or the project or undertaking; or

(2) the closing or layoff constitutes a strike or constitutes a lockout not intended to evade the requirements of this Act. Nothing in this Act shall require an employer to serve written notice pursuant to section 3(a) of this Act when permanently replacing a person who is deemed to be an economic striker under the National Labor Relations Act: Provided, That nothing in this Act shall be deemed to validate or invalidate any judicial or administrative ruling relating to the hiring of permanent replacements for economic strikers under the National Labor Relations Act.

§ 2104. Administration and enforcement of requirements

(a) Civil actions against employers

(1) Any employer who orders a plant closing or mass layoff in violation of section 3 of this Act shall be liable to each aggrieved employee who suffers an employment loss as a result of such closing or layoff for—

(A) back pay for each day of violation at a rate of compensation not less than the higher of—

(i) the average regular rate received by such employee during the last 3 years of the employee's employment; or

(ii) the final regular rate received by such employee; and

(B) benefits under an employee benefit plan described in section 3(3) of the Employee Retirement Income Security Act of 1974, including the cost of medical expenses incurred during the employment loss which would have been covered under an employee benefit plan if the employment loss had not occurred.

Such liability shall be calculated for the period of the violation, up to a maximum of 60 days, but in no event for more than one-half the number of days the employee was employed by the employer.

(2) The amount for which an employer is liable under paragraph (1) shall be reduced by—

(A) any wages paid by the employer to the employee for the period of the violation;

(B) any voluntary and unconditional payment by the employer to the employee that is not required by any legal obligation; and

(C) any payment by the employer to a third party or trustee (such as premiums for health benefits or payments to a defined contribution pension plan) on behalf of and attributable to the employee for the period of the violation.

In addition, any liability incurred under paragraph (1) with respect to a defined benefit pension plan may be reduced by crediting the employee with service for all purposes under such a plan for the period of the violation.

(3) Any employer who violates the provisions of section 3 with respect to a unit of local government shall be subject to a civil penalty of not more than $500 for each day of such violation, except that such penalty shall not apply if the employer pays to each aggrieved employee the amount for which the employer is liable to that employee within 3 weeks from the date the employer orders the shutdown or layoff.

(4) If an employer which has violated this chapter proves to the satisfaction of the court that the act or omission that violated this chapter was in good faith and that the employer had reasonable grounds for believing that the act or omission was not a violation of this chapter the court may, in its discretion, reduce the amount of the liability or penalty provided for in this section.

(5) A person seeking to enforce such liability, including a representative of employees or a unit of local government aggrieved under paragraph (1) or (3), may sue either for such person or for other persons similarly situated, or both, in any district court of the United States for any district in which the violation is alleged to have occurred, or in which the employer transacts business.

(6) In any such suit, the court, in its discretion, may allow the prevailing party a reasonable attorney's fee as part of the costs.

(7) For purposes of this subsection, the term, "aggrieved employee" means an employee who has worked for the employer ordering the plant closing or mass layoff and who, as a result of the failure by the employer to comply with section 2102 of this title did not receive timely notice either directly or through his or her representative as required by section 3.

(b) Exclusivity of remedies

The remedies provided for in this section shall be the exclusive remedies for any violation of this Act. Under this Act, a Federal court shall not have authority to enjoin a plant closing or mass layoff.

§ 2105. Procedures in addition to other rights of employees

The rights and remedies provided to employees by this Act are in addition to, and not in lieu of, any other contractual or statutory rights and remedies of the employees, and are not intended to alter or affect such rights and remedies, except that the period of notification required by this chapter shall run concurrently with any period of notification required by contract or by any other statute.

§ 2106. Procedures encouraged where not required

It is the sense of Congress that an employer who is not required to comply with the notice requirements of section 3 of this Act should, to the extent possible, provide notice to its employees about a proposal to close a plant or permanently reduce its workforce.

§ 2107. Authority to prescribe regulations

(a) The Secretary of Labor shall prescribe such regulations as may be necessary to carry out this Act. Such regulations shall, at a minimum, include interpretative regulations describing the methods by which employers may provide for appropriate service of notice as required by this chapter.

(b) The mailing of notice to an employee's last known address or inclusion of notice in the employee's paycheck will be considered acceptable methods for fulfillment of the employer's obligation to give notice to each affected employee under this Act.

§ 2108. Effect on other laws

The giving of notice pursuant to this Act, if done in good faith compliance with this Act, shall not constitute a violation of the National Labor Relations Act or the Railway Labor Act.

§ 2109. Report on employment and international competitiveness

Two years after the date of enactment of this Act, the Comptroller General shall submit to the Committee on Small Business of both the House and Senate, the Committee on Labor and Human Resources, and the Committee on Education and Labor a report containing a detailed and objective analysis of the effect of this Act on employers (especially small- and medium-sized businesses), the economy (international competitiveness), and employees (in terms of levels and conditions of employment). The Comptroller General shall assess both costs and benefits, including the effect on productivity, competitiveness, unemployment rates and compensation, and worker retraining and readjustment.

BANKRUPTCY ACT

11 U.S.C. §§ 101–1330, 1501, 15101–151326

Sec. 362 Automatic stay

* * *

(b) The filing of a petition under section 301, 302, or 303 of this title, or of an application under section 5(a)(3) of the Securities Investor Protection Act of 1970 (15 U.S.C. 78eee(a)(3)), does not operate as a stay—

* * *

(4) under paragraph (1), (2), (3), or (6) of subsection (a) of this section, of the commencement or continuation of an action or proceeding by a governmental unit or any organization exercising authority under the Convention on the Prohibition of the Development, Production, Stockpiling and Use of Chemical Weapons and on Their Destruction, opened for signature on January 13, 1993, to enforce such governmental unit's or organization's police and regulatory power, including the enforcement of a judgment other than a money judgment, obtained in an action or proceeding by the governmental unit to enforce such governmental unit's or organization's police or regulatory power;

Sec. 503 Allowance of administrative expenses

(a) An entity may timely file a request for payment of an administrative expense, or may tardily file such request if permitted by the court for cause.

(b) After notice and a hearing, there shall be allowed, administrative expenses, other than claims allowed under section 502(f) of this title, including—

(1)(A) the actual, necessary costs and expenses of preserving the estate, including wages, salaries, or commissions for services rendered after the commencement of the case;

* * *

Sec. 507 Priorities

(a) The following expenses and claims have priority in the following order:

(1) First, administrative expenses allowed under section 503(b) of this title, and any fees and charges assessed against the estate under chapter 123 of title 28.

(2) Second, unsecured claims allowed under section 502(f) of this title.

(3) Third, allowed unsecured claims for wages, salaries, or commissions, including vacation, severance and sick leave pay—

    (A) earned by an individual within 90 days before the date of the filing of the petition or the date of the cessation of the debtor's business, whichever occurs first; but only

    (B) to the extent of $2,000 for each such individual.

(4) Fourth, allowed unsecured claims for contributions to an employee benefit

    (A) arising from services rendered within 180 days before the date of the filing of the petition or the date of the cessation of the debtor's business, whichever occurs first; but only

    (B) for each such plan, to the extent of—

        (i) the number of employees covered by such plan multiplied by $2,000; less

        (ii) the aggregate amount paid to such employees under paragraph (3) of this subsection, plus the aggregate amount paid by the estate on behalf of such employees to any other employee benefit plan.

* * *

(7) Seventh, allowed unsecured claims of governmental units, only to the extent that such claims are for—

* * *

    (D) an employment tax on a wage, salary, or commission of a kind specified in paragraph (3) of this subsection earned from the debtor before the date of the filing of the petition, whether or not actually paid before such date, for which a return is last due, under applicable law or under any extension, after three years before the date of the filing of the petition;

* * *

SEC. 1113 Rejection of collective bargaining agreements

(a) The debtor in possession, or the trustee if one has been appointed under the provisions of this chapter, * * * may assume or reject a collective bargaining agreement only in accordance with the provisions of this section.

(b)(1) Subsequent to filing a petition and prior to filing an application seeking rejection of a collective bargaining agreement, the debtor in possession or trustee (hereinafter in this section "trustee" shall include a debtor in possession), shall—

> (A) make a proposal to the authorized representative of the employees covered by such agreement, based on the most complete and reliable information available at the time of such proposal, which provides for those necessary modifications in the employees benefits and protections that are necessary to permit the reorganization of the debtor and assures that all creditors, the debtor and all of the affected parties are treated fairly and equitably; and

> (B) provide, subject to subsection (d)(3), the representative of the employees with such relevant information as is necessary to evaluate the proposal.

(2) During the period beginning on the date of the making of a proposal provided for in paragraph (1) and ending on the date of the hearing provided for in subsection (d)(1), the trustee shall meet, at reasonable times, with the authorized representative to confer in good faith in attempting to reach mutually satisfactory modifications of such agreement.

(c) The court shall approve an application for rejection of a collective bargaining agreement only if the court finds that—

> (1) the trustee has, prior to the hearing, made a proposal that fulfills the requirements of subsection (b)(1);

> (2) the authorized representative of the employees has refused to accept such proposal without good cause; and

> (3) the balance of the equities clearly favors rejection of such agreement.

* * *

(d) * * *

(3) The court may enter such protective orders, consistent with the need of the authorized representative of the employee to evaluate the trustee's proposal and the application for rejection, as may be necessary to prevent disclosure of information provided to such representative where such disclosure could compromise the position of the debtor with respect to its competitors in the industry in which it is engaged.

(e) If during a period when the collective bargaining agreement continues in effect, and if essential to the continuation of the debtor's business, or in order to avoid irreparable damage to the estate, the court, after notice and a hearing, may authorize the trustee to implement interim changes in the terms, conditions, wages, benefits, or work rules provided by a collective bargaining agreement. Any hearing under this paragraph shall be scheduled in accordance with the needs of the trustee. The implementation of such interim changes shall not render the application for rejection moot.

(f) No provision of this title shall be construed to permit a trustee to unilaterally terminate or alter any provisions of a collective bargaining agreement prior to compliance with the provisions of this section.

SEC. 1114   **Payment of insurance benefits to retired employees**

(a) For purposes of this section, the term "retiree benefits" means payments to any entity or person for the purpose of providing or reimbursing payments for retired employees and their spouses and dependents, for medical, surgical, or hospital care benefits, or benefits in the event of sickness, accident, disability, or death under any plan, fund, or program (through the purchase of insurance or otherwise) maintained or established in whole or in part by the debtor prior to filing a petition commencing a case under this title.

(b)(1) For purposes of this section, the term "authorized representative" means the authorized representative designated pursuant to subsection (c) for persons receiving any retiree benefits covered by a collective bargaining agreement or subsection (d) in the case of persons receiving retiree benefits not covered by such an agreement.

(2) Committees of retired employees appointed by the court pursuant to this section shall have the same rights, powers, and duties as committees appointed under sections 1102 and 1103 of this title for the purpose of carrying out the purposes of sections 1114 and 1129 (a)(13) and, as permitted by the court, shall have the power to enforce the rights of persons under this title as they relate to retiree benefits.

(c)(1) A labor organization shall be, for purposes of this section, the authorized representative of those persons receiving any retiree benefits covered by any collective bargaining agreement to which that labor organization is signatory, unless (A) such labor organization elects not to serve as the authorized representative of such persons, or (B) the court, upon a motion by any party in interest, after notice and hearing, determines that different representation of such persons is appropriate.

(2) In cases where the labor organization referred to in paragraph (1) elects not to serve as the authorized representative of those persons receiving any retiree benefits covered by any collective bargaining agreement to which that labor organization is signatory, or in cases where the

court, pursuant to paragraph (1) finds different representation of such persons appropriate, the court, upon a motion by any party in interest, and after notice and a hearing, shall appoint a committee of retired employees if the debtor seeks to modify or not pay the retiree benefits or if the court otherwise determines that it is appropriate, from among such persons, to serve as the authorized representative of such persons under this section.

(d) The court, upon a motion by any party in interest, and after notice and a hearing, shall appoint a committee of retired employees if the debtor seeks to modify or not pay the retiree benefits or if the court otherwise determines that it is appropriate, to serve as the authorized representative, under this section, of those persons receiving any retiree benefits not covered by a collective bargaining agreement.

(e)(1) Notwithstanding any other provision of this title, the debtor in possession, or the trustee if one has been appointed under the provisions of this chapter (hereinafter in this section "trustee" shall include a debtor in possession), shall timely pay and shall not modify any retiree benefits, except that—

(A) the court, on motion of the trustee or authorized representative, and after notice and a hearing, may order modification of such payments, pursuant to the provisions of subsections (g) and (h) of this section, or

(B) the trustee and the authorized representative of the recipients of those benefits may agree to modification of such payments,

after which such benefits as modified shall continue to be paid by the trustee.

(2) Any payment for retiree benefits required to be made before a plan confirmed under section 1129 of this title is effective has the status of an allowed administrative expense as provided in section 503 of this title.

(f)(1) Subsequent to filing a petition and prior to filing an application seeking modification of the retiree benefits, the trustee shall—

(A) make a proposal to the authorized representative of the retirees, based on the most complete and reliable information available at the time of such proposal, which provides for those necessary modifications in the retiree benefits that are necessary to permit the reorganization of the debtor and assures that all creditors, the debtor and all of the affected parties are treated fairly and equitably; and

(B) provide, subject to subsection (k)(3), the representative of the retirees with such relevant information as is necessary to evaluate the proposal.

255

(2) During the period beginning on the date of the making of a proposal provided for in paragraph (1), and ending on the date of the hearing provided for in subsection (k)(1), the trustee shall meet, at reasonable times, with the authorized representative to confer in good faith in attempting to reach mutually satisfactory modifications of such retiree benefits.

(g) The court shall enter an order providing for modification in the payment of retiree benefits if the court finds that—

(1) the trustee has, prior to the hearing, made a proposal that fulfills the requirements of subsection (f);

(2) the authorized representative of the retirees has refused to accept such proposal without good cause; and

(3) such modification is necessary to permit the reorganization of the debtor and assures that all creditors, the debtor, and all of the affected parties are treated fairly and equitably, and is clearly favored by the balance of the equities;

except that in no case shall the court enter an order providing for such modification which provides for a modification to a level lower than that proposed by the trustee in the proposal found by the court to have complied with the requirements of this subsection and subsection (f): *Provided, however*, That at any time after an order is entered providing for modification in the payment of retiree benefits, or at any time after an agreement modifying such benefits is made between the trustee and the authorized representative of the recipients of such benefits, the authorized representative may apply to the court for an order increasing those benefits which order shall be granted if the increase in retiree benefits sought is consistent with the standard set forth in paragraph (3): *Provided further*, That neither the trustee nor the authorized representative is precluded from making more than one motion for a modification order governed by this subsection.

(h)(1) Prior to a court issuing a final order under subsection (g) of this section, if essential to the continuation of the debtor's business, or in order to avoid irreparable damage to the estate, the court, after notice and a hearing, may authorize the trustee to implement interim modifications in retiree benefits.

(2) Any hearing under this subsection shall be scheduled in accordance with the needs of the trustee.

(3) The implementation of such interim changes does not render the motion for modification moot.

(i) No retiree benefits paid between the filing of the petition and the time a plan confirmed under section 1129 of this title becomes effective shall be deducted or offset from the amounts allowed as claims for any benefits which remain unpaid, or from the amounts to be paid under the plan with respect to such claims for unpaid benefits, whether such claims for unpaid benefits are based upon or arise from a right to future unpaid benefits or from any benefits not paid as a result of modifications allowed pursuant to this section.

(j) No claim for retiree benefits shall be limited by section 502(b)(7) of this title.

(k)(1) Upon the filing of an application for modifying retiree benefits, the court shall schedule a hearing to be held not later than fourteen days after the date of the filing of such application. All interested parties may appear and be heard at such hearing. Adequate notice shall be provided to such parties at least ten days before the date of such hearing. The court may extend the time for the commencement of such hearing for a period not exceeding seven days where the circumstances of the case, and the interests of justice require such extension, or for additional periods of time to which the trustee and the authorized representative agree.

(2) The court shall rule on such application for modification within ninety days after the date of the commencement of the hearing. In the interests of justice, the court may extend such time for ruling for such additional period as the trustee and the authorized representative may agree to. If the court does not rule on such application within ninety days after the date of the commencement of the hearing, or within such additional time as the trustee and the authorized representative may agree to, the trustee may implement the proposed modifications pending the ruling of the court on such application.

(3) The court may enter such protective orders, consistent with the need of the authorized representative of the retirees to evaluate the trustee's proposal and the application for modification, as may be necessary to prevent disclosure of information provided to such representative where such disclosure could compromise the position of the debtor with respect to its competitors in the industry in which it is engaged.

(*l*) This section shall not apply to any retiree, or the spouse or dependents of such retiree, if such retiree's gross income for the twelve months preceding the filing of the bankruptcy petition equals or exceeds $250,000, unless such retiree can demonstrate to the satisfaction of the court that he is unable to obtain health, medical, life, and disability coverage for himself, his spouse, and his dependents who would otherwise be covered by the employer's insurance plan, comparable to the coverage provided by the employer on the day before the filing of a petition under this title.

Sec. 1123 Contents of plan

* * *

(b) Subject to subsection (a) of this section, a plan may—

* * *

(4) provide for the sale of all or substantially all of the property of the estate, and the distribution of the proceeds of such sale among holders of claims or interests; * * *

Sec. 1129 Confirmation of plan

(a) The court shall confirm a plan only if all of the following requirements are met:

* * *

(13) The plan provides for the continuation after its effective date of payment of all retiree benefits, as that term is defined in section 1114 of this title, at the level established pursuant to subsection (e)(1)(B) or (g) of section 1114 of this title, at any time prior to confirmation of the plan, for the duration of the period the debtor has obligated itself to provide such benefits.

* * *

(2) afford a reasonable opportunity to any participant whose claim for benefits has been denied for a full and fair review by the appropriate named fiduciary of the decision denying the claim. * * *

Sec. 1140 Interference with protected rights

It shall be unlawful for any person to discharge, fine, suspend, expel, discipline, or discriminate against a participant or beneficiary for exercising any right to which he is entitled under the provisions of an employee benefit plan, this title, section 1201, or the Welfare and Pension Plans Disclosure Act, or for the purpose of interfering with the attainment of any right to which such participant may become entitled under the plan, this title, or the Welfare and Pension Plans Disclosure Act. It shall be unlawful for any person to discharge, fine, suspend, expel, or discriminate against any person because he has given information or has testified or is about to testify in any inquiry or proceeding relating to this Act or the Welfare and Pension Plans Disclosure Act. The provisions of section 1132 shall be applicable in the enforcement of this section.

PENSION LAW

(A provision of the Labor Management Relations Act)
29 U.S.C. § 186

SEC. 186 Restrictions on financial transactions

Payment or lending, etc., of money by employer or agent to employees, representatives, or labor organizations

(a) It shall be unlawful for any employer or association of employers * * * to pay, lend, or deliver, or agree to pay, lend, or deliver, any money or other thing of value—

(1) to any representative of any of his employees who are employed in an industry affecting commerce; or

(2) to any labor organization, or any officer or employee thereof, which represents, seeks to represent, or would admit to membership, any of the employees of such employer who are employed in an industry affecting commerce; * * *

* * *

(c) Exceptions

The provisions of this section shall not be applicable * * * (5) with respect to money or other thing of value paid to a trust fund established by such representative, for the sole and exclusive benefit of the employees of such employer, and their families and dependents (or of such employees, families, and dependents jointly with the employees of other employers making similar payments, and their families and dependents); *Provided,* That (A) such payments are held in trust for the purpose of paying, either from principal or income or both, for the benefit of employees, their families and dependents, for medical or hospital care, pensions on retirement or death of employees, compensation for injuries or illness resulting from occupational activity or insurance to provide any of the foregoing, or unemployment benefits or life insurance, disability and sickness insurance, or accident insurance; (B) the detailed basis on which such payments are to be made is specified in a written agreement with the employer, and employees and employers are equally represented in the administration of such fund, together with such neutral persons as the representatives of the employers and the representatives of employees may agree upon * * * and (C) such payments as are intended to be used for the purpose of providing pensions or annuities for employees are made to a separate trust which provides that the funds held therein cannot be used for any purpose other than paying such pensions or annuities; * * *

259

EMPLOYEE RETIREMENT INCOME SECURITY ACT

29 U.S.C. §§ 1001–1461

SUBTITLE A—GENERAL PROVISIONS

SEC. 1001 Congressional findings and declaration of policy

(a) Benefit plans as affecting interstate commerce and the Federal taxing power

The Congress finds that the growth in size, scope, and numbers of employee benefit plans in recent years has been rapid and substantial; that the operational scope and economic impact of such plans is increasingly interstate; that the continued well-being and security of millions of employees and their dependents are directly affected by these plans; that they are affected with a national public interest; that they have become an important factor affecting the stability of employment and the successful development of industrial relations; that they have become an important factor in commerce because of the interstate character of their activities, and of the activities of their participants, and the employers, employee organizations, and other entities by which they are established or maintained; that a large volume of the activities of such plans is carried on by means of the mails and instrumentalities of interstate commerce; that owing to the lack of employee information and adequate safeguards concerning their operation, it is desirable in the interests of employees and their beneficiaries, and to provide for the general welfare and the free flow of commerce, that disclosure be made and safeguards be provided with respect to the establishment, operation, and administration of such plans; that they substantially affect the revenues of the United States because they are afforded preferential Federal tax treatment; that despite the enormous growth in such plans many employees with long years of employment are losing anticipated retirement benefits owing to the lack of vesting provisions in such plans; that owing to the inadequacy of current minimum standards, the soundness and stability of plans with respect to adequate funds to pay promised benefits may be endangered; that owing to the termination of plans before requisite funds have been accumulated, employees and their beneficiaries have been deprived of anticipated benefits; and that it is therefore desirable in the interests of employees and their beneficiaries, for the protection of the revenue of the United States, and to provide for the free flow of commerce, that minimum standards be provided assuring the equitable character of such plans and their financial soundness.

(b) Protection of interstate commerce and beneficiaries by requiring disclosure and reporting, setting standards of conduct, etc., for fiduciaries

It is hereby declared to be the policy of this Act to protect interstate commerce and the interests of participants in employee benefit plans and their beneficiaries, by requiring the disclosure and reporting to participants and beneficiaries of financial and other information with respect thereto, by establishing standards of conduct, responsibility, and obligation for fiduciaries of employee benefit plans, and by providing for appropriate remedies, sanctions, and ready access to the Federal courts.

(c) Protection of interstate commerce, the Federal taxing power, and beneficiaries by vesting of accrued benefits, setting minimum standards of funding, requiring termination insurance

It is hereby further declared to be the policy of this Act to protect interstate commerce, the Federal taxing power, and the interests of participants in private pension plans and their beneficiaries by improving the equitable character and the soundness of such plans by requiring them to vest the accrued benefits of employees with significant periods of service, to meet minimum standards of funding, and by requiring plan termination insurance.

SEC. 1002 Definitions

For purposes of this title:

(1) The terms "employee welfare benefit plan" and "welfare plan" mean any plan, fund, or program which was heretofore or is hereafter established or maintained by an employer or by an employee organization, or by both, to the extent that such plan, fund, or program was established or is maintained for the purpose of providing for its participants or their beneficiaries, through the purchase of insurance or otherwise, (A) medical, surgical, or hospital care or benefits, or benefits in the event of sickness, accident, disability, death or unemployment, or vacation benefits, apprenticeship or other training programs, or day care centers, scholarship funds, or prepaid legal services, or (B) any benefit described in section 302(c) of the Labor Management Relations Act, 1947 (other than pensions on retirement or death, and insurance to provide such pensions).

(2)(A) Except as provided in subparagraph (B), the terms "employee pension benefit plan" and "pension plan" mean any plan, fund, or program which was heretofore or is hereafter established or maintained by an employer or by an employee organization, or by both, to the extent that by its express terms or as a result of surrounding circumstances such plan, fund, or program—

(i) provides retirement income to employees, or

(ii) results in a deferral of income by employees for periods extending to the termination of covered employment or beyond,

regardless of the method of calculating the contributions made to the plan, the method of calculating the benefits under the plan or the method of distributing benefits from the plan.

(B) The Secretary may by regulation prescribe rules consistent with the standards and purposes of this Act providing one or more exempt categories under which—

(i) severance pay arrangements, and

(ii) supplemental retirement income payments, under which the pension benefits of retirees or their beneficiaries are supplemented to take into account some portion or all of the increases in the cost of living (as determined by the Secretary of Labor) since retirement,

shall, for purposes of this title, be treated as welfare plans rather than pension plans. In the case of any arrangement or payment a principal effect of which is the evasion of the standards or purposes of this Act applicable to pension plans, such arrangement or payment shall be treated as a pension plan.

(3) The term "employee benefit plan" or "plan" means an employee welfare benefit plan or an employee pension benefit plan or a plan which is both an employee welfare benefit plan and an employee pension benefit plan. * * *

* * *

(21)(A) Except as otherwise provided in subparagraph (B), a person is a fiduciary with respect to a plan to the extent (i) he exercises any discretionary authority or discretionary control respecting management of such plan or exercises any authority or control respecting management or disposition of its assets, (ii) he renders investment advice for a fee or other compensation, direct or indirect, with respect to any moneys or other property of such plan, or has any authority or responsibility to do so, or (iii) he has any discretionary authority or discretionary responsibility in the administration of such plan. Such term includes any person designated under section 405(c)(1)(B).

(B) If any money or other property of an employee benefit plan is invested in securities issued by an investment company registered under the Investment Company Act of 1940, such investment shall not by itself cause such investment company or such investment company's investment adviser or principal underwriter to be deemed to be a fiduciary or a party in interest as those terms are defined in this subchapter, except insofar as such investment company or its investment adviser or principal underwriter acts in connection with an employee benefit plan covering employees of the investment company, the investment adviser, or its principal underwriter. Nothing contained in this subparagraph shall limit the duties imposed on such investment company, investment adviser, or principal underwriter by any other law.

Sec. 1003 Coverage

(a) * * * [T]his title shall apply to any employee benefit plan if it is established or maintained—

(1) by any employer engaged in commerce or in any industry or activity affecting commerce; or

(2) by any employee organization or organizations representing employees engaged in commerce or in any industry or activity affecting commerce; or

(3) by both.

(b) The provisions of this subchapter shall not apply to any employee benefit plan if—

(1) such plan is a governmental plan * * *;

(2) such plan is a church plan * * *;

(3) such plan is maintained solely for the purpose of complying with applicable workmen's compensation laws or unemployment compensation or disability insurance laws;

(4) such plan is maintained outside of the United States primarily for the benefit of persons substantially all of whom are nonresident aliens; or

(5) such plan is an excess benefit plan.

* * *

Sec. 1021 Duty of disclosure and reporting

(a) Summary plan description and information to be furnished to participants and beneficiaries

The administrator of each employee benefit plan shall cause to be furnished in accordance with section 104(b) to each participant covered under the plan and to each beneficiary who is receiving benefits under the plan—

(1) a summary plan description described in section 102(a)(1) of this title; and

(2) the information described in sections 104(b)(3) and 105(a) and (c).

(b) Plan description, modifications and changes, and reports to be filed with Secretary of Labor

The administrator shall, in accordance with section 104(a), file with the Secretary—

(1) the summary plan description described in section 102(a)(1) of this title;

(2) a plan description containing the matter required in section 102(b) of this title.

(c) Terminal and supplementary reports

(1) Each administrator of an employee pension benefit plan which is winding up its affairs (without regard to the number of participants remaining in the plan) shall, in accordance with regulations prescribed by the Secretary, file such terminal reports as the Secretary may consider necessary. A copy of such report shall also be filed with the Pension Benefit Guaranty Corporation.

(2) The Secretary may require terminal reports to be filed with regard to any employee welfare benefit plan which is winding up its affairs in accordance with regulations promulgated by the Secretary.

* * *

(d) Notice of failure to meet minimum funding standards

(1) In general. If an employer maintaining a plan other than a multiemployer plan fails to make a required installment or other payment required to meet the minimum funding standard under section 302 to a plan before the 60th day following the due date for such installment or other payment, the employer shall notify each participant and beneficiary (including an alternate payee as defined in section 206(d)(3)(K) of this title) of such plan of such failure. Such notice shall be made at such time and in such manner as the Secretary may prescribe.

(2) Subsection not to apply if waiver pending. This subsection shall not apply to any failure if the employer has filed a waiver request under section 303 with respect to the plan year to which, the

required installment relates, except that if the waiver request is denied, notice under paragraph (1) shall be provided within 60 days after the date of such denial.

(3) Definitions. For purposes of this subsection, the terms "required installment" and "due date" have the same meanings given such terms by section 302(e).

* * *

SEC. 1025 Reporting of participant's benefit rights

(a) Statement furnished by administrator to participants and beneficiaries.

Each administrator of an employee pension benefit plan shall furnish to any plan participant or beneficiary who so requests in writing, a statement indicating, on the basis of the latest available information—

(1) the total benefits accrued, and

(2) the nonforfeitable pension benefits, if any, which have accrued, or the earliest date on which benefits will become nonforfeitable.

(b) One-per-year limit on reports

In no case shall a participant or beneficiary be entitled under this section to receive more than one report described in subsection (a) of this section during any one 12-month period.

(c) Individual statement furnished by administrator to participants setting forth information in administrator's Internal Revenue registration statement and notification of forfeitable benefits.

Each administrator required to register under section 6057 of the Internal Revenue Code of 1986 shall, before the expiration of the time prescribed for such registration, furnish to each participant described in subsection (a)(2)(C) of such section, an individual statement setting forth the information with respect to such participant required to be contained in the registration statement required by section 6057(a)(2) of such Code. Such statement shall also include a notice to the participant of any benefits which are forfeitable if the participant dies before a certain date.

(d) Plans to which more than one unaffiliated employer is required to contribute; regulations

Subsection (a) of this section shall apply to a plan to which more than one unaffiliated employer is required to contribute only to the extent provided in regulations prescribed by the Secretary in coordination with the Secretary of the Treasury.

* * *

SEC. 1052 Minimum participation standards

(a)(1)(A) No pension plan may require, as a condition of participation in the plan, that an employee complete a period of service with the employer or employers maintaining the plan extending beyond the later of the following dates—

   (i) the date on which the employee attains the age of 21; or

   (ii) the date on which he completes 1 year of service.

(B)(i) In the case of any plan which provides that after not more than 2 years of service each participant has a right to 100 percent of his accrued benefit under the plan which is nonforfeitable at the time such benefit accrues, clause (ii) of subparagraph (A) shall be applied by substituting "2 years of service" for "1 year of service".

* * *

SEC. 1053 Minimum vesting standards

(a) Nonforfeitability requirements

Each pension plan shall provide that an employee's right to his normal retirement benefit is nonforfeitable upon the attainment of normal retirement age and in addition shall satisfy the requirements of paragraphs (1) and (2) of this subsection.

   (1) A plan satisfies the requirements of this paragraph if an employee's rights in his accrued benefit derived from his own contributions are nonforfeitable.

   (2) Except as provided in paragraph (4), a plan satisfies the requirements of this paragraph if it satisfies the requirements of subparagraph (A) or (B).

      (A) A plan satisfies the requirements of this subparagraph if an employee who has completed at least 5 years of service has a nonforfeitable right to 100 percent of the employee's accrued benefit derived from employer contributions.

      (B) A plan satisfies the requirements of this subparagraph if an employee has a nonforfeitable right to a percentage of the employee's accrued benefit derived from employer contributions determined under the following table:

Years of service:	The nonforfeitable percentage is:
3	20
4	40
5	60
6	80
7 or more	100.

(C) A plan satisfies the requirements of this subparagraph if—

(i) the plan is a multiemployer plan (within the meaning of section 3(37)), and

(ii) under the plan—

(I) an employee who is covered pursuant to a collective bargaining agreement described in section 1002(37)(A)(ii) of this title and who has completed at least 10 years of service has a nonforfeitable right to 100 percent of the employee's accrued benefit derived from employer contributions.

* * *

Sec. 1054 Benefit accrual requirements

(a) Satisfaction of requirements by pension plans

Each pension plan shall satisfy the requirements of subsection (b)(3), and—

(1) in the case of a defined benefit plan, shall satisfy the requirements of subsection (b)(1) of this section; and

(2) in the case of a defined contribution plan, shall satisfy the requirements of subsection (b)(2) of this section.

(b) Enumeration of plan requirements

(1)(A) A defined benefit plan satisfies the requirements of this paragraph if the accrued benefit to which each participant is entitled upon his separation from the service is not less than—

(i) 3 percent of the normal retirement benefit to which he would be entitled at the normal retirement age if he commenced participation at the earliest possible entry age under the plan and served continuously until the earlier of age 65 or the normal retirement age specified under the plan, multiplied by

(ii) the number of years (not in excess of 33 ⅓) of his participation in the plan.

In the case of a plan providing retirement benefits based on compensation during any period, the normal retirement benefit to which a participant would be entitled shall be determined as if he continued to earn annually the average rate of compensation which he earned during consecutive years of service, not in excess of 10, for which his compensation was the highest. For purposes of this subparagraph, social security benefits and all other relevant factors used to compute benefits shall be treated as remaining constant as of the current year for all years after such current year.

* * *

(2)(A) A defined contribution plan satisfies the requirements of this paragraph if, under the plan, allocations to the employee's account are not ceased, and the rate at which amounts are allocated to the employee's account is not reduced, because of the attainment of any age.

(B) A plan shall not be treated as failing to meet the requirements of subparagraph (A) solely because the subsidized portion of any early retirement benefit is disregarded in determining benefit accruals.

* * *

Sec. 1056   Form and payment of benefits

(a) Commencement date for payment of benefits

Each pension plan shall provide that unless the participant otherwise elects, the payment of benefits under the plan to the participant shall begin not later than the 60th day after the latest of the close of the plan year in which—

> (1) the date on which the participant attains the earlier of age 65 or the normal retirement age specified under the plan,

> (2) occurs the 10th anniversary of the year in which the participant commenced participation in the plan, or

> (3) the participant terminates his service with the employer.

In the case of a plan which provides for the payment of an early retirement benefit, such plan shall provide that a participant who satisfied the service requirements for such early retirement benefit, but separated from the service (with any nonforfeitable right to an accrued benefit) before satisfying the age requirement for such early retirement benefit, is entitled upon satisfaction of such age requirement to receive a benefit not less than the benefit to which he would be entitled at the normal retirement age, actuarially reduced under regulations prescribed by the Secretary of the Treasury.

(b) Decrease in plan benefits by reason of increases in benefit levels under Social Security Act or Railroad Retirement Act of 1937

If—

(1) a participant or beneficiary is receiving benefits under a pension plan, or

(2) a participant is separated from the service and has nonforfeitable rights to benefits,

a plan may not decrease benefits of such a participant by reason of any increase in the benefit levels payable under title II of the Social Security Act or the Railroad Retirement Act of 1937, or any increase in the wage base under such title II, if such increase takes place after the date of the enactment of this Act, or (if later) the earlier of the date of first entitlement of such benefits or the date of such separation.

(c) Forfeiture of accrued benefits derived from employer contributions

No pension plan may provide that any part of a participant's accrued benefit derived from employer contributions (whether or not otherwise nonforfeitable) is forfeitable solely because of withdrawal by such participant of any amount attributable to the benefit derived from contributions made by such participant. The preceding sentence shall not apply (1) to the accrued benefit of any participant unless, at the time of such withdrawal, such participant has a nonforfeitable right to at least 50 percent of such accrued benefit, or (2) to the extent that an accrued benefit is permitted to be forfeited in accordance with section 203(a)(3)(D)(iii).

(d) Assignment or alienation of plan benefits

(1) Each pension plan shall provide that benefits provided under the plan may not be assigned or alienated.

(2) For the purposes of paragraph (1) of this subsection, there shall not be taken into account any voluntary and revocable assignment of not to exceed 10 percent of any benefit payment, or of any irrevocable assignment or alienation of benefits executed before the date of the enactment of this Act. The preceding sentence shall not apply to any assignment or alienation made for the purposes of defraying plan administration costs. For purposes of this paragraph a loan made to a participant or beneficiary shall not be treated as an assignment or alienation if such loan is secured by the participant's accrued nonforfeitable benefit and is exempt from the tax imposed by section 4975 of the Internal Revenue Code of 1986 (relating to tax on prohibited transactions) by reason of section 4975(d)(1) of such code.

(3)(A) Paragraph (1) shall apply to the creation, assignment, or recognition of a right to any benefit payable with respect to a participant pursuant to a domestic relations order, except that paragraph (1) shall not apply if the order is determined to be a qualified domestic relations order. Each pension plan shall provide for the payment of benefits in accordance with the applicable requirements of any qualified domestic relations order.

(B) For purposes of this paragraph—

(i) the term "qualified domestic relations order" means a domestic relations order—

(I) which creates or recognizes the existence of an alternate payee's right to, or assigns to an alternate payee the right to, receive all or a portion of the benefits payable with respect to a participant under a plan,

* * *

(ii) the term "domestic relations order" means any judgment, decree, or order (including approval of a property settlement agreement) which—

(I) relates to the provision of child support, alimony payments, or marital property rights to a spouse, former spouse, child, or other dependent of a participant, and

(II) is made pursuant to a State domestic relations law (including a community property law). * * *

Sec. 1082 Minimum funding standards

(a) Avoidance of accumulated funding deficiency

(1) Every employee pension benefit plan subject to this part shall satisfy the minimum funding standard (or the alternative minimum funding standard under section 305) for any plan year to which this part applies. A plan to which this part applies shall have satisfied the minimum funding standard for such plan for a plan year if as of the end of such plan year the plan does not have an accumulated funding deficiency.

* * *

(9) For purposes of this part, a determination of experience gains and losses and a valuation of the plan's liability shall be made not less frequently than once every 3 years, except that such determination shall be made more frequently to the extent required in particular cases under regulations prescribed by the Secretary of the Treasury.

(10) For purposes of this part, any contributions for a plan year made by an employer after the last day of such plan year, but not later than 2½ months after such day, shall be deemed to have been made on such last day. For purposes of this paragraph, such 2½ month period may be extended for not more than 6 months under regulations prescribed by the Secretary of the Treasury.

Sec. 1083 Variance from minimum funding standard

(a) Waiver of requirements in event of business hardship

If an employer, or in the case of a multiemployer plan, 10 percent or more of the number of employers contributing to or under the plan are unable to satisfy the minimum funding standard for a plan year without temporary substantial business hardship (substantial business hardship in the case of a multiemployer plan) and if application of the standard would be adverse to the interests of plan participants in the aggregate, the Secretary of the Treasury may waive the requirements of section 302(a) of this title for such year with respect to all or any portion of the minimum funding standard other than the portion thereof determined under section 302(b)(2)(C) of this title. The Secretary of the Treasury shall not waive the minimum funding standard with respect to a plan for more than 3 of any 15 (5 of any 15 in the case of a multiemployer plan) consecutive plan years. The interest rate used for purposes of computing the amortization charge described in subsection (b)(2)(C) of this section for any plan year shall be—

(1) in the case of a plan other than a multiemployer plan, the greater of (A) 150 percent of the Federal mid-term rate (as in effect under section 1274 of the Internal Revenue Code of 1986 for the 1st month of such plan year), or (B) the rate of interest used under the plan in determining costs (including adjustments under section 302(b)(5)(B) of this title), and

(2) in the case of a multiemployer plan, the rate determined under section 6621(b) of such Code.

(b) Matters considered in determining business hardship

For purposes of this part, the factors taken into account in determining temporary substantial business hardship (substantial business hardship in the case of a multiemployer plan) shall include (but shall not be limited to) whether—

(1) the employer is operating at an economic loss,

(2) there is substantial unemployment or underemployment in the trade or business and in the industry concerned,

(3) the sales and profits of the industry concerned are depressed or declining, and

(4) it is reasonable to expect that the plan will be continued only if the waiver is granted.

* * *

Sec. 1103   Establishment of trust

(a) Benefit plan assets to be held in trust;   authority of trustees

Except as provided in subsection (b), all assets of an employee benefit plan shall be held in trust by one or more trustees. Such trustee or trustees shall be either named in the trust instrument or in the plan instrument described in section 402(a) or appointed by a person who is a named fiduciary, and upon acceptance of being named or appointed, the trustee or trustees shall have exclusive authority and discretion to manage and control the assets of the plan, except to the extent that—

(1) the plan expressly provides that the trustee or trustees are subject to the direction of a named fiduciary who is not a trustee, in which case the trustees shall be subject to proper directions of such fiduciary which are made in accordance with the terms of the plan and which are not contrary to this Act, or

(2) authority to manage, acquire, or dispose of assets of the plan is delegated to one or more investment managers pursuant to section 402(c)(3).

(b) Exceptions

The requirements of subsection (a) of this section shall not apply—

(1) to any assets of a plan which consist of insurance contracts or policies issued by an insurance company qualified to do business in a State;

(2) to any assets of such an insurance company or any assets of a plan which are held by such an insurance company;

(3) to a plan—

(A) some or all of the participants of which are employees described in section 401(c)(1) of the Internal Revenue Code of 1986; or

(B) which consists of one or more individual retirement accounts described in section 408 of the Internal Revenue Code of 1986;

to the extent that such plan's assets are held in one or more custodial accounts which qualify under section 401(f) or 408(h) of the Internal Revenue Code of 1986, whichever is applicable.

(4) to a plan which the Secretary exempts from the requirement of subsection (a) of this section and which is not subject to any of the following provisions of this chapter—

(A) part 2 of this subtitle,

(B) part 3 of this subtitle, or

(C) title IV of the Act; or

(5) to a contract established and maintained under section 403(b) of the Internal Revenue Code of 1986 to the extent that the assets of the contract are held in one or more custodial accounts pursuant to section 403(b)(7) of the Internal Revenue Code of 1986.

(6) Any plan, fund or program under which an employer, all of whose stock is directly or indirectly owned by employees, former employees or their beneficiaries, proposes through an unfunded arrangement to compensate retired employees for benefits which were forfeited by such employees under a pension plan maintained by a former employer prior to the date such pension plan became subject to this Act.

(c) Assets of plan not to inure to benefit of employer; allowable purposes of holding plan assets

(1) Except * * *, the assets of a plan shall never inure to the benefit of any employer and shall be held for the exclusive purposes of providing benefits to participants in the plan and their beneficiaries and defraying reasonable expenses of administering the plan.

* * *

(d) Termination of plan

* * *

(2) The assets of a welfare plan which terminates shall be distributed in accordance with the terms of the plan, except as otherwise provided in regulations of the Secretary.

SEC. 1104   Fiduciary duties

(a) Prudent man standard of care

(1) Subject to sections 403(c) and (d), 4042, and 4044, a fiduciary shall discharge his duties with respect to a plan solely in the interest of the participants and beneficiaries and—

(A) for the exclusive purpose of:

(i) providing benefits to participants and their beneficiaries; and

(ii) defraying reasonable expenses of administering the plan;

(B) with the care, skill, prudence, and diligence under the circumstances then prevailing that a prudent man acting in a like capacity and familiar with such matters would use in the conduct of an enterprise of a like character and with like aims;

(C) by diversifying the investments of the plan so as to minimize the risk of large losses, unless under the circumstances it is clearly prudent not to do so; and

(D) in accordance with the documents and instruments governing the plan insofar as such documents and instruments are consistent with the provisions of this title and title IV.

(2) In the case of an eligible individual account plan (as defined in section 407(d)(3)), the diversification requirement of paragraph (1)(C) and the prudence requirement (only to the extent that it requires diversification) of paragraph (1)(B) is not violated by acquisition or holding of qualifying employer real property or qualifying employer securities (as defined in section 407(d)(4) and (5)).

* * *

Sec. 1106 Prohibited transactions

(a) Transactions between plan and party in interest

Except as provided in section 408:

(1) A fiduciary with respect to a plan shall not cause the plan to engage in a transaction, if he knows or should know that such transaction constitutes a direct or indirect—

(A) sale or exchange, or leasing, of any property between the plan and a party in interest;

(B) lending of money or other extension of credit between the plan and a party in interest;

(C) furnishing of goods, services, or facilities between the plan and a party in interest;

(D) transfer to, or use by or for the benefit of, a party in interest, of any assets of the plan; or

(E) acquisition, on behalf of the plan, of any employer security or employer real property in violation of section 407(a).

(2) No fiduciary who has authority or discretion to control or manage the assets of a plan shall permit the plan to hold any employer security or employer real property if he knows or should know that holding such security or real property violates section 407(a).

(b) Transactions between plan and fiduciary

A fiduciary with respect to a plan shall not—

(1) deal with the assets of the plan in his own interest or for his own account,

(2) in his individual or in any other capacity act in any transaction involving the plan on behalf of a party (or represent a party) whose interests are adverse to the interests of the plan or the interests of its participants or beneficiaries, or

(3) receive any consideration for his own personal account from any party dealing with such plan in connection with a transaction involving the assets of the plan.

* * *

SEC. 1107 **Limitation with respect to acquisition and holding of employer securities and employer real property by certain plans**

(a) Percentage limitation

Except as otherwise provided in this section and section 414:

(1) A plan may not acquire or hold—

(A) any employer security which is not a qualifying employer security, or

(B) any employer real property which is not qualifying employer real property.

(2) A plan may not acquire any qualifying employer security or qualifying employer real property, if immediately after such acquisition the aggregate fair market value of employer securities and employer real property held by the plan exceeds 10 percent of the fair market value of the assets of the plan.

(3)(A) After December 31, 1984, a plan may not hold any qualifying employer securities or qualifying employer real property (or both) to the extent that the aggregate fair market value of such securities and property determined on December 31, 1984, exceeds 10 percent of the greater of—

(i) the fair market value of the assets of the plan, determined on December 31, 1984, or

(ii) the fair market value of the assets of the plan determined on January 1, 1975.

(B) Subparagraph (A) of this paragraph shall not apply to any plan which on any date after December 31, 1974; and before January 1, 1985, did not hold employer securities or employer real property (or both) the aggregate fair market value of which determined on such date exceeded 10 percent of the greater of

(i) the fair market value of the assets of the plan, determined on such date, or

(ii) the fair market value of the assets of the plan determined on January 1, 1975.

(4)(A) After December 31, 1979, a plan may not hold any employer securities or employer real property in excess of the amount specified in regulations under subparagraph (B). This subparagraph shall not apply to a plan after the earliest date after December 31, 1974, on which it complies with such regulations.

(B) Not later than December 31, 1976, the Secretary shall prescribe regulations which shall have the effect of requiring that a plan divest itself of 50 percent of the holdings of employer securities and employer real property which the plan would be required to divest before January 1, 1985, under paragraph (2) or subsection (c) of this section (whichever is applicable).

* * *

Sec. 1108   Exemptions from prohibited transactions

* * *

(c) Fiduciary benefits and compensation not prohibited by 29 USCS § 1106

Nothing in section 406 shall be construed to prohibit any fiduciary from—

(1) receiving any benefit to which he may be entitled as a participant or beneficiary in the plan, so long as the benefit is computed and paid on a basis which is consistent with the terms of the plan as applied to all other participants and beneficiaries;

(2) receiving any reasonable compensation for services rendered, or for the reimbursement of expenses properly and actually incurred, in the performance of his duties with the plan; except that no person so serving who already receives full-time pay from an employer or an association of employers, whose employees are participants in the plan, or from an employee organization whose members are participants in such plan shall receive compensation from such plan, except for reimbursement of expenses properly and actually incurred; or

(3) serving as a fiduciary in addition to being an officer, employee, agent, or other representative of a party in interest.

Sec. 1109   Liability for breach of fiduciary duty

(a) Any person who is a fiduciary with respect to a plan who breaches any of the responsibilities, obligations, or duties imposed upon fiduciaries by this subchapter shall be personally liable to make good to such plan any losses to the plan resulting from each such breach, and to restore to such plan any profits of such fiduciary which have been made through use of assets of the plan by the fiduciary, and shall be subject to such other equitable or remedial relief as the court may deem appropriate, including removal of such fiduciary. A fiduciary may also be removed for a violation of section 411 of this Act.

(b) No fiduciary shall be liable with respect to a breach of fiduciary duty under this subchapter if such breach was 'committed before he became a fiduciary or after he ceased to be a fiduciary.

Sec. 1132   Civil enforcement

(a) Persons empowered to bring a civil action

A civil action may be brought—

(1) by a participant or beneficiary—

(A) for the relief provided for in subsection (c) of this section, or

(B) to recover benefits due to him under the terms of his plan, to enforce his rights under the terms of the plan, or to clarify his rights to future benefits under the terms of the plan;

(2) by the Secretary, or by a participant, beneficiary or fiduciary for appropriate relief under section 409;

(3) by a participant, beneficiary, or fiduciary (A) to enjoin any act or practice which violates any provision of this subchapter or the terms of the plan, or (B) to obtain other appropriate equitable relief (i) to redress such violations or (ii) to enforce any provisions of this subchapter or the terms of the plan;

(4) by the Secretary, or by a participant, or beneficiary for appropriate relief in the case of a violation of 105(c);

(5) except as otherwise provided in subsection (b) of this section, by the Secretary (A) to enjoin any act or practice which violates any provision of this subchapter, or (B) to obtain other appropriate equitable relief (i) to redress such violation or (ii) to enforce any provision of this subchapter; or

(6) by the Secretary to collect any civil penalty under paragraph (2), (4), (5), (6), or (7) of subsection (c) or under subsection (i) or (*l*).

* * *

(b) Plans qualified under Internal Revenue Code; maintenance of actions involving delinquent contributions

(1) In the case of a plan which is qualified under section 401(a), 403(a), or 405(a) of the Internal Revenue Code of 1986 (or with respect to which an application to so qualify has been filed and has

not been finally determined) the Secretary may exercise his authority under subsection (a)(5) of this section with respect to a violation of, or the enforcement of, parts 2 and 3 of this subtitle (relating to participation, vesting, and funding) only if—

(A) requested by the Secretary of the Treasury, or

(B) one or more participants, beneficiaries, or fiduciaries, of such plan request in writing (in such manner as the Secretary shall prescribe by regulation) that he exercise such authority on their behalf. In the case of such a request under this paragraph he may exercise such authority only if he determines that such violation affects, or such enforcement is necessary to protect, claims of participants or beneficiaries to benefits under the plan.

(2) The Secretary shall not initiate an action to enforce section 515.

* * *

(c) Administrator's refusal to supply requested information; penalty for failure to provide annual report in complete form

(1) Any administrator (A) who fails to meet the requirements of paragraph (1) or (4) of section 606 with respect to a participant or beneficiary, or (B) who fails or refuses to comply with a request for any information which such administrator is required by this subchapter to furnish to a participant or beneficiary (unless such failure or refusal results from matters reasonably beyond the control of the administrator) by mailing the material requested to the last known address of the requesting participant or beneficiary within 30 days after such request may in the court's discretion be personally liable to such participant or beneficiary in the amount of up to $100 a day from the date of such failure or refusal, and the court may in its discretion order such other relief as it deems proper.

(2) The Secretary may assess a civil penalty against any plan administrator of up to $1,000 a day from the date of such plan administrator's failure or refusal to file the annual report required to be filed with the Secretary under section 101(b)(4). For purposes of this paragraph, an annual report that has been rejected under section 104(a)(4) for failure to provide material information shall not be treated as having been filed with the Secretary.

(3) Any employer maintaining a plan who fails to meet the notice requirement of section 101(d) with respect to any participant or beneficiary may in the court's discretion be liable to such participant or beneficiary in the amount of up to $100 a day from the date

of such failure, and the court may in its discretion order such other relief as it deems proper.

* * *

(d) Status of employee benefit plan as entity

(1) An employee benefit plan may sue or be sued under this subchapter as an entity. Service of summons, subpoena, or other legal process of a court upon a trustee or an administrator of an employee benefit plan in his capacity as such shall constitute service upon the employee benefit plan. In a case where a plan has not designated in the summary plan description of the plan an individual as agent for the service of legal process, service upon the Secretary shall constitute such service. The Secretary, not later than 15 days after receipt of service under the preceding sentence, shall notify the administrator or any trustee of the plan of receipt of such service.

(2) Any money judgment under this subchapter against an employee benefit plan shall be enforceable only against the plan as an entity and shall not be enforceable against any other person unless liability against such person is established in his individual capacity under this title.

(e) Jurisdiction

(1) Except for actions under subsection (a)(1)(B) of this section, the district courts of the United States shall have exclusive jurisdiction of civil actions under this title brought by the Secretary or by a participant, beneficiary, or fiduciary, or any person referred to in section 101(f)(1). State courts of competent jurisdiction and district courts of the United States shall have concurrent jurisdiction of actions under paragraphs (1)(B) and (7) of subsection (a) of this section.

(2) Where an action under this title is brought in a district court of the United States, it may be brought in the district where the plan is administered, where the breach took place, or where a defendant resides or may be found, and process may be served in any other district where a defendant resides or may be found.

(f) Amount in controversy; citizenship of parties

The district courts of the United States shall have jurisdiction, without respect to the amount in controversy or the citizenship of the parties, to grant the relief provided for in subsection (a) of this section in any action.

(g) Attorney's fees and costs; awards in actions involving delinquent contributions

(1) In any action under this subchapter (other than an action described in paragraph (2)) by a participant, beneficiary, or fiduciary, the court in its discretion may allow a reasonable attorney's fee and costs of action to either party.

(2) In any action under this subchapter by a fiduciary for or on behalf of a plan to enforce section 515 of this title in which a judgment in favor of the plan is awarded, the court shall award the plan—

> (A) the unpaid contributions,
>
> (B) interest on the unpaid contributions,
>
> (C) an amount equal to the greater of—
>
>> (i) interest on the unpaid contributions, or
>>
>> (ii) liquidated damages provided for under the plan in an amount not in excess of 20 percent (or such higher percentage as may be permitted under Federal or State law) of the amount determined by the court under subparagraph (A),
>
> (D) reasonable attorney's fees and costs of the action, to be paid by the defendant, and
>
> (E) such other legal or equitable relief as the court deems appropriate.

For purposes of this paragraph, interest on unpaid contributions shall be determined by using the rate provided under the plan, or, if none, the rate prescribed under section 6621 of the Internal Revenue Code of 1986.

(h) Service upon Secretary of Labor and Secretary of Treasury

A copy of the complaint in any action under this title by a participant, beneficiary, or fiduciary (other than an action brought by one or more participants or beneficiaries under subsection (a)(1)(B) of this section which is solely for the purpose of recovering benefits due such participants under the terms of the plan) shall be served upon the Secretary and the Secretary of the Treasury by certified mail. Either Secretary shall have the right in his discretion to intervene in any action, except that the Secretary of the Treasury may not intervene in any action under part 4 of this subtitle. If the Secretary brings an action under subsection (a) of this section on behalf of a participant or beneficiary, he shall notify the Secretary of the Treasury.

(i) Administrative assessment of civil penalty

In the case of a transaction prohibited by section 406 by a party in interest with respect to a plan to which this part applies, the Secretary may assess a civil penalty against such party in interest. The amount of such penalty may not exceed 5 percent of the amount involved in each such transaction (as defined in section 4975(f)(4) of the Internal Revenue Code of 1986) for each year or part thereof during which the prohibited transaction continues, except that, if the transaction is not corrected (in such manner as the Secretary shall prescribe in regulations which shall be consistent with section 4975(f)(5) of such code) within 90 days after notice from the Secretary (or such longer period as the Secretary may permit), such penalty may be in an amount not more than 100 percent of the amount involved. This subsection shall not apply to a transaction with respect to a plan described in section 4975(e)(1) of such code.

(j) Direction and control of litigation by Attorney General

In all civil actions under this subchapter, attorneys appointed by the Secretary may represent the Secretary (except as provided in section 518(a) of Title 28), but all such litigation shall be subject to the direction and control of the Attorney General.

(k) Jurisdiction of actions against the Secretary of Labor

Suits by an administrator, fiduciary, participant, or beneficiary of an employee benefit plan to review a final order of the Secretary, to restrain the Secretary from taking any action contrary to the provisions of this Act, or to compel him to take action required under this title, may be brought in the district court of the United States for the district where the plan has its principal office, or in the United States District Court for the District of Columbia.

(l) Civil penalties on violations by fiduciaries

(1) In the case of—

(A) any breach of fiduciary responsibility under (or other violation of) part 4 by a fiduciary, or

(B) any knowing participation in such a breach or violation by any other person,

the Secretary shall assess a civil penalty against such fiduciary or other person in an amount equal to 20 percent of the applicable recovery amount.

(2) For purposes of paragraph (1), the term "applicable recovery amount" means any amount which is recovered from a fiduciary or other person with respect to a breach or violation described in paragraph (1)—

(A) pursuant to any settlement agreement with the Secretary, or

(B) ordered by a court to be paid by such fiduciary or other person to a plan or its participants and beneficiaries in a judicial proceeding instituted by the Secretary under subsection (a)(2) or (a)(5) of this section.

(3) The Secretary may, in the Secretary's sole discretion, waive or reduce the penalty under paragraph (1) if the Secretary determines in writing that—

    (A) the fiduciary or other person acted reasonably and in good faith, or

    (B) it is reasonable to expect that the fiduciary or other person will not be able to restore all losses to the plan without severe financial hardship unless such waiver or reduction is granted.

(4) The penalty imposed on a fiduciary or other person under this subsection with respect to any transaction shall be reduced by the amount of any penalty or tax imposed on such fiduciary or other person with respect to such transaction under subsection (i) of this section and section 4975 of the Internal Revenue Code of 1986.

SEC. 1133 Claims procedure

In accordance with regulations of the Secretary, every employee benefit plan shall—

    (1) provide adequate notice in writing to any participant or beneficiary whose claim for benefits under the plan has been denied, setting forth the specific reasons for such denial, written in a manner calculated to be understood by the participant. . . .

SEC. 1140 Interference with protected rights

It shall be unlawful for any person to discharge, fine, suspend, expel, discipline, or discriminate against a participant or beneficiary for exercising any right to which he is entitled under the provisions of an employee benefit plan, this title, section 3001, or the Welfare and Pension Plans Disclosure Act [29 U.S.C. 301 et seq.], or for the purpose of interfering with the attainment of any right to which such participant may become entitled under the plan, this subchapter, or the Welfare and Pension Plans Disclosure Act. It shall be unlawful for any person to discharge, fine suspend, expel, or discriminate against any person because he has given information or has testified or is about to testify in any inquiry or proceeding relating to this Act or the Welfare and Pension Plans Disclosure Act. It shall be unlawful for any person to discharge, fine, suspend, expel, or discriminate against any person because he has given information or has testified or is about to testify in any inquiry or proceeding relating to this Act or the Welfare and Pension Plans Disclosure Act. The provisions of section 502 shall be applicable in the enforcement of this section.

SEC. 1144 **Other laws**

(a) Supersedure; effective date

Except as provided in subsection (b) of this section, the provisions of this title and title IV shall supersede any and all State laws insofar as they may now or hereafter relate to any employee benefit plan described in section 4(a) and not exempt under section 4(b) of this title....

(b) Construction and application

(1) This section shall not apply with respect to any cause of action which arose, or any act or omission which occurred, before January 1, 1975.

(2)(A) Except as provided in subparagraph (B), nothing in this title shall be construed to exempt or relieve any person from any law of any State which regulates insurance, banking, or securities.

(B) Neither an employee benefit plan described in section 4(a), which is not exempt under section 4(b) (other than a plan established primarily for the purpose of providing death benefits), nor any trust established under such a plan, shall be deemed to be an insurance company or other insurer, bank, trust company, or investment company or to be engaged in the business of insurance or banking for purposes of any law of any State purporting to regulate insurance companies, insurance contracts, banks, trust companies, or investment companies.

* * *

SEC. 1161 **Plans must provide continuation coverage to certain individuals**

(a) In general

The plan sponsor of each group health plan shall provide, in accordance with this part, that each qualified beneficiary who would lose coverage under the plan as a result of a qualifying event is entitled, under the plan, to elect, within the election period, continuation coverage under the plan.

* * *

SEC. 1162 **Continuation coverage**

For purposes of section 601 of this title the term "continuation coverage" means coverage under the plan which meets the following requirements:

(1) Type of benefit coverage

The coverage must consist of coverage which, as of the time the coverage is being provided, is identical to the coverage provided under the plan to similarly situated beneficiaries under the plan with respect to whom a qualifying event has not occurred. If coverage is modified under the plan for any group of similarly situated beneficiaries, such coverage shall also be modified in the same manner for all individuals who are qualified beneficiaries under the plan pursuant to this part in connection with such group.

(2) Period of coverage

The coverage must extend for at least the period beginning on the date of the qualifying event and ending not earlier than the earliest of the following:

(A) Maximum required period.—

(i) General rule for terminations and reduced hours.— In the case of a qualifying event described in section 603(2) of this title, except as provided in clause (ii), the date which is 18 months after the date of the qualifying event.

(ii) Special rule for multiple qualifying events.—If a qualifying event (other than a qualifying event described in section 603(6) of this title) occurs during the 18 months after the date of a qualifying event described in section 603(2) of this title, the date which is 36 months after the date of the qualifying event described in section 603(2) of this title.

(iii) Special rule for certain bankruptcy proceedings.— In the case of a qualifying event described in section 603(6) of this title (relating to bankruptcy proceedings), the date of the death of the covered employee or qualified beneficiary (described in section 607(3)(C)(iii)) of this title, or in the case of the surviving spouse or dependent children of the covered employee, 36 months after the date of the death of the covered employee.

(iv) General rule for other qualifying events.—In the case of a qualifying event not described in section 603(2) or 603(6) of this title, the date which is 36 months after the date of the qualifying event.

* * *

(3) Premium requirements

The plan may require payment of a premium for any period of continuation coverage,

* * *

(4) No requirement of insurability

The coverage may not be conditioned upon, or discriminate on the basis of lack of, evidence of insurability.

* * *

SEC. 1163   Qualifying event

For purposes of this part, the term "qualifying event" means, with respect to any covered employee, any of the following events which, but for the continuation coverage required under this part, would result in the loss of coverage of a qualified beneficiary:

(1) The death of the covered employee.

(2) The termination (other than by reason of such employee's gross misconduct), or reduction of hours, of the covered employee's employment.

(3) The divorce or legal separation of the covered employee from the employee's spouse.

(4) The covered employee becoming entitled to benefits under title XVIII of the Social Security Act.

(5) A dependent child ceasing to be a dependent child under the generally applicable requirements of the plan.   * * *

SEC. 1302   Pension Benefit Guaranty Corporation

(a) Establishment within Department of Labor

There is established within the Department of Labor a body corporate to be known as the Pension Benefit Guaranty Corporation.   In carrying out its functions under this title, the corporation shall be administered by the chairman of the board of directors in accordance with policies established by the board.   The purposes of this title, which are to be carried out by the corporation, are—

(1) to encourage the continuation and maintenance of voluntary private pension plans for the benefit of their participants,

(2) to provide for the timely and uninterrupted payment of pension benefits to participants and beneficiaries under plans to which this subchapter applies, and

(3) to maintain premiums established by the corporation under section 4006 at the lowest level consistent with carrying out its obligations under this subchapter.

* * *

SEC. 1306 Premium rates

(a) Schedules for premium rates and bases for application; establishment, coverage, etc.

(1) The corporation shall prescribe such schedules of premium rates and bases for the application of those rates as may be necessary to provide sufficient revenue to the fund for the corporation to carry out its functions under this title.

* * *

(3)(A) * * * [T]he annual premium rate payable to the corporation by all plans for basic benefits guaranteed under this title is—

(i) in the case of a single-employer plan, for plan years beginning after December 31, 1990, an amount equal to the sum of $19 plus the additional premium (if any) determined under subparagraph (E).

* * *

(E)(i) The additional premium determined under this subparagraph with respect to any plan for any plan year shall be an amount equal to the amount determined under clause (ii) divided by the number of participants in such plan as of the close of the preceding plan year.

(ii) The amount determined under this clause for any plan year shall be an amount equal to $9.00 for each $1,000 (or fraction thereof) of unfunded vested benefits under the plan as of the close of the preceding plan year.

(iii) For purposes of clause (ii)—

(I) Except as provided in subclause (II) or (III), the term "unfunded vested benefits" means the amount which would be the unfunded current liability (within the meaning of section 302(d)(8)(A)) if only vested benefits were taken into account.

(II) The interest rate used in valuing vested benefits for purposes of subclause (I) shall be equal to the applicable percentage of the annual yield on 30-year Treasury securities for the month preceding the month in which the plan year begins.

(iv)(I) Except as provided in this clause, the aggregate increase in the premium payable with respect to any participant by reason of this subparagraph shall not exceed $34.

* * *

SEC. 1322 **Single-employer plan benefits guaranteed**

(a) Nonforfeitable benefits

Subject to the limitations contained in subsection (b) of this section, the corporation shall guarantee, in accordance with this section, the payment of all nonforfeitable benefits (other than benefits becoming nonforfeitable solely on account of the termination of a plan) under a single-employer plan which terminates at a time when this title applies to it. [Section 1322a guarantees benefits under multi-employer plans.]

SEC. 1344 **Allocation of assets**

* * *

(d) Distribution of residual assets; restrictions on reversions pursuant to recently amended plans; assets attributable to employee contributions; calculation of remaining assets

(1) Subject to paragraph (3), any residual assets of a single-employer plan may be distributed to the employer if—

(A) all liabilities of the plan to participants and heir beneficiaries have been satisfied,

(B) the distribution does not contravene any provision of law, and

(C) the plan provides for such a distribution in these circumstances.

(2)(A) In determining the extent to which a plan provides for the distribution of plan assets to the employer for purposes of paragraph (1)(C), any such provision, and any amendment increasing the amount which may be distributed to the employer, shall not be treated as effective before the end of the fifth calendar year following the date of the adoption of such provision or amendment.

(B) A distribution to the employer from a plan shall not be treated as failing to satisfy the requirements of this paragraph if the plan has been in effect for fewer than 5 years and the plan has provided for such a distribution since the effective date of the plan.

(C) Except as otherwise provided in regulations of the Secretary of the Treasury, in any case in which a transaction described in section 208 occurs, subparagraph (A) shall continue to apply separately with respect to the amount of any assets transferred in such transaction.

(D) For purposes of this subsection, the term "employer" includes any member of the controlled group of which the employer is a member. For purposes of the preceding sentence, the term "controlled group" means any group treated as a single employer under subsection (b), (c), (m) or (*o*) of section 414 of the Internal Revenue Code of 1986.

(3)(A) Before any distribution from a plan pursuant to paragraph (1), if any assets of the plan attributable to employee contributions remain after satisfaction of all liabilities described in subsection (a) of this section, such remaining assets shall be equitably distributed to the participants who made such contributions or their beneficiaries (including alternate payees, within the meaning of section 206(d)(3)(K)).

(B) For purposes of subparagraph (A), the portion of the remaining assets which are attributable to employee contributions shall be an amount equal to the product derived by multiplying—

(i) the market value of the total remaining assets, by

(ii) a fraction—

(I) the numerator of which is the present value of all portions of the accrued benefits with respect to participants which are derived from participants' mandatory contributions (referred to in subsection (a)(2) of this section), and

(II) the denominator of which is the present value of all benefits with respect to which assets are allocated under paragraphs (2) through (6) of subsection (a).

(C) For purposes of this paragraph, each person who is, as of the termination date—

(i) a participant under the plan, or

(ii) an individual who has received, during the 3-year period ending with the termination date, a distribution from the plan of such individual's entire nonforfeitable benefit in the form of a single sum distribution in accordance with section 203(e) or in the form of irrevocable commitments purchased by the plan from an insurer to provide such nonforfeitable benefit, shall be treated as a participant with respect to the termination, if all or part of the nonforfeitable benefit with respect to such person is or was attributable to participants' mandatory contributions (referred to in subsection (a)(2)).

OLDER WORKERS BENEFIT PROTECTION ACT

Pub.L. No. 101–433, 104 Stat. 978 (1990)

TITLE I—OLDER WORKERS BENEFIT PROTECTION

SECTION 101. FINDING

The Congress finds that, as a result of the decision of the Supreme Court in Public Employees Retirement System of Ohio v. Betts, 109 S.Ct. 256 (1989), legislative action is necessary to restore the original congressional intent in passing and amending the Age Discrimination in Employment Act of 1967 (29 U.S.C. 621 et seq.), which was to prohibit discrimination against older workers in all employee benefits except when age-based reductions in employee benefit plans are justified by significant cost considerations.

SECTION 102. DEFINITION

Section 11 of the Age Discrimination in Employment Act of 1967 (29 U.S.C. 630) is amended by adding at the end of the following new subsection:

"(1) The term 'compensation, terms, conditions, or privileges of employment' encompasses all employee benefits, including such benefits provided pursuant to a bona fide employee benefit plan.".

SECTION 103. LAWFUL EMPLOYMENT PRACTICES

Section 4 of the Age Discrimination in Employment Act of 1967 (29 U.S.C. 623) is amended—

(1) in subsection (f), by striking paragraph (2) and inserting the following new paragraph:

"(2) to take any action otherwise prohibited under subsection (a), (b), (c), or (e) of this section—

"(A) to observe the terms of a bona fide seniority system that is not intended to evade the purposes of this Act, except that no such seniority system shall require or permit the involuntary retirement of any individual specified by section 12(a) because of the age of such individual; or

"(B) to observe the terms of a bona fide employee benefit plan—

"(i) where, for each benefit or benefit package, the actual amount of payment made or cost incurred on behalf of an older worker is no less than that made or incurred on

289

behalf of a younger worker, as permissible under section 1625.10, title 29, Code of Federal Regulations (as in effect on June 22, 1989); or

"(ii) that is a voluntary early retirement incentive plan consistent with the relevant purpose or purposes of this Act.

Notwithstanding clause (i) or (ii) of subparagraph (B), no such employee benefit plan or voluntary early retirement incentive plan shall excuse the failure to hire any individual, and no such employee benefit plan shall require or permit the involuntary retirement of any individual specified by section 12(a), because of the age of such individual. An employer, employment agency, or labor organization acting under subparagraph (A), or under clause (i) or (ii) of subparagraph (B), shall have the burden of proving that such actions are lawful in any civil enforcement proceeding brought under this Act; or

(2) by redesignating the second subsection (i) as subsection (j); and

(3) by adding at the end the following new subsections:

"(k) A seniority system or employee benefit plan shall comply with this Act regardless of the date of adoption of such system or plan.

"(*l*) Notwithstanding clause (i) or (ii) of subsection (f)(2)(B)—

"(1) It shall not be a violation of subsection (a), (b), (c), or (e) solely because—

"(A) an employee pension benefit plan (as defined in section 3(2) of the Employee Retirement Income Security Act of 1974 (29 U.S.C. 1002(2))) provides for the attainment of a minimum age as a condition of eligibility for normal or early retirement benefits; or

"(B) a defined benefit plan (as defined in section 3(35) of such Act) provides for—

"(i) payments that constitute the subsidized portion of an early retirement benefit; or

"(ii) social security supplements for plan participants that commence before the age and terminate at the age (specified by the plan) when participants are eligible to receive reduced or unreduced old-age insurance benefits under title II of the Social Security Act (42 U.S.C. 401 et seq.), and that do not exceed such old-age insurance benefits.

"(2)(A) It shall not be a violation of subsection (a), (b), (c), or (e) solely because following a contingent event unrelated to age—

"(i) the value of any retiree health benefits received by an individual eligible for an immediate pension; and

"(ii) the value of any additional pension benefits that are made available solely as a result of the contingent event unrelated to age and following which the individual is eligible for not less than an immediate and unreduced pension,

are deducted from severance pay made available as a result of the contingent event unrelated to age.

"(B) For an individual who receives immediate pension benefits that are actuarially reduced under subparagraph (A)(i), the amount of the deduction available pursuant to subparagraph (A)(i) shall be reduced by the same percentage as the reduction in the pension benefits.

"(C) For purposes of this paragraph, severance pay shall include that portion of supplemental unemployment compensation benefits (as described in section 501(c)(17) of the Internal Revenue Code of 1986) that—

"(i) constitutes additional benefits of up to 52 weeks;

"(ii) has the primary purpose and effect of continuing benefits until an individual becomes eligible for an immediate and unreduced pension; and

"(iii) is discontinued once the individual becomes eligible for an immediate and unreduced pension.

"(D) For purposes of this paragraph, the term 'retiree health benefits' means benefits provided pursuant to a group health plan covering retirees, for which (determined as of the contingent event unrelated to age)—

"(i) the package of benefits provided by the employer for the retirees who are below age 65 is at least comparable to benefits provided under title XVIII of the Social Security Act (42 U.S.C. 1395 et seq.); and

"(ii) the package of benefits provided by the employer for the retirees who are age 65 and above is at least comparable to that offered under a plan that provides a benefit package with one-fourth the value of benefits provided under title XVIII of such Act.

"(E)(i) If the obligation of the employer to provide retiree health benefits is of limited duration, the value for each individual shall be calculated at a rate of $3,000 per year for benefit years before age 65 and $750 per year for benefit years beginning at age 65 and above.

"(ii) If the obligation of the employer to provide retiree health benefits is of unlimited duration, the value for each individual shall be calculated at a rate of $48,000 for individuals below age 65, and $24,000 for individuals age 65 and above.

"(iii) The values described in clauses (i) and (ii) shall be calculated based on the age of the individual as of the date of the contingent event unrelated to age. The values are effective on the date of enactment of this subsection, and shall be adjusted on an annual basis, with respect to a contingent event that occurs subsequent to the first year after the date of enactment of this subsection, based on the medical component of the Consumer Price Index for all-urban consumers published by the Department of Labor.

"(iv) If an individual is required to pay a premium for retiree health benefits, the value calculated pursuant to this subparagraph shall be reduced by whatever percentage of the overall premium the individual is required to pay.

"(F) If an employer that has implemented a deduction pursuant to subparagraph (A) fails to fulfill the obligation described in subparagraph (E), any aggrieved individual may bring an action for specific performance of the obligation described in subparagraph (E). The relief shall be in addition to any other remedies provided under Federal or State law.

"(3) It shall not be a violation of subsection (a), (b), (c), or (e) solely because an employer provides a bona fide employee benefit plan or plans under which long-term disability benefits received by an individual are reduced by any pension benefits (other than those attributable to employee contributions)—

"(A) paid to the individual that the individual voluntarily elects to receive; or

"(B) for which an individual who has attained the later of age 62 or normal retirement age is eligible.".

* * *

TITLE II—WAIVER OF RIGHTS OR CLAIMS

SECTION 201. WAIVER OF RIGHTS OR CLAIMS

Section 7 of the Age Discrimination in Employment Act of 1967 (29 U.S.C. 626) is amended by adding at the end the following new subsection:

"(f)(1) An individual may not waive any right or claim under this Act unless the waiver is knowing and voluntary. Except as provided in paragraph (2), a waiver may not be considered knowing and voluntary unless at a minimum—

"(A) the waiver is part of an agreement between the individual and the employer that is written in a manner calculated to be understood by such individual, or by the average individual eligible to participate;

"(B) the waiver specifically refers to rights or claims arising under this Act;

"(C) the individual does not waive rights or claims that may arise after the date the waiver is executed;

"(D) the individual waives rights or claims only in exchange for consideration in addition to anything of value to which the individual already is entitled;

"(E) the individual is advised in writing to consult with an attorney prior to executing the agreement;

"(F)(i) the individual is given a period of at least 21 days within which to consider the agreement; or

"(ii) if a waiver is requested in connection with an exit incentive or other employment termination program offered to a group or class of employees, the individual is given a period of at least 45 days within which to consider the agreement;

"(G) the agreement provides that for a period of at least 7 days following the execution of such agreement, the individual may revoke the agreement, and the agreement shall not become effective or enforceable until the revocation period has expired;

"(H) if a waiver is requested in connection with an exit incentive or other employment termination program offered to a group or class of employees, the employer (at the commencement of the period specified in subparagraph (F)) informs the individual in writing in a manner calculated to be understood by the average individual eligible to participate, as to—

"(i) any class, unit, or group of individuals covered by such program, any eligibility factors for such program, and any time limits applicable to such program; and

"(ii) the job titles and ages of all individuals eligible or selected for the program, and the ages of all individuals in the same job classification or organizational unit who are not eligible or selected for the program.

"(2) A waiver in settlement of a charge filed with the Equal Employment Opportunity Commission, or an action filed in court by the individual or the individual's representative, alleging age discrimination of a kind prohibited under section 4 or 15 may not be considered knowing and voluntary unless at a minimum—

"(A) subparagraphs (A) through (E) of paragraph (1) have been met; and

"(B) the individual is given a reasonable period of time within which to consider the settlement agreement.

"(3) In any dispute that may arise over whether any of the requirements, conditions, and circumstances set forth in subparagraph (A), (B), (C), (D), (E), (F), (G), or (H) of paragraph (1), or subparagraph (A) or (B) of paragraph (2), have been met, the party asserting the validity of a waiver shall have the burden of proving in a court of competent jurisdiction that a waiver was knowing and voluntary pursuant to paragraph (1) or (2).

"(4) No waiver agreement may affect the Commission's rights and responsibilities to enforce this Act. No waiver may be used to justify interfering with the protected right of an employee to file a charge or participate in an investigation or proceeding conducted by the Commission.".

†